I0800489

IMAGES
of America

COCOA AND ROCKLEDGE

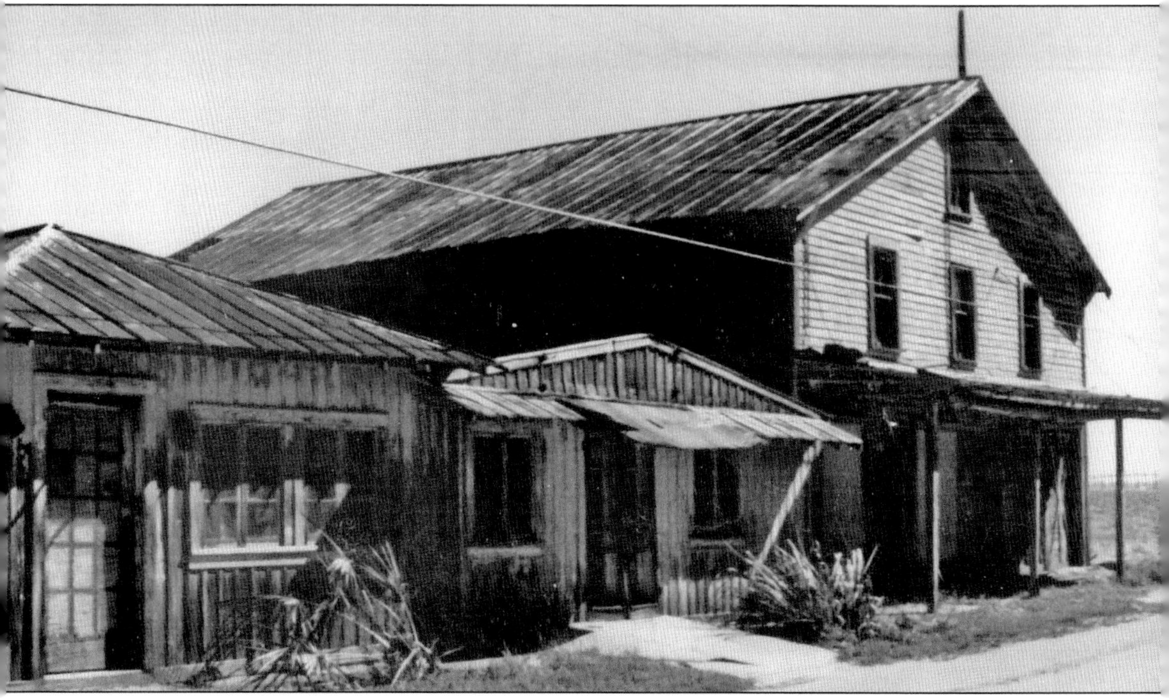

Shown here are the Hub Williams buildings at City Point, Florida. The structure at the far left is Hub's Inn Restaurant, famous for 50 miles in all directions. Nellie M. Williams started the restaurant by serving fresh fish that her husband had caught the night before. Nelly Rowe Lynch acquired the business from her parents. Cleo Phillips then ran the restaurant until it closed due to a lack of parking. (Courtesy Mosquito Beaters collection.)

ON THE COVER: Winter tourists admire a large alligator on the grounds of the Indian River Hotel in Rockledge. The alligator is very likely dead and his mouth tied shut with two or three ropes, but the tourists are still giving him plenty of room. (Courtesy Mosquito Beaters collection.)

IMAGES
of America

COCOA AND ROCKLEDGE

Alma Clyde Field, Ada Edmiston Parrish,
and George Leland "Speedy" Harrell

ARCADIA
PUBLISHING

ISBN 978-0-7385-5334-4

Published by Arcadia Publishing
Charleston, South Carolina

Printed in the United States of America

Library of Congress Catalog Card Number: 2007935230

For all general information contact Arcadia Publishing at:
Telephone 843-853-2070
Fax 843-853-0044
E-mail sales@arcadiapublishing.com
For customer service and orders:
Toll-Free 1-888-313-2665

Visit us on the Internet at www.arcadiapublishing.com

This book is dedicated to the stout-hearted settlers
who worked so hard to carve the central Brevard area
from the jungle and its unlimited mosquitoes.

Contents

ACKNOWLEDGMENTS

This book would not have been possible without the support and contributions of the following people: Don Ball, the Brevard County Historical Commission, June Dixon, the Florida Historical Society, June Gettings Geiger, Lois Dixon Gray, Lowell Gray, Kay Kelly Grooms, Bob Gross, Marion Paterson Jackson, Renee Lamarr, Charles Wilson LaRoche, Kay Wylie Nix, Rick Nix, Tom Norwood, Paul Pruett, Charles Reed, Ashley Morgan Ringo, Bob Roth, Joyce Roth, Irvin Rubin, Mitchell Sayers, Wanda Speir, Marilu Shepard Thistle, the volunteer staff of Alma Clyde Field Library of Florida History, Charles Augustus Vuille, Virginia Eastmoore Washbon, Barbara West, Debra Wynne, Nick Wynne, and Joanne Youngblood.

In addition, numerous unnamed others suggested ideas and sources for photographs. Thank you all.

The Central Brevard Mosquito Beaters made their photographic archives available to the authors and encouraged us to proceed with this volume.

INTRODUCTION

Many people find it ironic that the area now regarded as Greater Cocoa-Rockledge, located on the east coast of Florida, and St. Augustine, the oldest city in the country, are just 115 miles apart in distance but more than three centuries apart in time.

Juan Ponce de Leon in fact bypassed Cape Canaveral and this inland section. He noted the landmass, with reeds growing on the promontory and the presence of natives, but declined to stop and become acquainted. He sailed north to present-day St. Augustine, possibly in search of the fabled Fountain of Youth.

Although Spanish conquerors tended to stay north of the Indian River Lagoon, the Ais Indians continued to inhabit the coastline and to carry on with their hunting and fishing culture. When the British took possession of Florida in 1763, they, unlike the Spanish before them, moved south. Around modern-day Daytona Beach and New Smyrna, sugar plantations were developed, but these were never as successful as British plantations in the colonies to the north. When the Spanish regained control of the peninsula in 1783, colonization efforts south of St. Augustine ground to a halt. In 1821, the United States took ownership of Florida, and the hunger of Americans for land pushed settlement southward into present-day Brevard County. The original owners, the Ais Indians, were long gone, and only the recently arrived Seminoles were there to oppose them. Due to long-running conflicts between the Seminoles and Americans during the first half of the 19th century, settlement of the Indian River area proceeded at a slow pace.

Native Americans, invalids, hunters, sportsmen, soldiers, adventurers, and people who needed to make themselves scarce were drawn to this mosquito-infested, overgrown coast. As time went by, the inhabitants were joined by those seeking new beginnings after the Civil War. Communities were formed to take advantage of the waterways—especially the Indian and St. Johns Rivers—since overland travel, though possible, was very difficult.

In 1891, a visitor wrote that Rockledge as the "choicest jewel set in the coquina coast." In its early days, Rockledge was a winter resort patronized by sportsmen, socialites, and tourists, who found lodgings at three major hotels lining the river shore and in the cottages of Barton Avenue. Guests who came for the season were entertained by orchestras imported from New York and enjoyed elaborate meals, hunting and fishing parties, boat races, and other amusements. Wealthy visitors often decided to establish a second home in Rockledge. Early visitors came by steamboats or sailboats until railroads arrived in the 1890s to augment river travel. The only church at the time, Rockledge Presbyterian, was located near the hotels, and the seasonal visitors swelled the congregation. According to James F. Mitchell, a Scotsman who wrote back to the *Chambers' Journal* in Edinburgh describing early life in Rockledge, the village had a population of 2,000 in winter but only 200 in summer.

Cocoa, Rockledge's sister city, was less involved with early tourists and more interested in developing its commercial potential. Despite years of continued change, it has remained the commercial center for both communities. Merchants in the early times called it "the City of Progress." Indeed it did possess an impressive business section, which centered on Willard Street but later shifted to Brevard Avenue, and merchants concentrated on supplying the needs of grove owners and farmers in the surrounding area. Banks, sales emporiums, business-class hotels, and other enterprises flourished until a fire destroyed most of the northern part of town in the 1890s. The proprietors pitched in and replaced—better than ever—many of the buildings that were damaged or destroyed.

Growth in both Cocoa and Rockledge came in a tremendous spurt in the 1950s, when Cape Canaveral was selected as "America's Gateway to Space." Cocoa and Rockledge grew accordingly—providing residences and commercial services for those brought here by the space program.

One

EARLY TIMES

Cephas Bailey Magruder was given the honor of naming his hometown. A veteran of the Civil War, he was known locally as Major Magruder. He regarded his homestead, located on the coquina buffs of the Indian River, as at the "end of my personal rainbow" and gave his hometown the same name as his home: Rock Ledge.

Cocoa is the only place so named in the country—possibly the world. Several stories have circulated about the origin. One is that a much longer name was submitted to the U.S. Postal Service, but was rejected because of excessive length. A group of cronies sitting around the traditional cracker barrel at the general store got news of the rejection, and one of the men, eyeing the just-arrived shipment of Baker's Cocoa, suggested that *Cocoa* might do just fine. The name was accepted, approved, and adopted.

The Census of Florida of 1885 documented that the Cocoa and Rockledge residents of that time had been born in Florida, other states, Canada, and Europe. Most of the heads of households described themselves as fruit growers or farmers. There were also construction workers such as carpenters, painters, and laborers. Hotel and boarding housekeepers, merchants, seamstresses, and a lawyer or two were listed by name. On the survey was the name of the only minister: a black man living in Cocoa.

When the railroad hugging the East Coast arrived in the 1890s, the focus of the Cocoanuts and Rockledgers became more global. The Spanish American War of 1898 fired the imaginations of the local residents, and many volunteered to serve in the conflict, though few were called to action.

Near the end of the 19th century, both communities were incorporated by the State of Florida—Rockledge in 1887 and Cocoa in 1895.

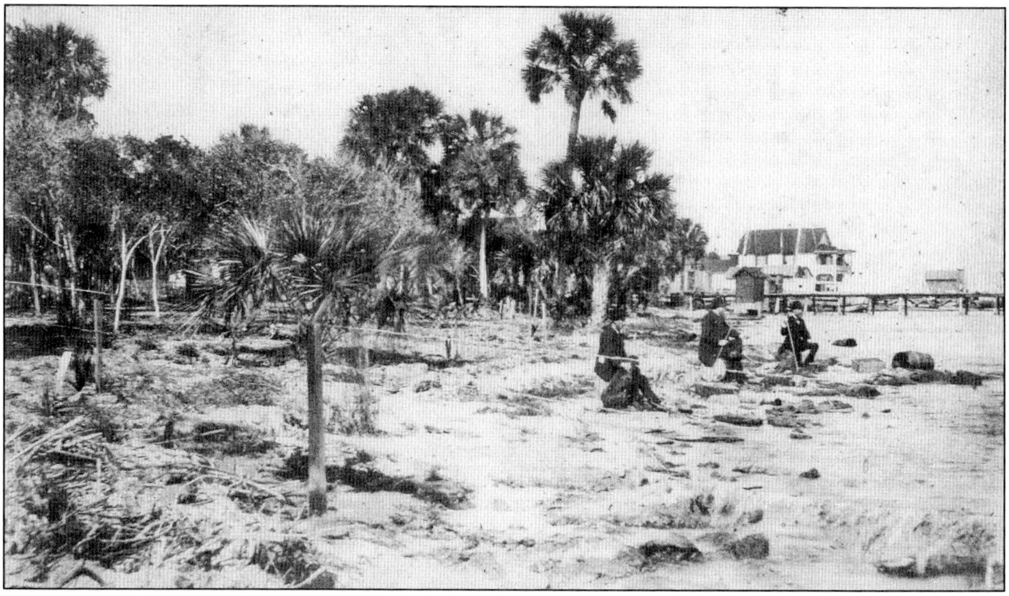

This view looks north from the present location of the E. P. Porcher House. Tourists found it a convenient spot to admire the Indian River. Albert Taylor built his house in the background, on the present location of the civic center and Taylor Park.

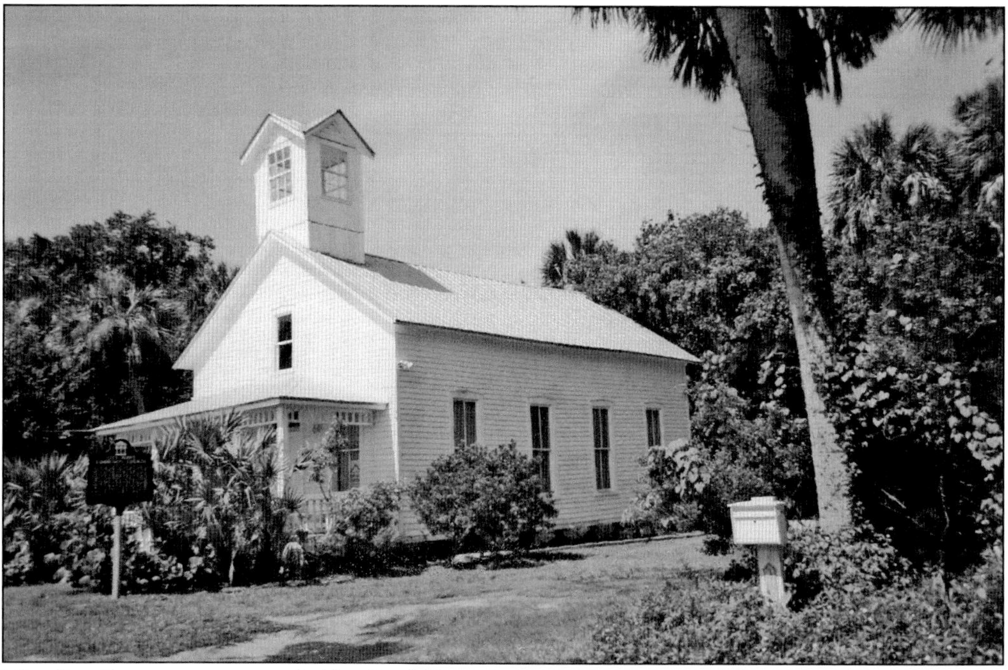

The City Point area was settled by Civil War veterans, Northerners, laborers, and those seeking a healthy climate. In 1885, a board of trustees was formed to construct a public building. The board was William Sharpe, George Holmes, A. L. Hatch, John Sanders, and George Chester. J. C. Norwood donated the land; A. L. Hatch designed the building; John Sanders was the builder. The structure was completed on November 1, 1885.

Ann Brockett Ball preserved this photograph of her grandfather Alexander A. Stewart and his family standing in their sugar cane field at Bonaventure. Kate (left) and Caldwell R. "Clad" Stewart were the children of Alexander A. and Maria Stewart. The elder Stewart became the first clerk of the court of Brevard County. His name appears on most early county documents, but his photograph is rare. (Courtesy Don Ball.)

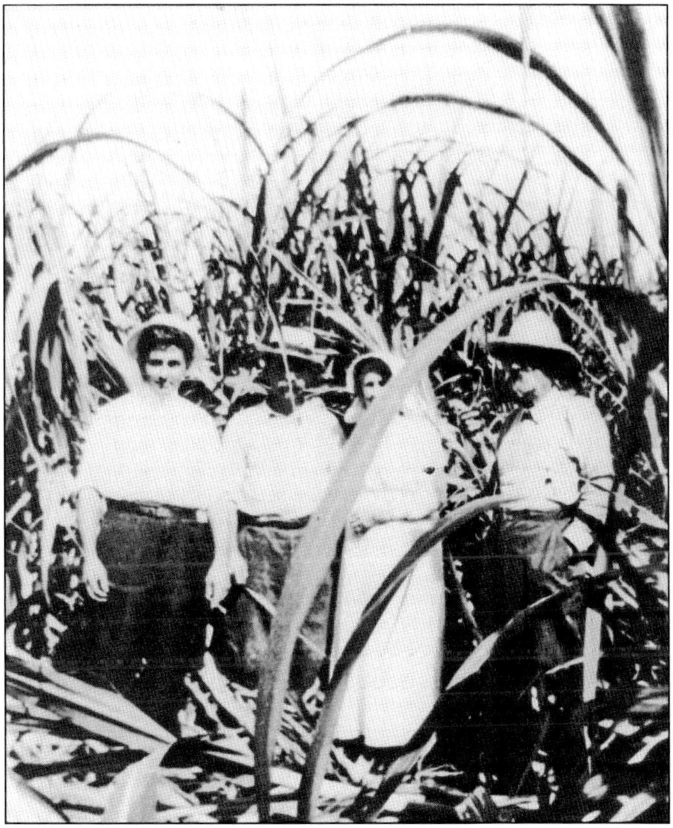

J. M. Sanders's store stood on Willard Street in Cocoa, near the first city dock. Its merchandise consisted of the basics every pioneer family needed.

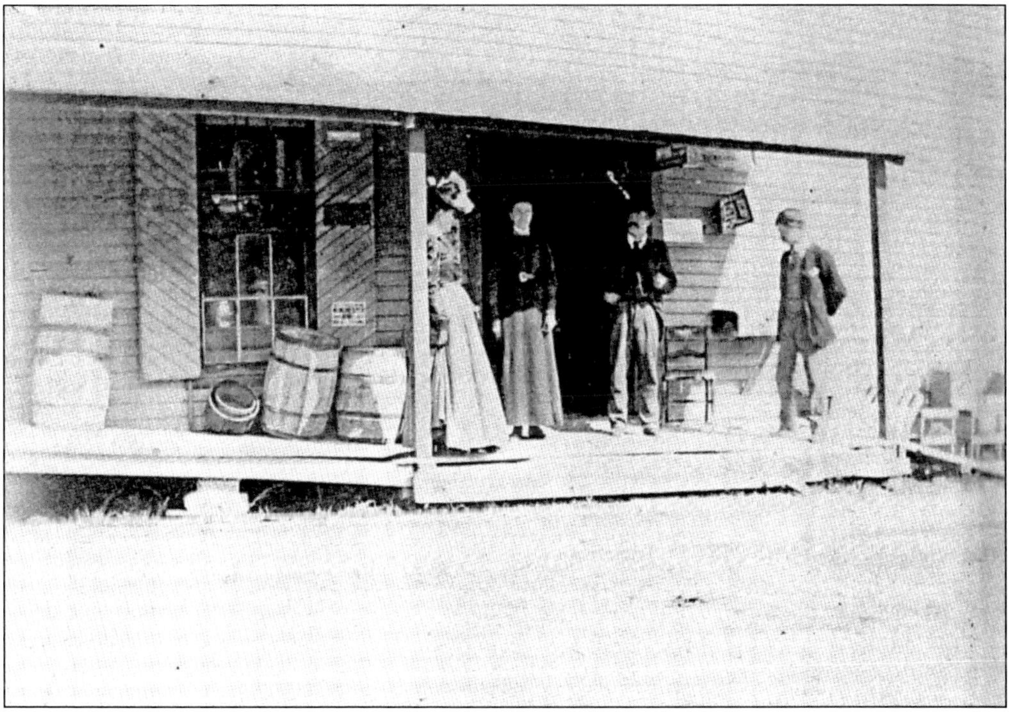

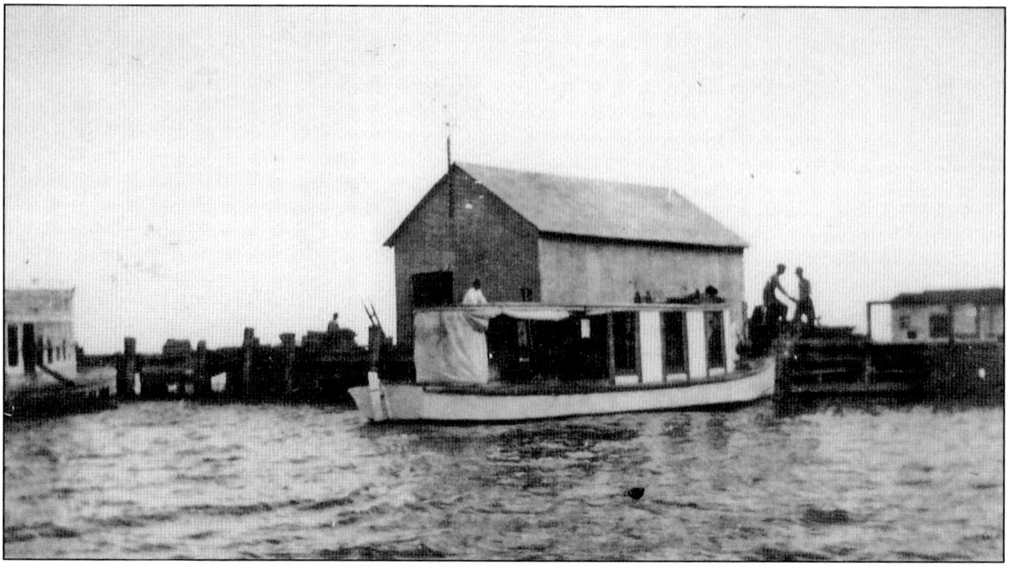

The Cocoa city dock was situated at the end of Willard Street. Cocoa was a regular stopping point for steamboat traffic along the Indian River. The dock also served the people of Merritt Island who came to town in their boats.

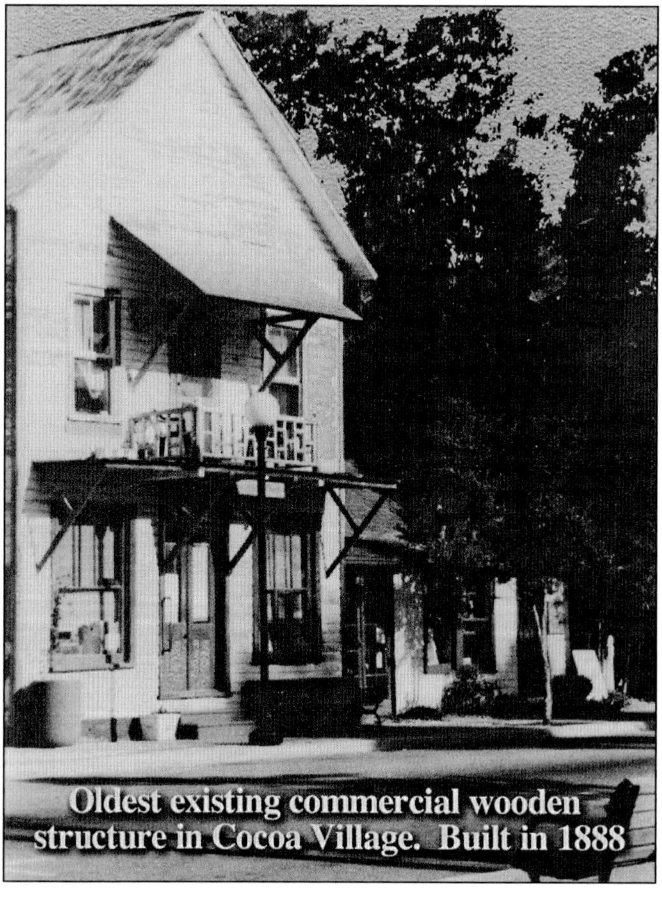

This two-story wooden building that housed Julia Roberts O'Brien's dressmaking shop in early times took a four-block ride from 415 Delannoy Avenue to a new site on Florida Avenue in April 2006. Built in 1888, it was the only wooden structure on Delannoy to survive the fire that devastated Cocoa Village in the 1890s. It now bears the distinction of being the city's oldest commercial building. Before being bought by new owners from Orlando, it was last used as an art studio. Coincidentally, the new owners are also named Roberts and are originally from this area. They plan to return the frame building as near to its original glory as possible.

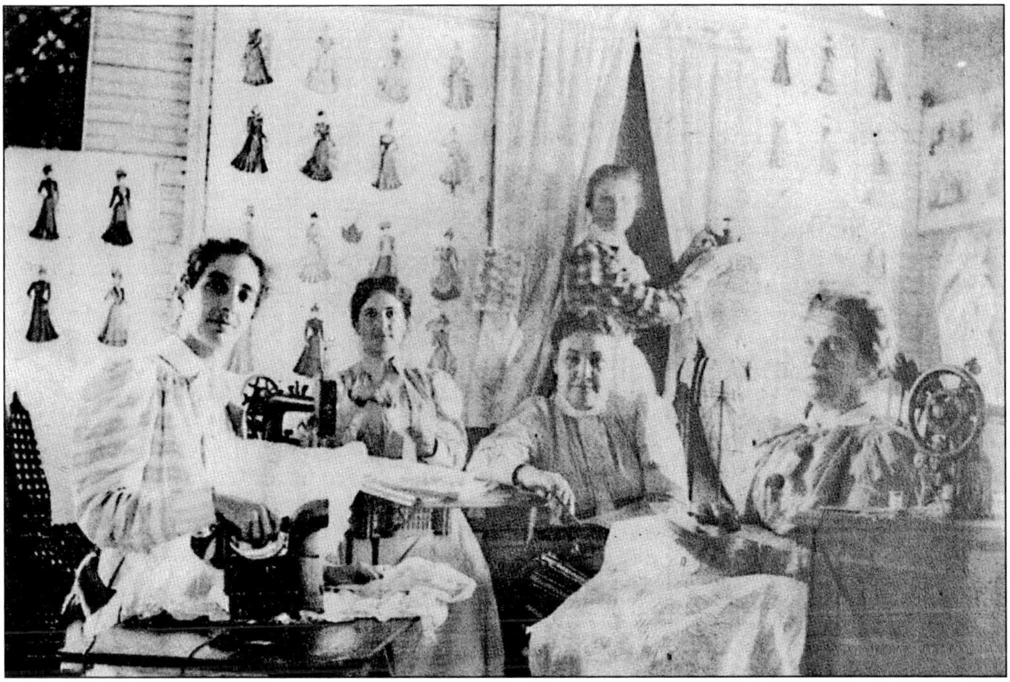

Shown here is the interior of Julia Roberts O'Brien's dressmaking shop on Delannoy Avenue. The main mission of the shop was to teach dressmaking. It was not a factory.

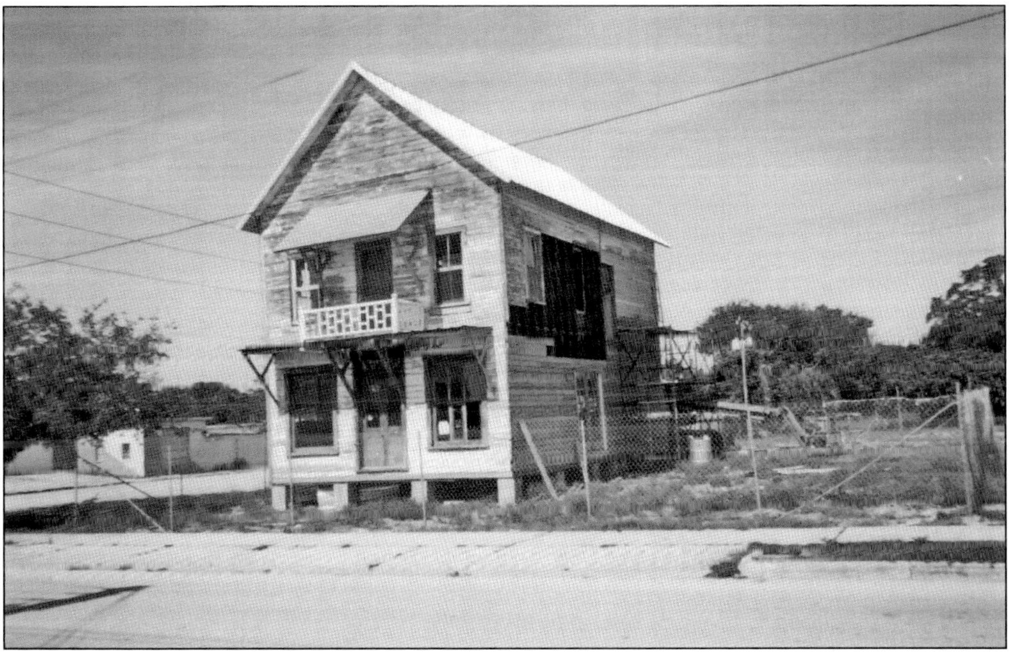

Cocoa's oldest commercial wooden building stands at its new location on Florida Avenue. The present owners plan to restore it to its original condition.

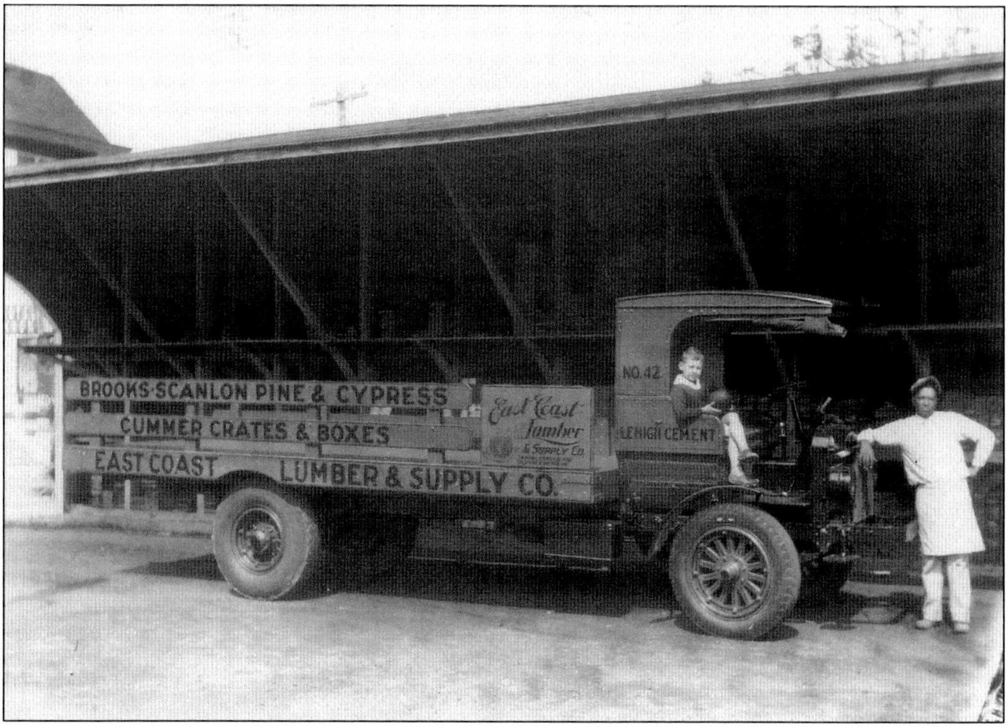

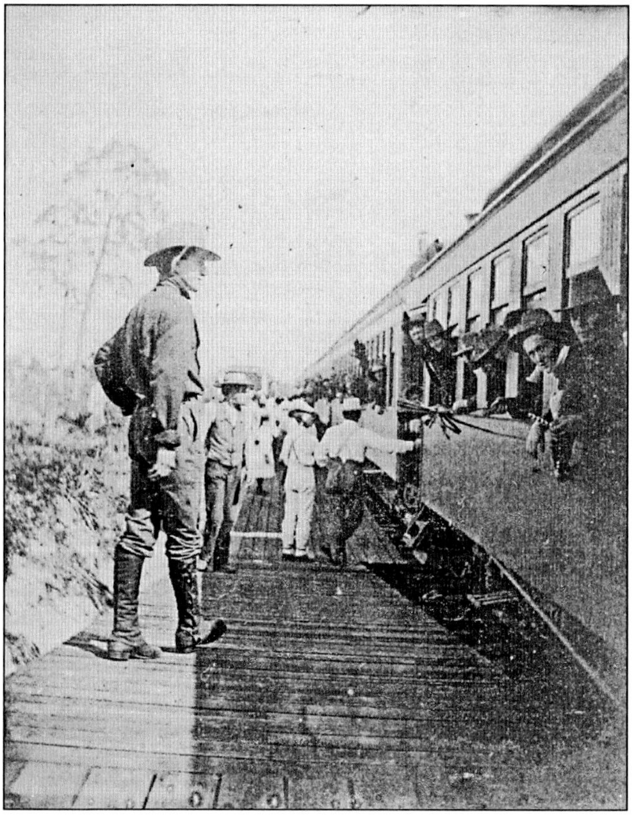

The East Coast Lumber and Supply Company was formed on July 12, 1901, and has served its Cocoa customers for more than 100 years.

The Spanish American War of 1898 was the first conflict to capture the patriotic enthusiasm of the settlers. Rumors were rampant. Men rushed to Titusville to join the Indian River Guard, Company C, 5th Battalion, expecting to be trained and deployed to Cuba. The women, feeling left out and useless, decided to feed the troop trains coming through loaded with soldiers headed for Miami and other points. The men were not called to serve, but the catering services of the women of Cocoa were greatly appreciated.

Cocoa, Florida
October 1, 1895

Pursuant to a call published (30) thirty days in the "Cocoa and Rockledge News" a newspaper published weekly at Cocoa, Florida, a meeting of citizens convened at Wootens Store building--recently occupied by S. S. Jones (the place designated in aforesaid call) for the purpose of incorporating the town of Cocoa. Upon motion at 8:00 P. M. J. M. Sanders was named and elected as Chairman of the meeting and W. L. Hughlett elected Secretary. Upon carefully reviewing a list of qualified electors furnished and certified to by E. W. Hall the County tax collector, it was found that there resided in the proposed incorporate limits fifty-nine (59) qualified electors.

The Chairman announced that it would be necessary to have two-thirds or forty (40) of such qualified electors present.

Accordingly the roll of electors was called and the following answered to their names.

1. R. N. Andrews
2. L. S. Andrews
3. T. F. Bell
4. Joseph Brown
5. Sanuel Childs
6. J. P. Cropen
7. Edwin Dunn
8. L. T. Daniel
9. Fred Fisher
10. W. A. Heaton
11. W. L. Hughlett
12. Wm. Hindle
13. R. B. Holmes
14. E. C. Johnson
15. Wm. Jarvis
16. S. S. Jones
17. Frank Lipp
18. A. S. Magruder
19. G. J. Merceir
20. M. M. McLeod
21. Jas. McNeil
22. B. Nail
23. A. O. Paine
24. W. G. Paterson
25. S. Shean
26. J. M. Sanders
27. A. A. Taylor
28. S. F. Travis
29. Wm. Tennel
30. J. F. Wooten
31. J. L. Wilson
32. H. M. Hill
33. Theo. Demro
34. A. Habernicht
35. E. Stiling
36. A. G. Weinberg
37. Ed. Arnold
38. Henry Whipple
39. J. C. Shaw
40. S. P. Taylor
41. David R. Johnson

The Chairman announced that the required two-thirds were present and that the meeting would proceed to business.

S. F. Travis offered the following

Resolved "That the Corporate name of our proposed town be "Cocoa," carried.

S. F. Travis offered the following

Resolved "That we adopt a seal of the size of an american silver dollar on which shall be the words

"Town of Cocoa, Florida" - carried.

The incorporation papers for the City of Cocoa are presented here and on the following two pages.

Resolved that the following metes and bounds shall be the territorial limits of the proposed town of Cocoa, to wit: Begin on section line dividing sections 32 and 33, quarter of a mile due north of the S. W. Corner of Section 33 aforesaid in Township 24 south of range 36 east; from this point run due east along the 1/4 section line to Channel of Indian River; thence northerly along the Channel of Indian River to a point on or opposite the center section line of section 28 township 24 South range 36 east; from this point run due West along said center line of section 28 to the section line dividing sections 28 and 29, thence run due South along the section line dividing sections 28 and 29 and sections 32 and 33 to point of commencement, which is 1/4 of a mile North of the S. W. Corner of Section 33, township and range before mentioned

Resolution carried.

S. F. Travis offered the following

Resolved "That we proceed to choose a Mayor and five aldermen and that the Chairman appoint tellers to receive the vote.

Resolution carried and Chairman appointed S. S. Jones, W. G. Paterson, and M. M. McLeod tellers. Chairman then announced that nominations were in order. Nominations as follows were then made and seconded

For Mayor	W. L. Hughlett
For Aldermen	J. M. Sanders
	J. F. Wooten
	A. A. Tayler
	S. F. Travis
	Ed. Stiling

The tellers having received the votes reported the following with the number of votes opposite their names as being elected

For Mayor	W. L. Hughlett	36 Votes
For Aldermen	J. M. Sanders	36 Votes
	J. F. Wooten	36 Votes
	A. A. Taylor	37 Votes
	Ed. Stiling	35 Votes
	S. F. Travis	36 Votes

For Clerk and Treasurer

R. N. Andrews was nominated, received 36 votes electing him without opposition.

The papers also included the names of the city officers and recorded the votes they received in the city election.

For Marshall & Collector

Geo. L. Lynch was nominated, received 31 votes, elected, without opposition.

For Assessor

E. C. Johnson was nominated, received 33 Votes, elected, without opposition. S. F. Travis, Notary Public, then swore in W. L. Hughlett as Mayor.

W. L. Hughlett as Mayor then swore in J. M. Sanders, J. F. Wooten, A. A. Tayler, Ed. Stiling, S. F. Travis, as Aldermen.

The business of the meeting having been concluded by motion it was adjourned.

s/W. L. Hughlett
Mayor

Aldermen
s/J. M. Sanders
s/J. F. Wooten
s/A. A. Tayler
s/S. F. Travis
s/Edward Stiling

s/R. N. Andrews
Clerk

Some of the city officials became state officers and the descendants of those named in the papers of incorporation are still well-known local names.

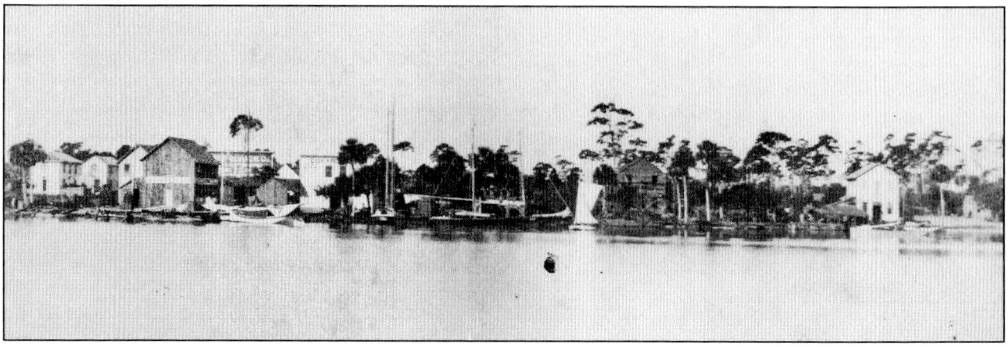

In contrast to the earlier desolate view of the Indian River shoreline, the scene had become quite impressive by the 1890s.

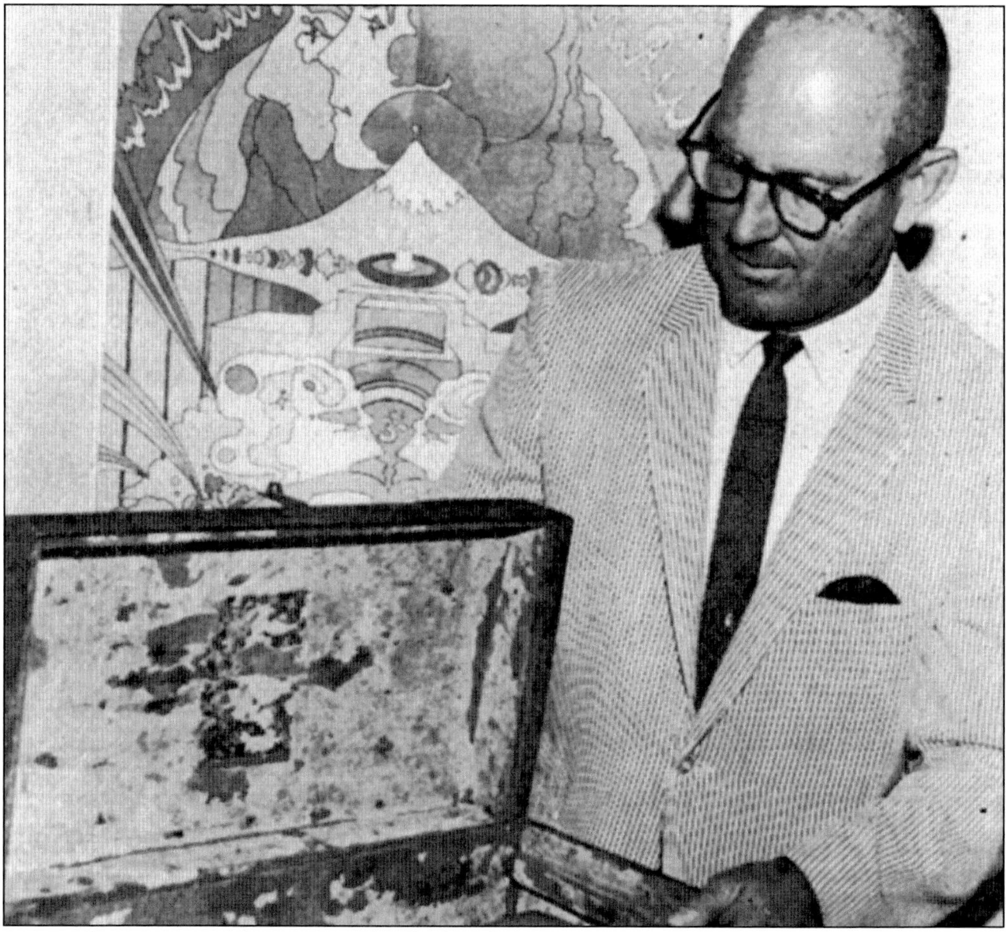

Mrs. Robert L. Dixon (Nancy Jane), who lived just north of Cocoa at City Point, was the first postmistress. Mail was brought down the St. Johns River and then overland to Nancy Jane's home. She stored the mail in a small trunk that served as the first post office. Some say she kept it under her bed. During an 1876 fire that destroyed her home and most everything in her vicinity, the mail and stamps were saved when her daughter waded out into the Indian River carrying the makeshift post office. Settlers could travel by sailboat to her home, pick up their mail, and deposit more for the next boat.

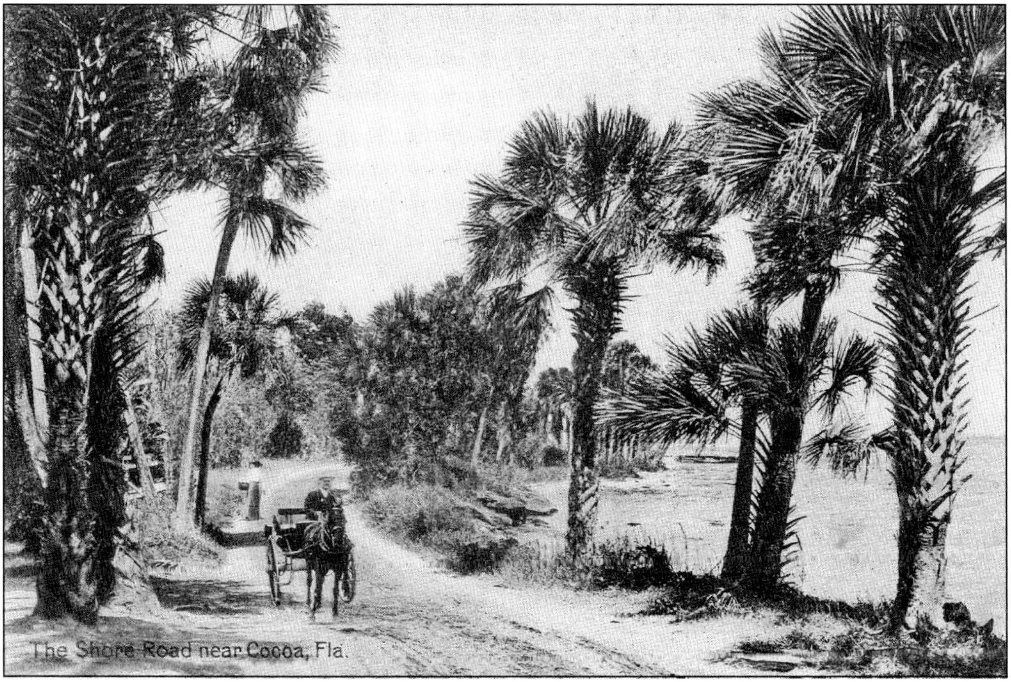

The River Road connecting Cocoa and Rockledge was originally a dirt Native American trail. Because it followed the Indian River shoreline, it was convenient for the early settlers who homesteaded there.

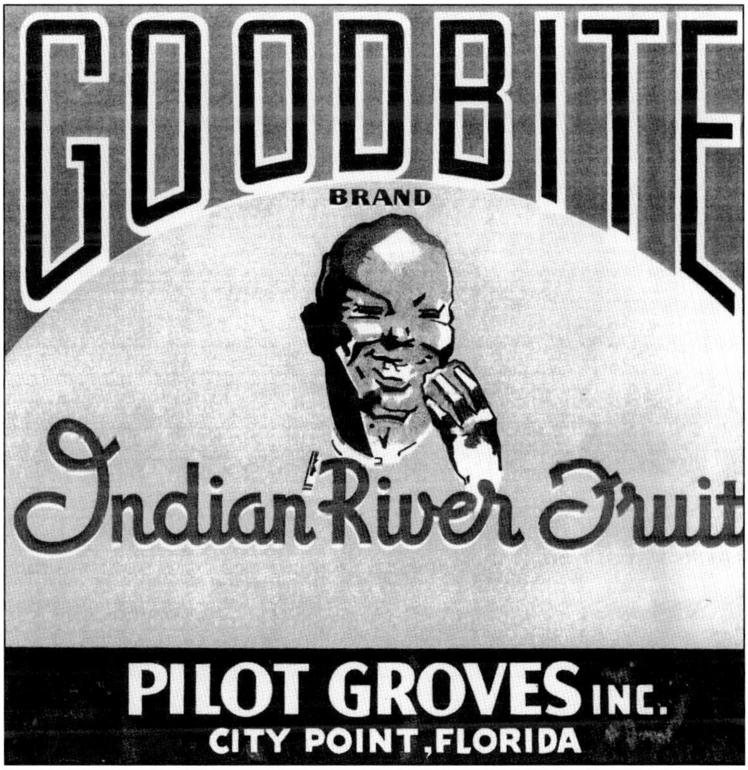

This label would be placed on the ends of citrus-fruit boxes awaiting shipment north. Pilot Groves was owned by the Pinkerton family.

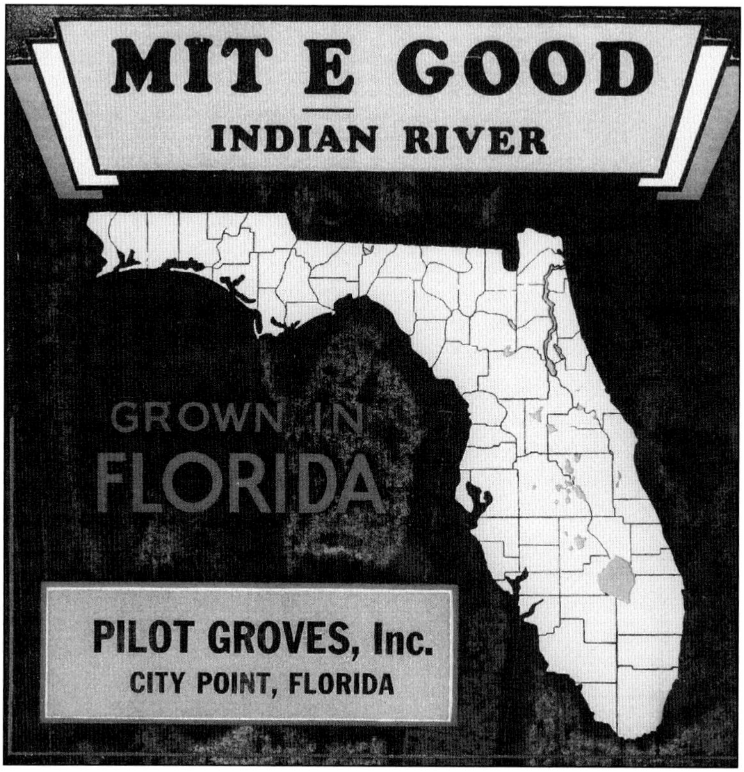

Mit E Good was another brand of Pilot Groves citrus. These labels were printed in vibrant hues—the more colorful the better.

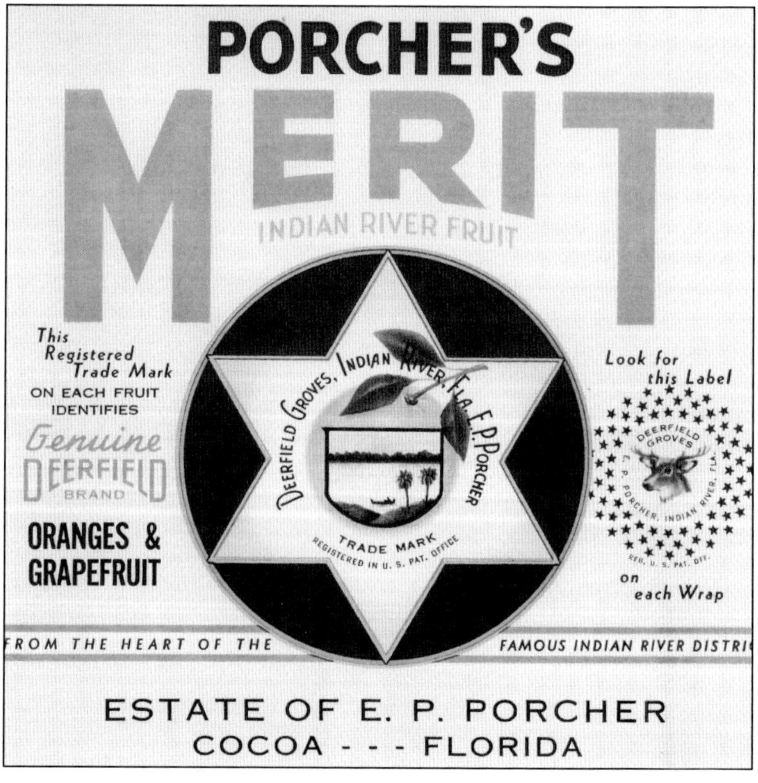

The E. P. Porcher estate's Merit brand was one of several citrus brands packed by the Porcher packinghouse, located over the river north of the Porcher House in Cocoa Village.

One

FRONTENAC TO PEACHTREE STREET

Frontenac is the farthest north of the small communities covered in this book. These small communities had their own identities, but Cocoa was the nearest large town where residents could shop for essentials such as drugs, hardware, and lumber.

Sharpes, a small village on the west bank of the Indian River, is the next community when traveling south. It had a post office served by boat until the Flagler Railroad was built approximately one mile west of the river. Continuing south, one approaches the City Point community. City Point was also situated on the river and included a post office and general store. Boats could dock at the back or, in the early days, the front of the general store, since most travel at the time was by boat.

The town of Cocoa is located south of City Point. Peachtree Street was chosen as the separation point for the communities, since it was the site of the Cocoa passenger railroad depot and is the dividing point for the town's north-south street numbering system.

BREVARD COUNTY DIRECTORY (1926-27) 21

FRONTENAC

On the main line of the F. E. C. Railway, 2 miles north of Sharpes, and also on the Dixie Highway. The nearest post office is Sharpes.

Atkinson Jas (Thilda) r E C Brinks
Beckham David C (Lina) section formn F E C Ry
Brinks Edw C (Martha A) dairy
Brinks Hazel r E C Birnks
*Brown Wardell (Jennie) lab
*Corens Wm (Mattie) lab
*Dawes Chas (Mary) lab
*Gibson Hiram lab
*Gray Chester (Rose) lab
*James Jas (Tommie) lab
McCarty Clarence r E C Brinks
*Nicholson Rose
Pickett Willie E (wid Edw) r A R Wilson
*Robertson Wiley (Maggie) lab
*Small Jos (Stewie) lab
*Taylor Jas lab r Hiram Gibson
Wilson Almeda (wid Albert S) r A R Wilson
Wilson A Ross gro and fill sta Dixie Hwy

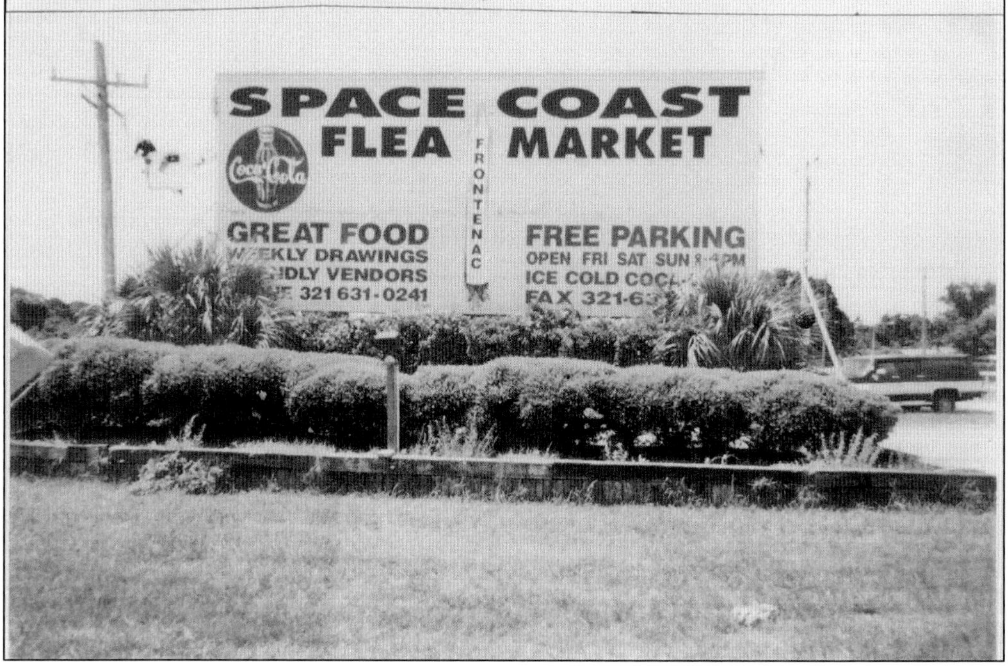

When Billy Wilson and Ralph Christian started a flea market in Frontenac, many people looked for the village on maps, to no avail. The map companies called the Cocoa Chamber of Commerce and Cocoa Post Office to find out where Frontenac was located so it could be added.

SHARPES

Located 6 miles north from the center of Cc on the main line of the F. E. C. Ry. and on the Dixie Highway, famous for its numerous ci groves. Mrs. Lydia N. Blackburn, acting postmas Sharpes Public School—Eloise Swinson, teacher

*Anderson Frank (Matilda) lab
Anthony W Earl (Iona; Brevard Ne-Hi Bottling
Ard Edwin J (Johanna) fruit grower r J D Schul
Arwood Jas C (Eliz) fruit grower
*Austin Saml cook T L Salter
Black Bernard real est r F H Black
Black Dorothea student r F H Black
Black Fred H (Addie) real est
Blackburn Anna r S W Blackburn
Blackburn Grover C (Lydia) formn A H Smith
Blackburn Lydia N Mrs asst postmaster
Blackburn Stanley W lab
Brevard Ne-Hi Bottle Co Sharpes bottle mfrs
Breavrd Ne-Hi Bottle Co Sharpes
Bright Side Inn W J Spafford prop
Carhart Norman chauf Mrs Ella Taylor
Carroll Alva E Mrs
Carroll John student r Mrs A E Carroll
Carroll Margt student r Mrs A E Carroll
Carroll N Ray (Lottie) fruit grower r Mrs A E roll
*Collins Nathan (Alice) lab
*Collins Neda r Nathan Collins
*Collins Thomas lab r Nathan Collins
Cooper Benj F student r Mrs A E Carroll
Cooper Elzey Mrs r Mrs A E Carroll
Cox Walter clk City Drug Store Cocoa
*Davis Jas lab
Eustace Edyth r H K Eustace
Eustace H Kaigh (Edyth) lecturer
Faber Barbara (wid Albert)
Faber Chas W gardener r Mrs Barbara Faber
Faber Geo B (Bertha) fruit grower
Faber Wm student r G B Faber
Foster Ellsworth carp A H Smith
*Gaines Henry lab Indian River Dairy Co
Grandview Place (Jos Tilley) furn rms
Hardee John R (Jewell; Brevard Ne-Hi Bottle C
Haskell John student r J R Hardee
Hidell Max (Florence; Poinsett Garage Cocoa Brentwood Heights
Hill Wm J (Nellie) fruit grower

Seen here is a listing of Sharpes residents from a 1926–1927 *Polk's Directory*. Since the U.S. Census provided a head count every 10 years, the area residents relied on city directories in the meantime.

SHARPES—Contd

Hoffman Hardy r Otto Hoffman

Hoffman Lydia r Otto Hoffman

Hoffmann Otto (Maria) genl contr h Brentwood Heights

Holmes Geo W (Gertrude) phys

*Howard Jacob (Hattie) lab

INDIAN RIVER DAIRY CO, T L Salter Mgr Wholesale and Retail Pure Milk, Cream, Buttermilk, Butter, Eggs and Milk Fed Poultry, A Modern Dairy Plant Using and Supplying The Products From Its Own Herds

Jenkins Chas R (Emma V; Sharpes Grocery Co)

Jenkins Chas R jr (Charlotte; Sharpes Grocery Co) r C R Jenkins

Klein Gus A fruit grower

*Littlejohn Robt lab Indian River Dairy Co

Lynch Frank K (Kath) fruit grower

Mack Chas W (Lena) state bee inspr

Mack Paul C student r C W Mack

Massey Edw milker Indian River Dairy Co

Massey Rufus milker Indian River Dairy Co

Massey Thos r T L Salter

*Moore Geo (Carrie) lab

*Moore Orluster lab r Geo Moore

Nichols Alice W (wid Chas L)

Nichols Bruce W marine eng r W A Spiller

Nichols Grace A clk Am Ry Exp Co r W A Spiller

Nichols John G (Mary)

Nichols Porter B (Bertha) carp

*Norman Robt lab

Nyman John A (Alma) fruit grower

O'Brien Cath Mrs r F K Lynch

Ollif Lee F student r Mrs W F Ollif

Ollif Williette F (wid Lee)

Petty John

Peckinpaugh Wm

Pierson Floyd H student r J R Pierson

Seen here is a listing of Sharpes residents from a 1926–1927 directory. Many small communities were scattered nearby so that it was helpful to be able to tell where a particular friend of family lived by consulting the directory.

Pierson Joshua R (Ora) fruit grower
Pinkerton Sherwood fruit grower
*Pitman Alonzo lab
*Pollock Alex (Elisha) lab
*Pollock Mattie H r Alex Pollock
*Pollock Rosa L r Alex Pollock
Post Office Mrs Lydia N Blackburn asst postmaster
Ritter Geo S (Cath) fruit grower
*Robinson Zeke (Barbara) lab
SALTER T LLOYD, Mgr Indian River Dairy Co
Schultz Julius D fruit grower
Sharpes Grocery Co (C R Jenkins, C R Jenkins jr) genl mdse
Sharpes Public School Eloise Swinson tchr
Sheets Thos J (Lucy) carp
*Sherman Edw (Nellie) lab
Shippee Wm A r Ellsworth Foster
Smith Norman D (Nellie) carp r W J Hill
Spafford Alma student r W J Spafford
Spafford Edith student r W J Spafford
Spafford Wm J (Lyda; Bright-Side Inn)
*Spikes Henry (Cath) lab
Spiller Wm A (Ada) fruit grower
Swinson Edw hlpr Indian River Dairy Co
Swinson Eloise tchr Sharpes Public School r J I Swinson
Swinson Emery U S Army r J I Swinson
Swinson Jas I (Emma) mail carrier
Swinson Ruth student r J I Swinson
Taylor Ella (wid T J)
Thomas Nell C (wid G F)
Thomas Verna student r Mrs N C Thomas
Thompson Josiah (Cecile) real est
Tilley Aaron W (Minnie) carp
Tilley Esther r Jos Tilley
Tilley Jos (Grandview Place) carp
Tilley Susan M r Jos Tilley
*Ulmer Adam lab r Geo Moore
Watkins Elvira Mrs tchr r W A Spiller
Watkins Paul C real est r W A Spiller
Windell Arth (Minnie) genl contr
Yoerk Louis H

Seen here is a listing of Sharpes residents from a 1926–1927 directory. The *Polk Directory* still provides information to the local residents and businesses.

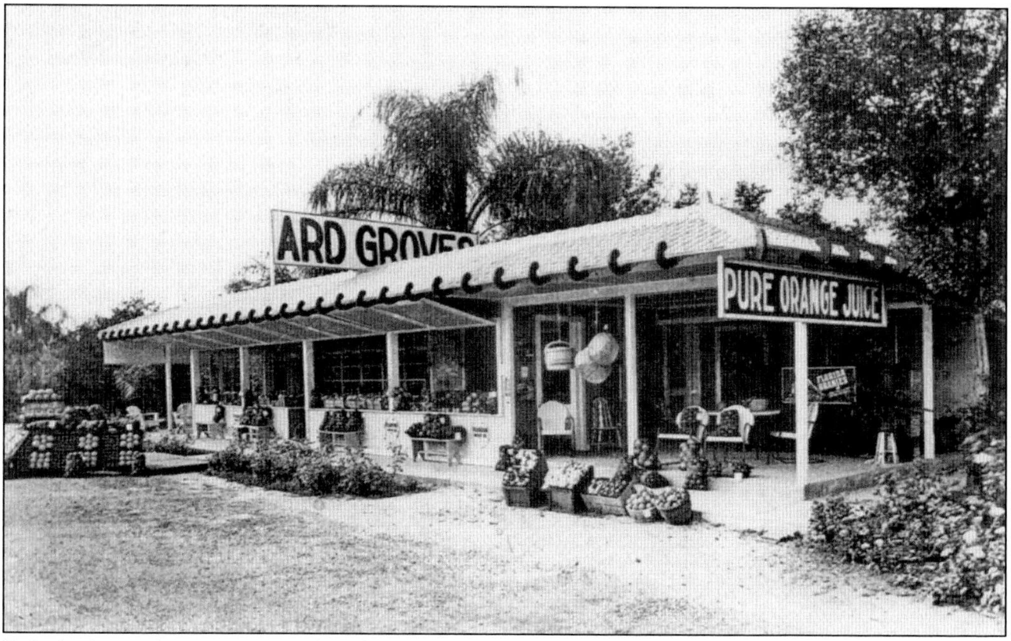

E. J. Ard was the proprietor of Ard Groves, located on U.S. Route 1 in North Cocoa. The Ard family specialized in growing, selling, packing, and shipping the famous Indian River tree-ripened fruit—oranges, grapefruits, and tangerines. Many tourists gathered at fruit stands such as this to compare citrus from other areas with Indian River varieties. When the Indian River varieties proved superior, they asked the stand owners to ship orders north to their friends and neighbors.

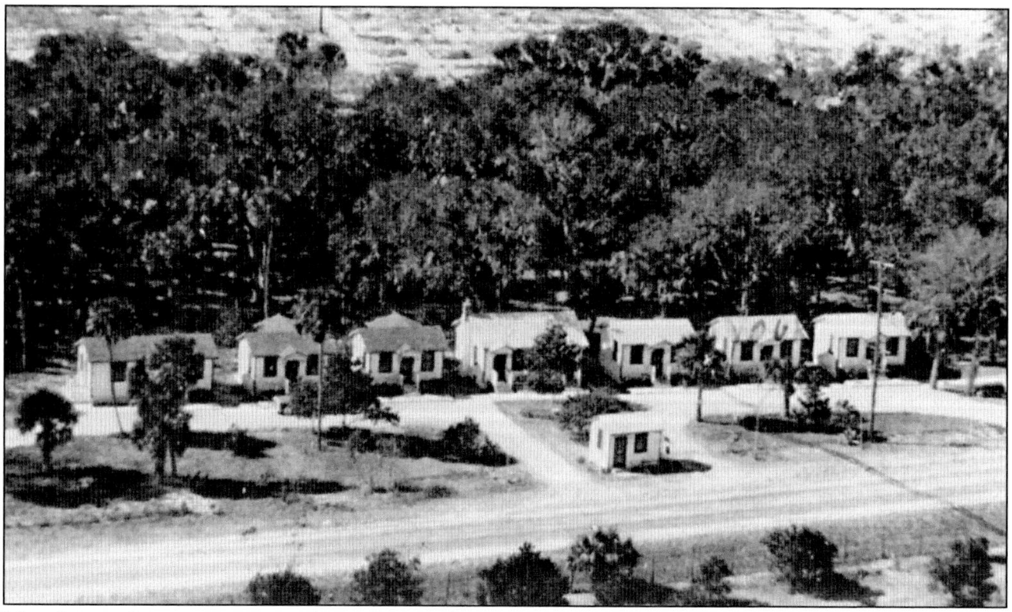

New Jersey Court was situated on the northwest corner of U.S. Route 1 and Cross Road. It was one of the old-style tourist courts for early automobile tourists in Florida.

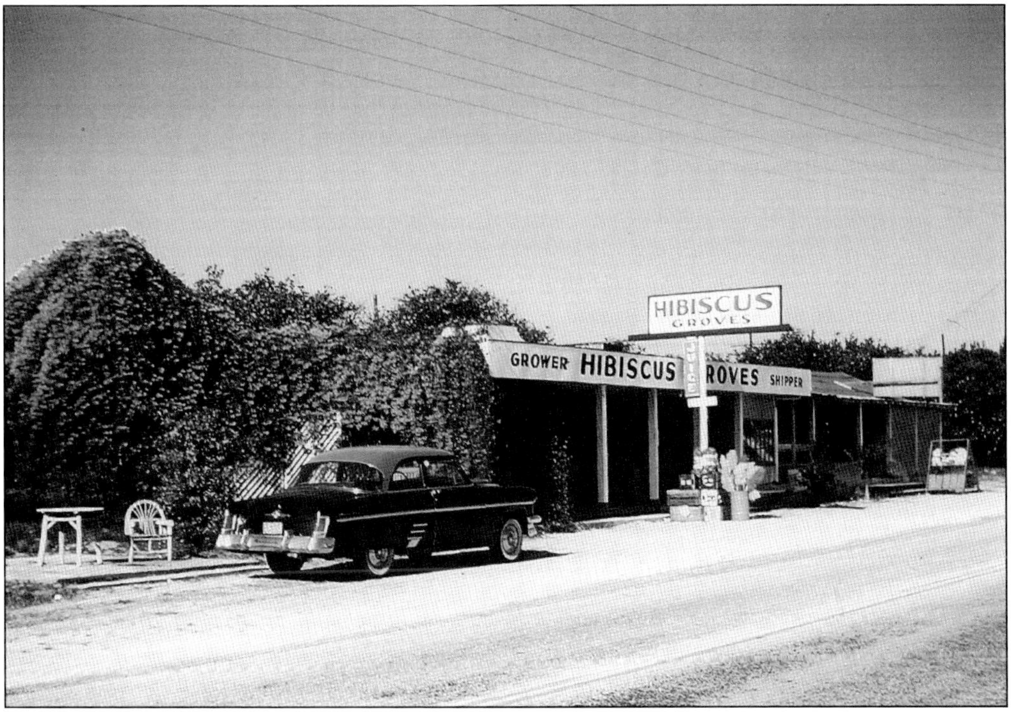

Hibiscus Grove, located at the end of Beverly Road in North Cocoa, was one of many fruit stands along U.S. Route 1. The blooming vine covering the end of the building is called flame vine.

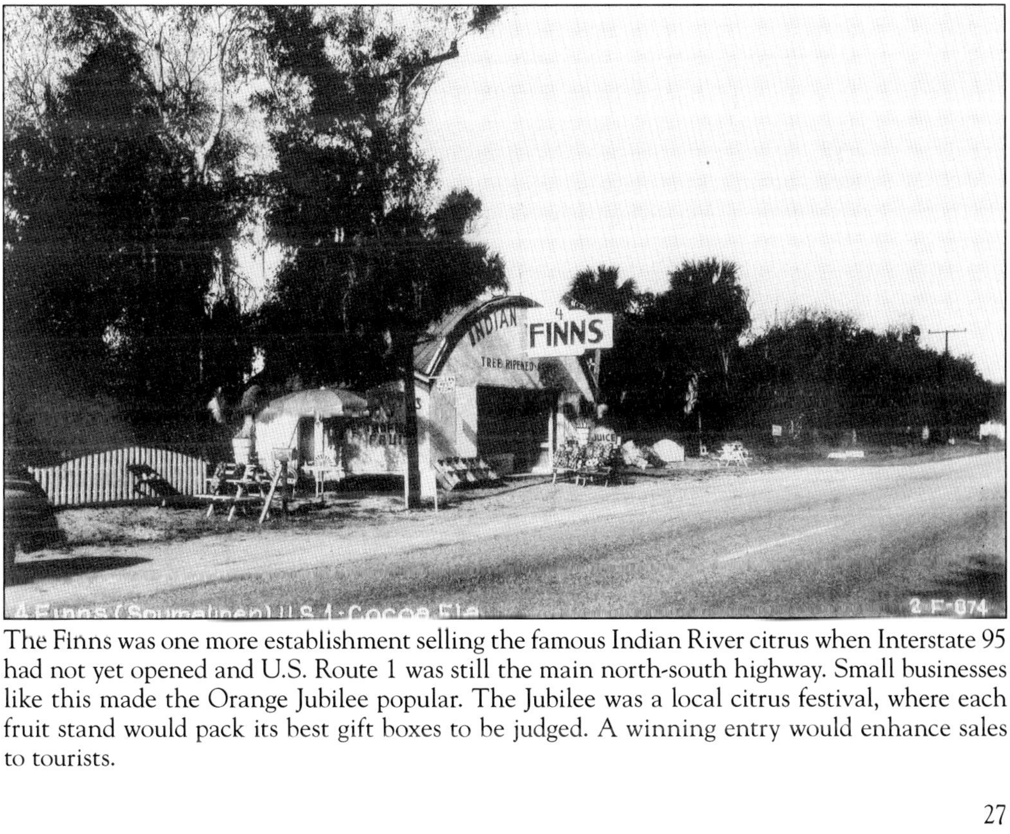

The Finns was one more establishment selling the famous Indian River citrus when Interstate 95 had not yet opened and U.S. Route 1 was still the main north-south highway. Small businesses like this made the Orange Jubilee popular. The Jubilee was a local citrus festival, where each fruit stand would pack its best gift boxes to be judged. A winning entry would enhance sales to tourists.

CITY POINT

On the main line of the F. E. C. Railway and on the new Dixie Highway, adjoining the Cocoa city limits to the north. The industries are fruit growing and fishing. Mrs. Anna M. Abney postmaster. City Point Community Church; *A. M. E. Church, Rev. D. J. Gaynor pastor; *Mt. Carmel Baptist Church, Rev. J. W. Driskel pastor.

*A M E Church Rev D J Gaynor pastor
Abney Anna M (wid R W) postmaster
Abney Bros (L P and R W) genl mdse
Abney Lawrence R (Abney Bros) r Mrs Anna M Abney
Abney Robt W (Abney Bros) r Mrs Anna M Abney
Arwood J C fruit grower
*Betts Benj lab r Chas Betts
*Betts Chas (Bessie) lab
*Betts John lab r Chas Betts
*Betts Wm lab r Chas Betts
Bovard Geo fruit grower
Bovard Orr B fruit grower
*Butler Simon (Mabel) lab
Chancey John J carp
Chancey S C Mrs r J J Chancey
City Point Community Church
*Clark Geo (Pauline) lab r Geo Miller
*Collins Albert r Thos Collins
*Collins Aneta r Thos Collins
*Collins Thos (Alice) lab

CITY POINT—Contd
Cox Geo r W T Cox
Cox W T fruit grower
Cox Walter r W T Cox
Curran John T farmer
Dixon A L
Dixon Adam S
Dixon R Leonard
Dixon Zack
Drinkwater A C fruit grower
*Driskel J W Rev pastor Mt Carmel Baptist Church
Fox Ralph (Mattie) lab r R A Tillis
*Gaynor D J Rev pastor A M E Church
Graham Jessie
Hendry Ewart chiropractor r Snell Hendry
Hendry Harold florist r Snell Hendry
Hendry Snell florist
HIDELL F E (Florence; Poinsett Garage, Cocoa, Fla), h Brentwood Heights P O City Point, Fla

Seen here is a listing of City Point residents from a 1926–1927 directory. Not only were the names of residents and their occupations recorded, but the city dignitaries were also noted.

Houton Edith r N J Ribson
Hub's Inn (M J and Mrs N R Lynch) restr
*Johnson Kylo (Ellen) lab
Leverette Thos mech Williams Garage r John Williams
*Lindsey Frank (Alice)
Lynch Matthew J (Nellie R; Hub's Inn)
*McDonald David (Violet) lab
*Miller Geo (Grace) lab
*Miller Loomis (Reta) lab
*Moore Geo (Mattie) lab
*Mt Carmel Baptist Church Rev J W Driskel pastor
*Norman Robt gro
Nyman John A fruit grower
Post Office Mrs Anna M Abney postmaster
Powell Noah mech Williams Garage r John Willia
Ribson Nicholas J florist
Robins John A clk Cocoa P O
*Robinson Jacob (Stella) lab
*Robinson Jennie r Peter Robinson

---

*Robinson Peter (Hattie) lab
*Ross Edw (Bertha) lab
Royal Hulit waitress Hub's Inn r M S Lynch
Seely D M (Anna) fruit grower
Shailer Dewight (Florence) mech Williams Gar res Cocoa Fla
SMITH CHAS D (Lucy), V-Pres Brevard Cou Bank & Trust Co
*Smith Robt lab r Chas Betts
Stone Wm Prof (Flora)
*Summers Chas (Cummings) lab
*Summers Lottie lndrs r Chas Summers
Swinson Everett E (Jessie) fruit grower
Swinson Saml student r E E Swinson
*Thompson Wm (Ella) lab
Tillis R Arminios (Arline) section formn F E C
Townsend Eloise student r W O Townsend
Townsend Lloyd student r W O Townsend
Townsend Olive student r W O Townsend

Townsend Wm O (Laurie) fruit grower
*Tysinger Ernest lab r Hamp Tysinger
*Tysinger Hamp (Josephine) lab
*Tysinger Precious lab r Hamp Tysinger
Waite Geo W fruit grower
Williams Chas E garage and fill sta r Hub Willia
Williams Hub (Nellie M) whol and ret fish
Williams John mech Williams Garage
*Williams Lucy cook Hub's Inn
*Williams Theo cook Hub's Inn r Lucy Williams
*Young Alonzo (Ida) lab

Seen here is a listing of City Point residents from the 1926–1927 *Polk Directory*.

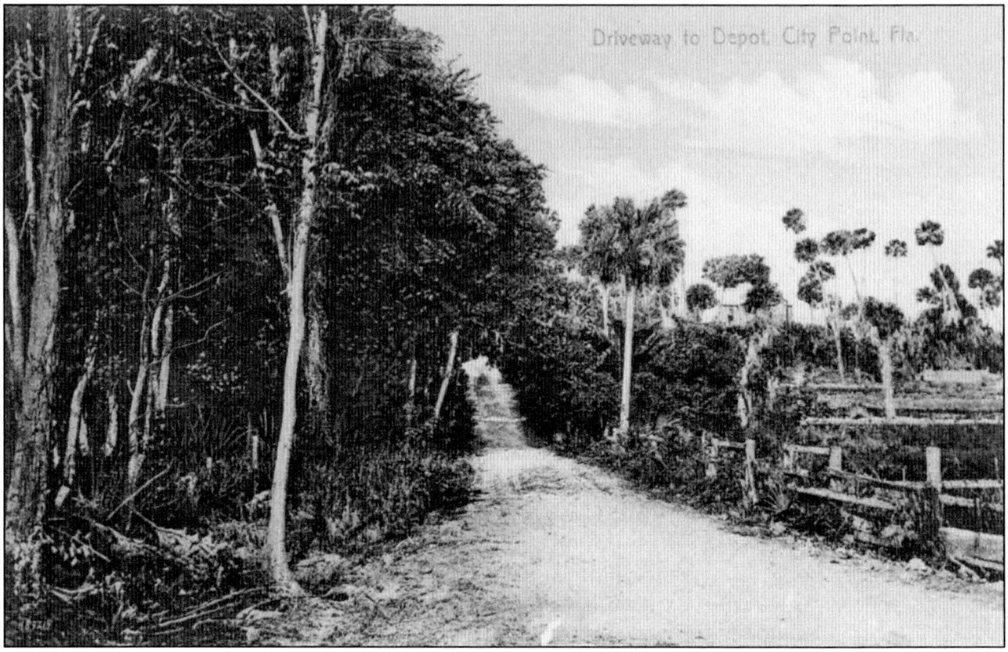

This postcard view depicts City Point Road, *c.* 1900.

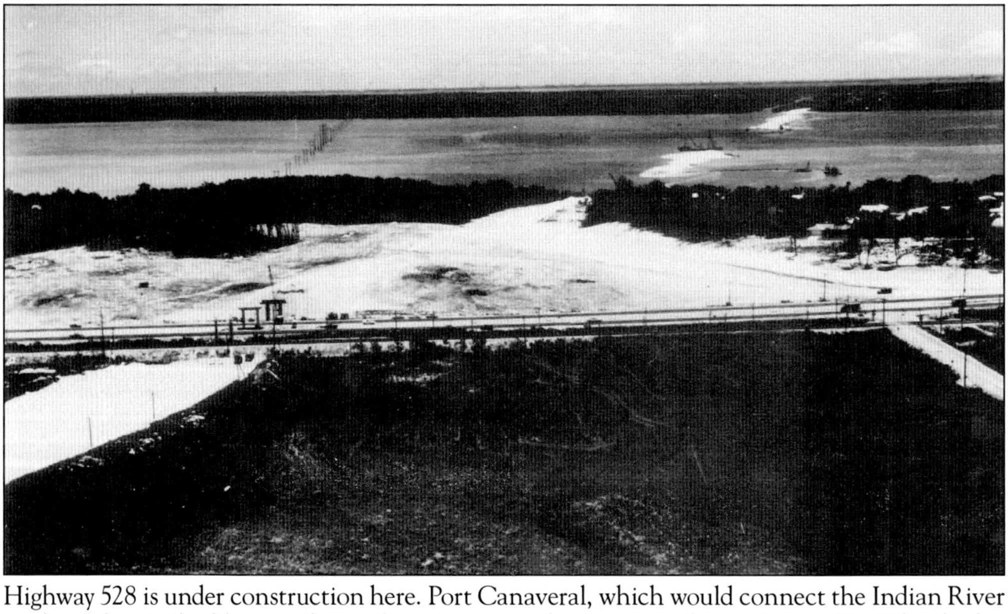
Highway 528 is under construction here. Port Canaveral, which would connect the Indian River to the Atlantic, had been a dream for many years, but was now becoming reality. The dredge started in the inland-waterway Indian River and cut across Merritt Island, placing the dirt for a road as shown. The Barge Canal is visible to the left of the white dirt in the upper portion of the image.

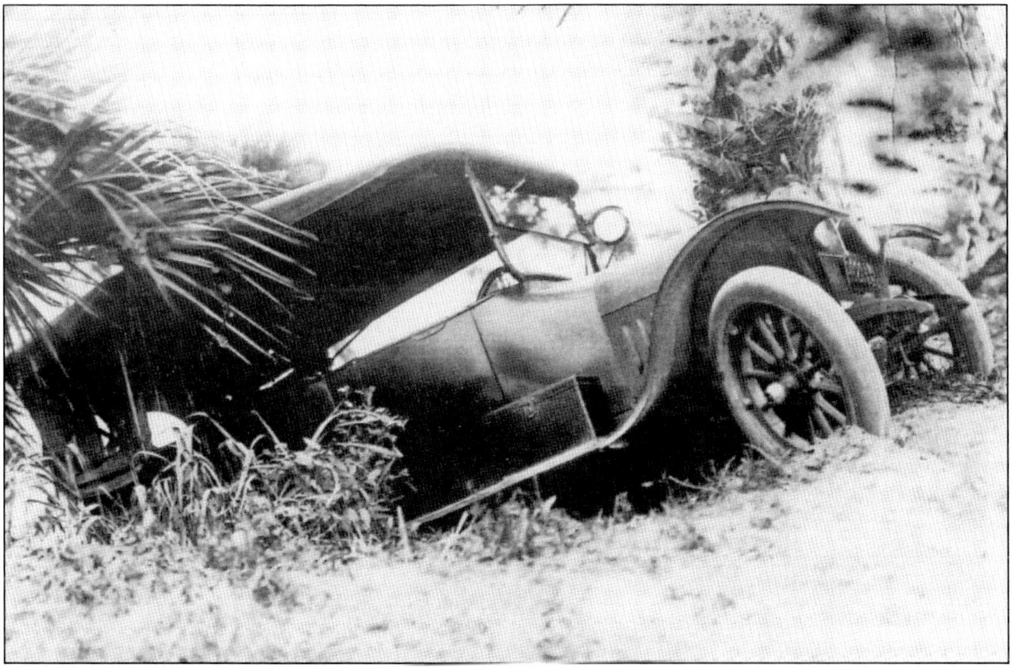

This photograph was taken in 1919. The car was parked in the driveway of the Packard home. Its brakes did not hold, and it rolled back across the road and down the bank.

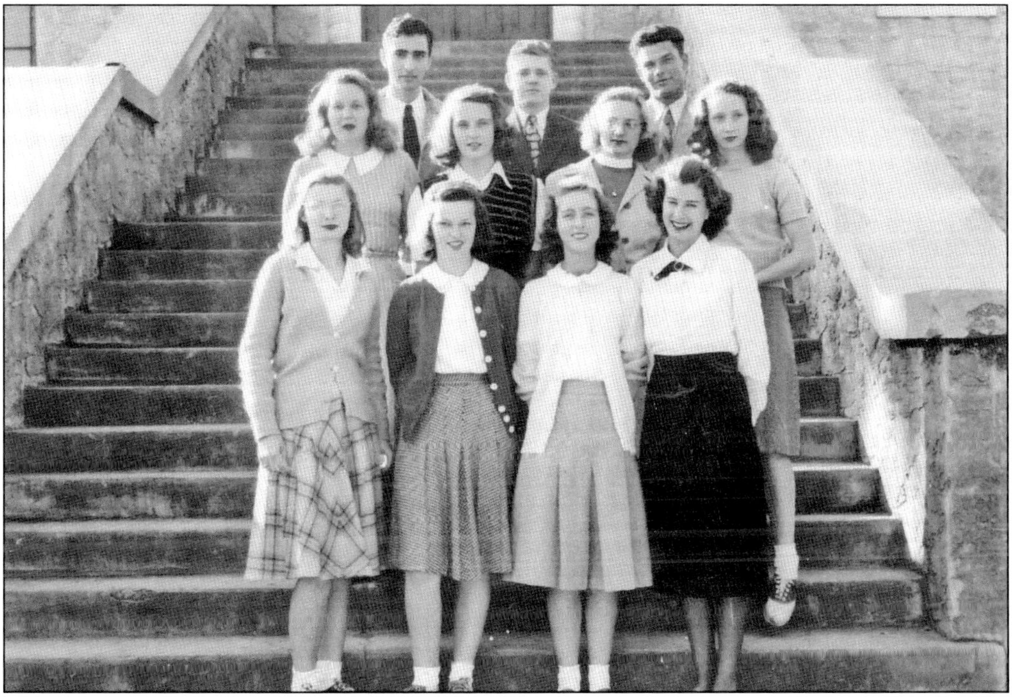

Posing for a portrait is the Cocoa High *Tiger* newspaper staff for the school year 1947–1948. Pictured from left to right are the following: (first row) Sally Hare, Patricia Fenner, Norma Jean Leighty, and Billie Jean Hill; (second row) Mary Sue Poole, June Gettings, Kaye Crisman, and Betty Jean Parker; (third row) Bill Bailey, Ray Dewey, and Murray Gay.

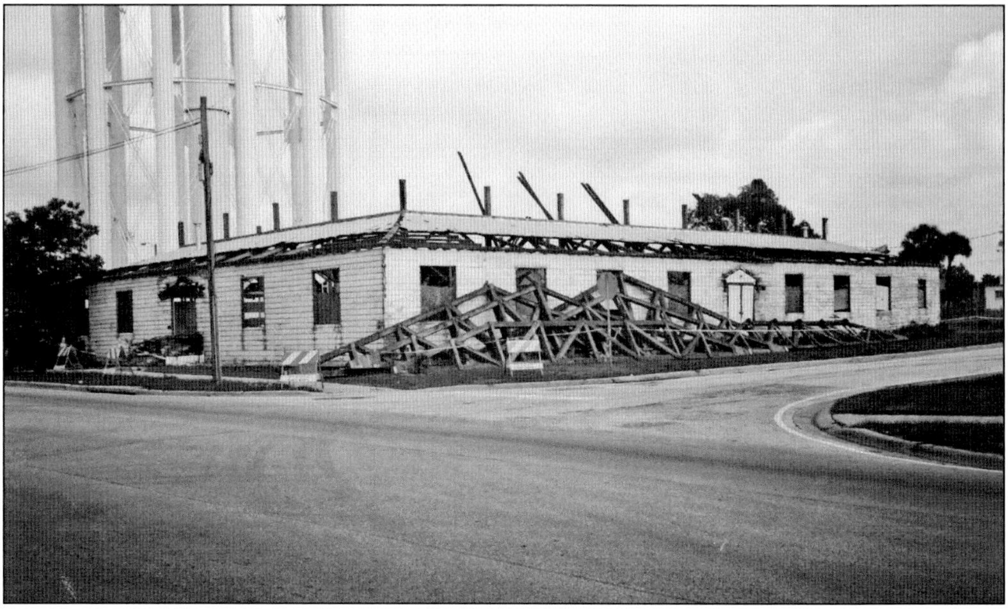

Another landmark was demolished when the building on the corner of Peachtree and First Streets outlived its usefulness. Erected by the Works Progress Administration in the mid-1930s, it served Cocoa High as a gymnasium and local civic clubs as headquarters. When Tex Beneke brought his band to town, it became a dance floor for the Orange Jubilee Ball. The building also housed fruit displays and served the youth as a gathering place called the Tiger Den.

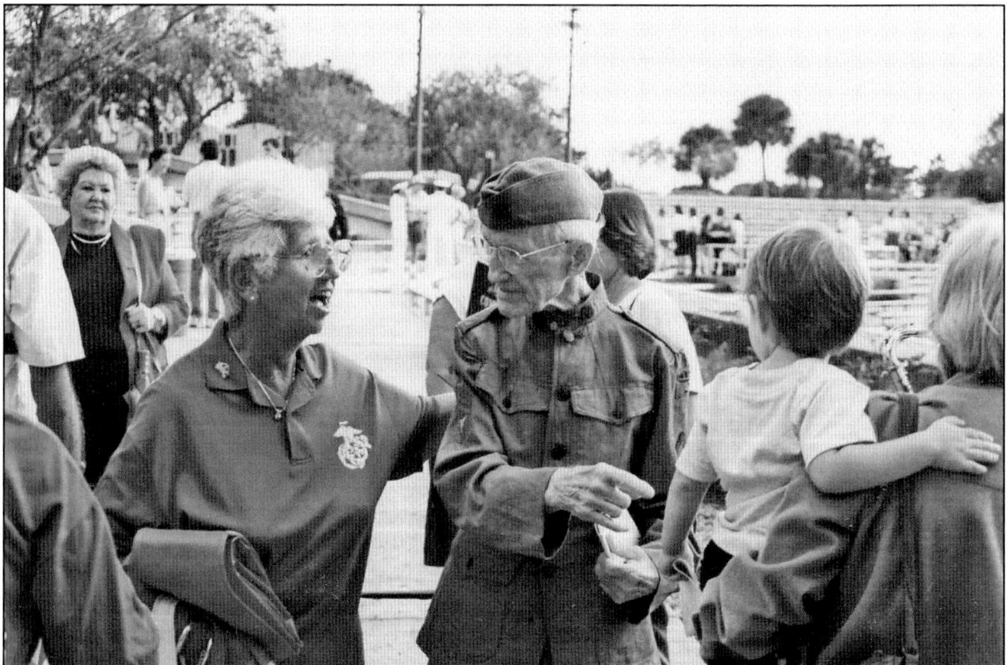

Rev. Leonard Vanderwater, onetime pastor of the Cocoa United Methodist Church, attends the 1995 Veterans Day celebration at Brevard Community College, Cocoa Campus, wearing his World War I uniform.

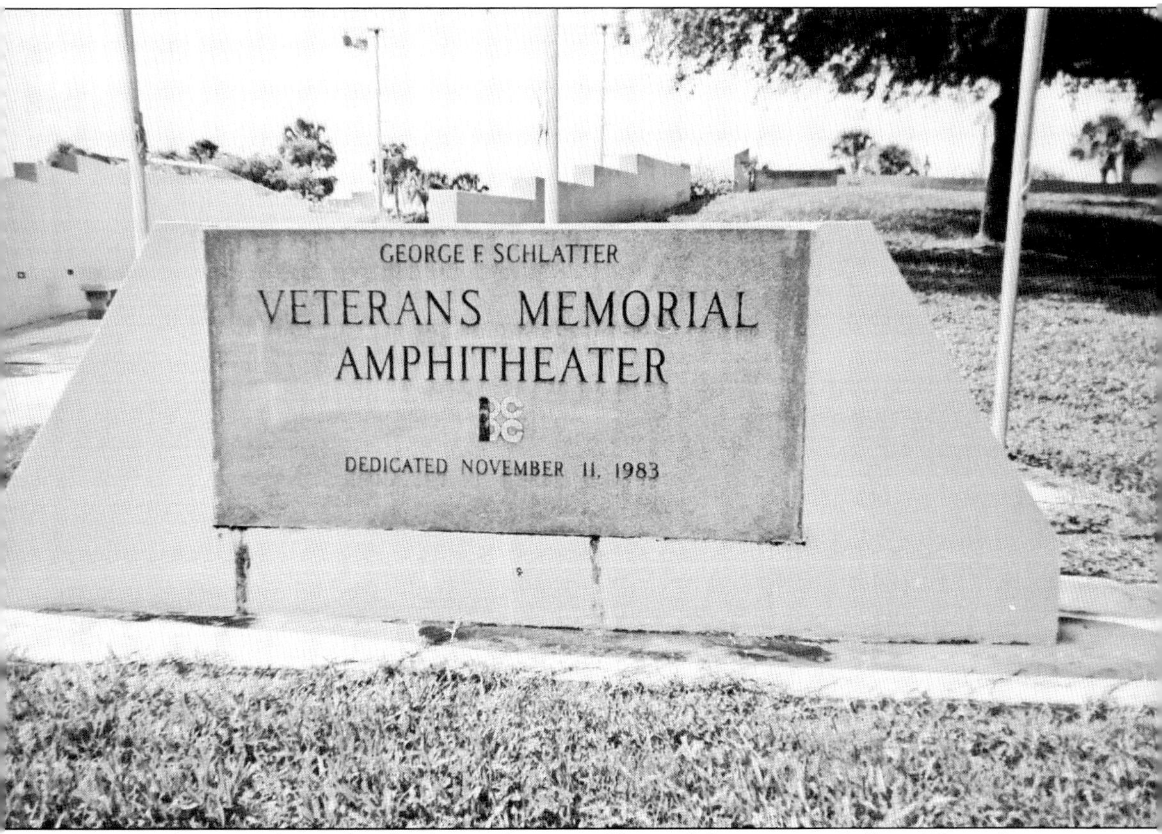

The Wall of Honor is located at the Cocoa Campus of Brevard Community College. The military home of record is here in Brevard County. Those listed on the wall made the ultimate sacrifice for their nation and their community as protectors of our freedom.

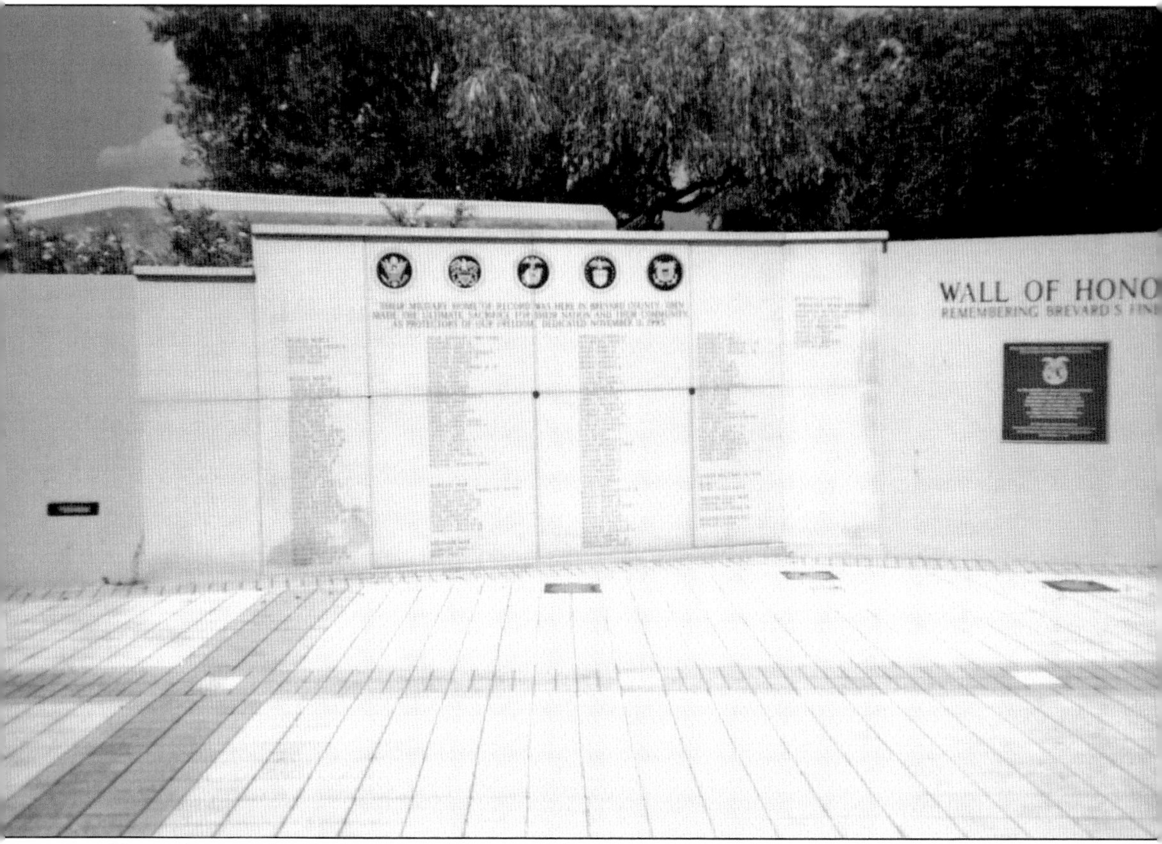

Shown here is the War Memorial at Brevard Community College (BBC).

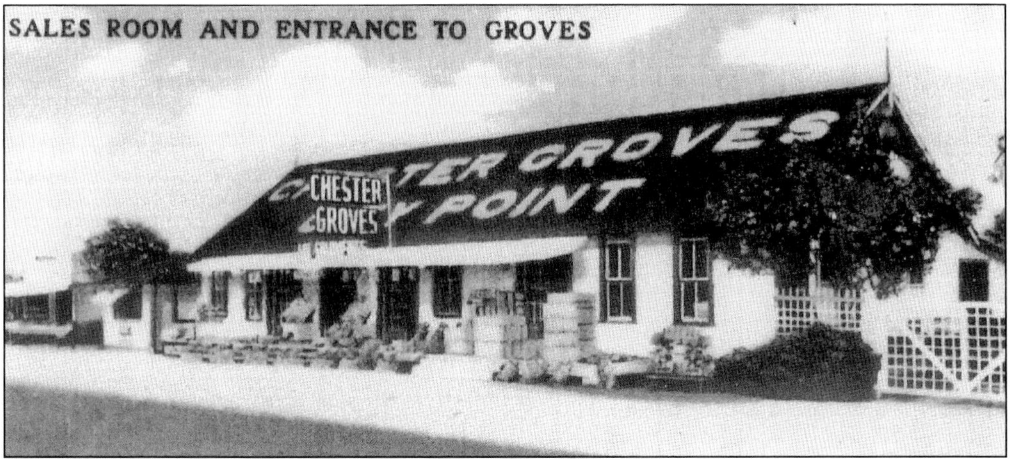

Chester Groves was one of the larger, private-order citrus shippers in the area. Thanksgiving and Christmas were the peaks of the season for shipping private orders. Employees would work late into the night prior to the holidays, processing the fruit for shipment.

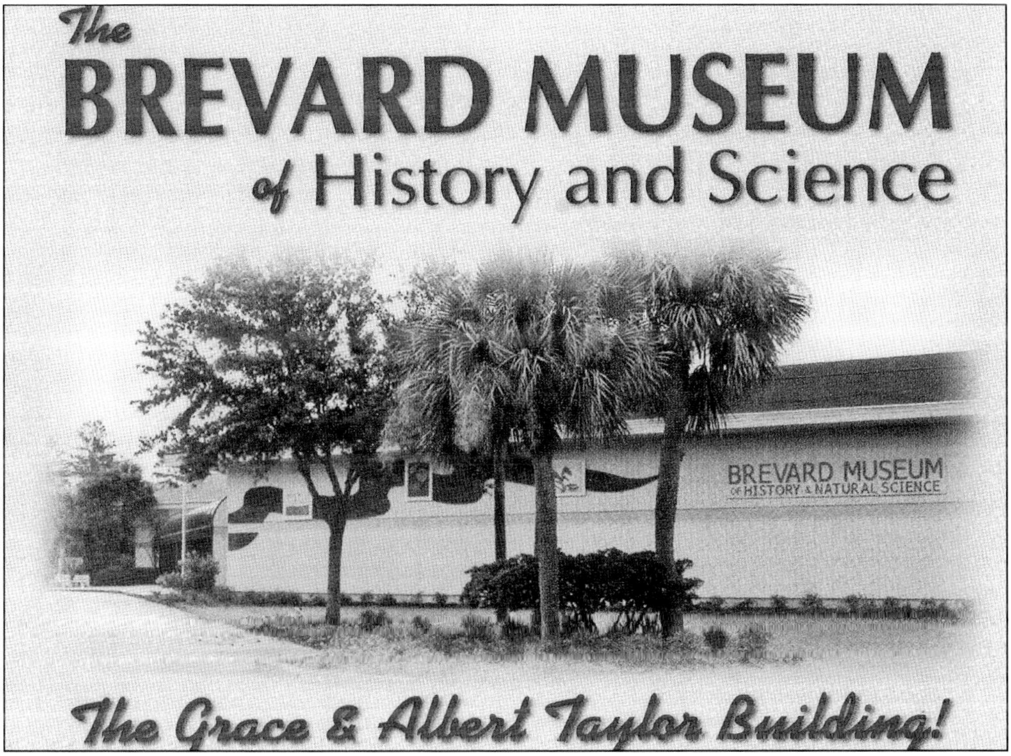

Albert Armer Taylor and his second wife, Grace Webster Taylor, were born in New York and Maine, respectively, but they both left a lasting impression on Cocoa and Rockledge. They had real estate interest in Cocoa, Merritt Island, Cocoa Beach, Vero Beach, and West Palm Beach, but their home was listed as 420 Delannoy Avenue. Upon their deaths, the Taylors left two public parks to area residents—one on the three-acre site of the former Taylor home on Delannoy and Harrison Streets in Cocoa, and the second on land surrounding the Taylor mausoleum in Rockledge. A large bequest financed the construction of the Taylor Wing of the Brevard Museum of History and Science on Michigan Avenue in Cocoa.

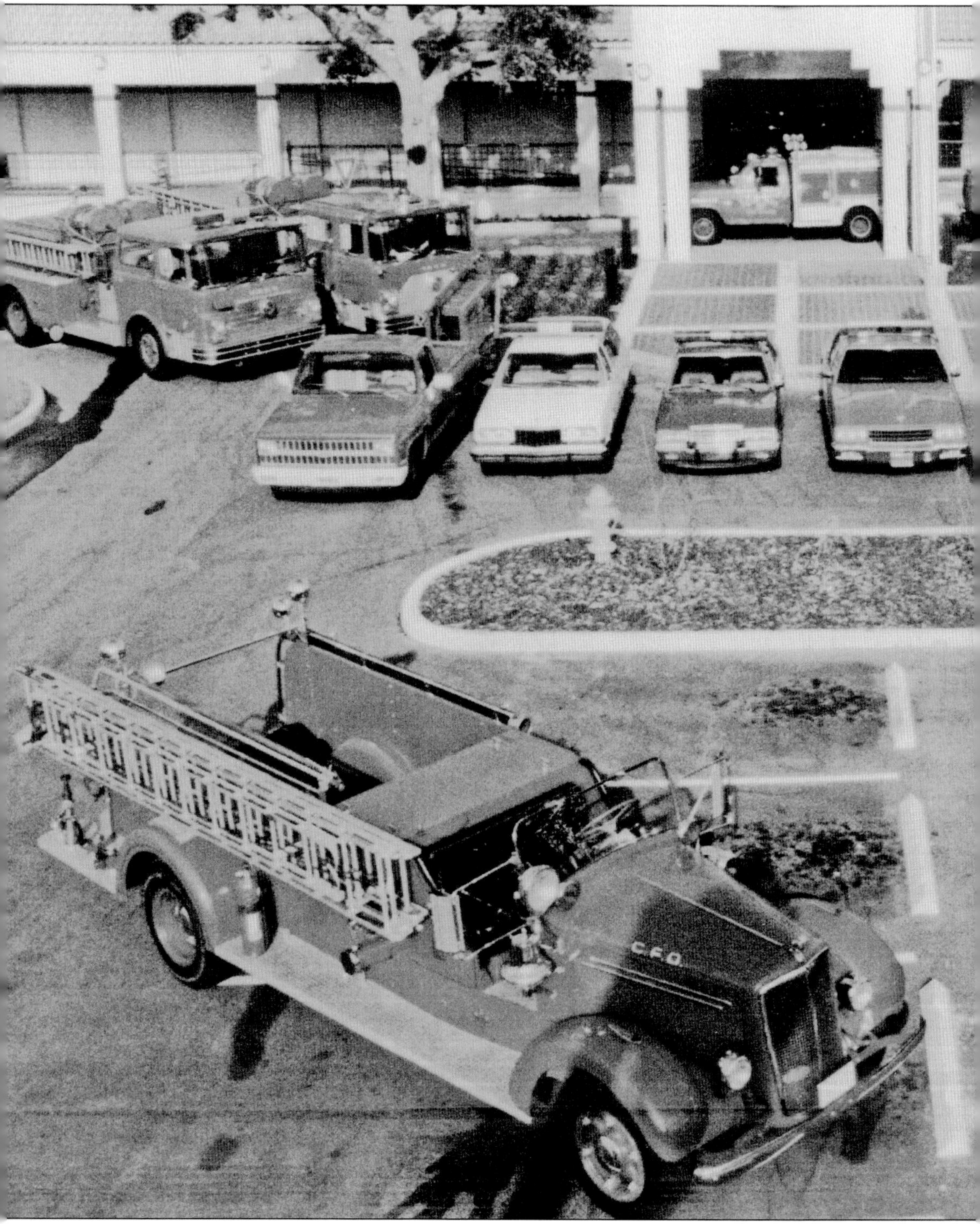

Coca's fire trucks are pictured on display in front of Cocoa's Central Brevard Library and Reference Center. The building was constructed by the *Cocoa Tribune*. After the *Tribune* was sold to the Gannett Corporation, additions were made and the *Florida Today* newspaper was started. When

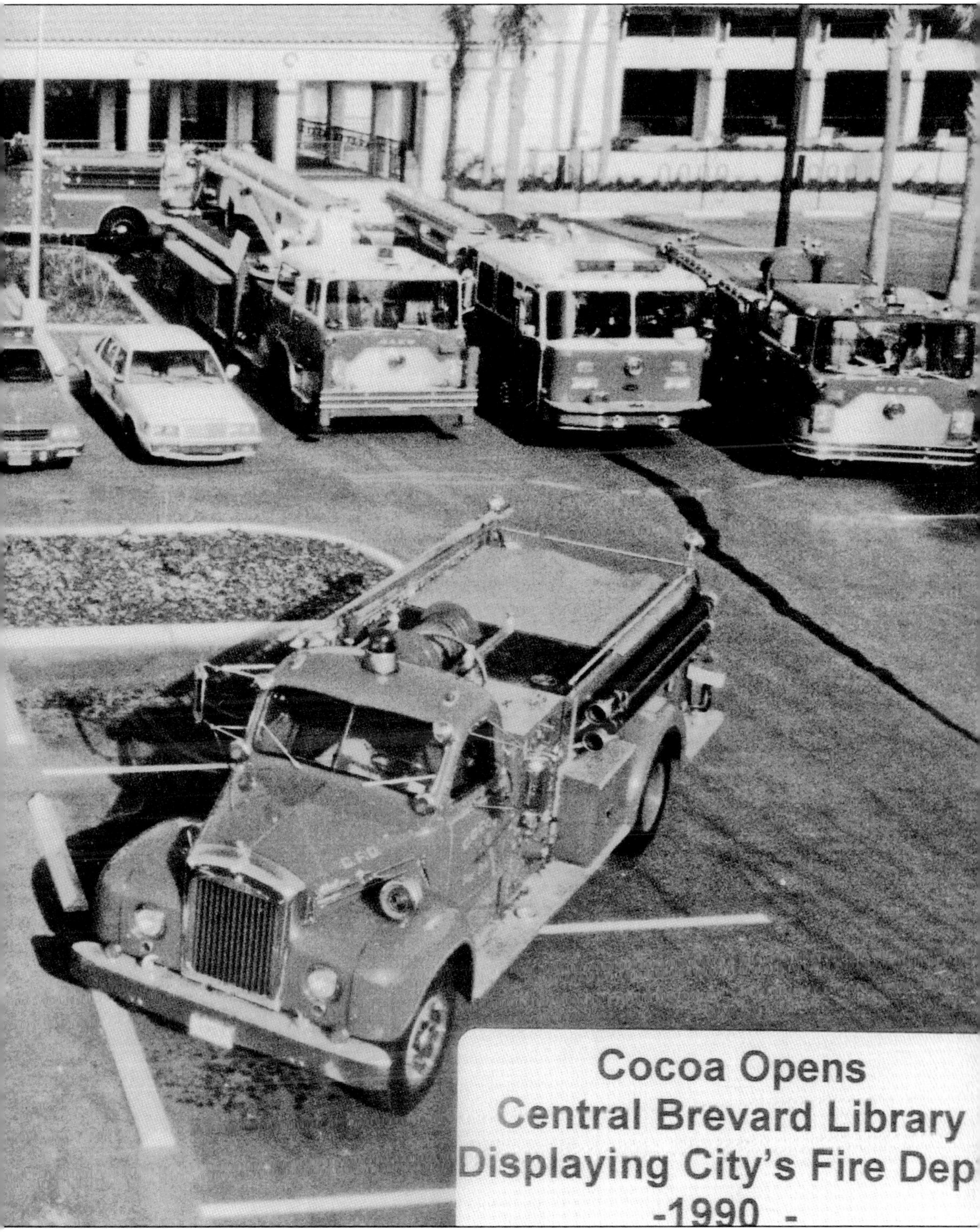

Gannett outgrew the location, Brevard County bought the property and remodeled it for a library in 1990.

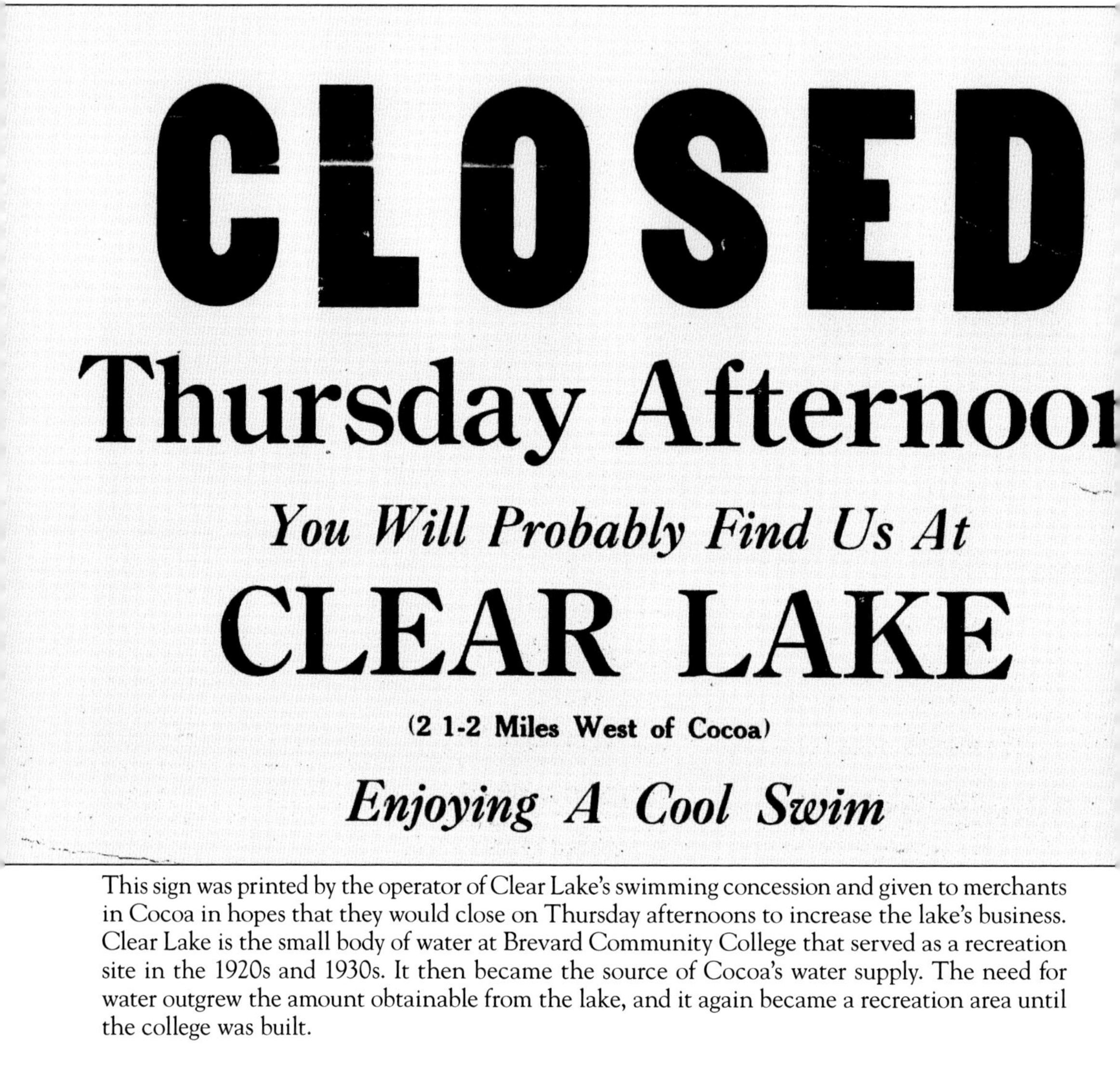

This sign was printed by the operator of Clear Lake's swimming concession and given to merchants in Cocoa in hopes that they would close on Thursday afternoons to increase the lake's business. Clear Lake is the small body of water at Brevard Community College that served as a recreation site in the 1920s and 1930s. It then became the source of Cocoa's water supply. The need for water outgrew the amount obtainable from the lake, and it again became a recreation area until the college was built.

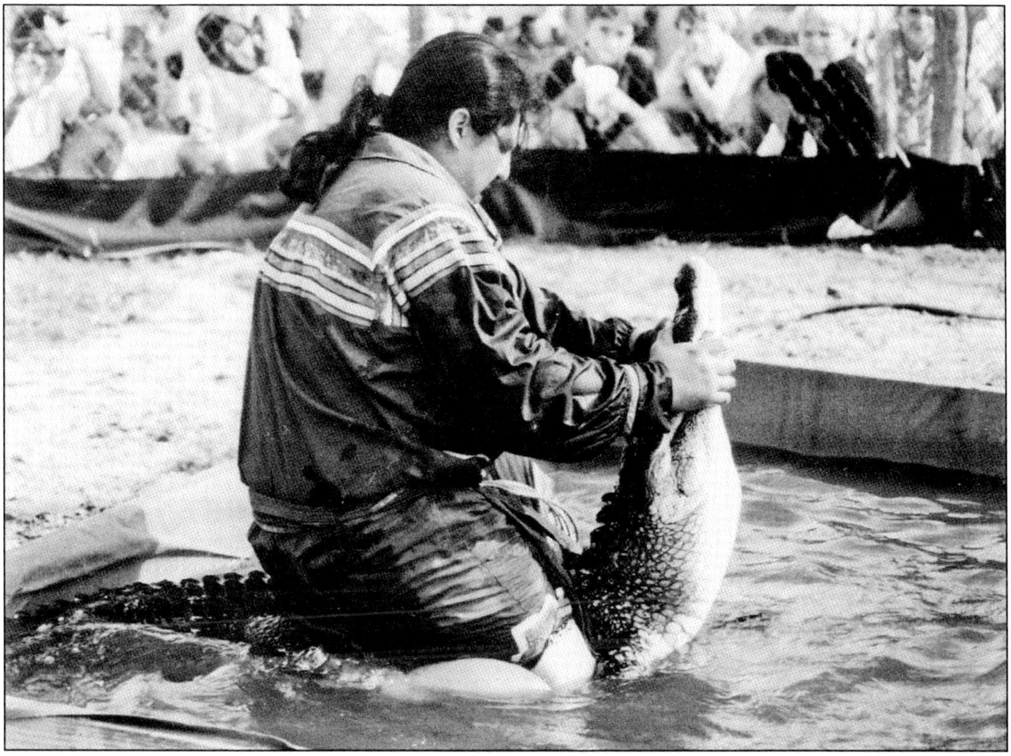

Patrick Smith, a Merritt Island Nobel Prize–nominated author, made friends with the Seminole Indians while writing his novels based on tribal life. He promoted the Brevard Junior College by hosting a festival with the Native Americans, who traveled to the Cocoa campus for two days. The Seminoles cooked their food, sold native dress and jewelry, and sang and danced to tribal music. They also demonstrated alligator wrestling and offered airboat rides on Clear Lake.

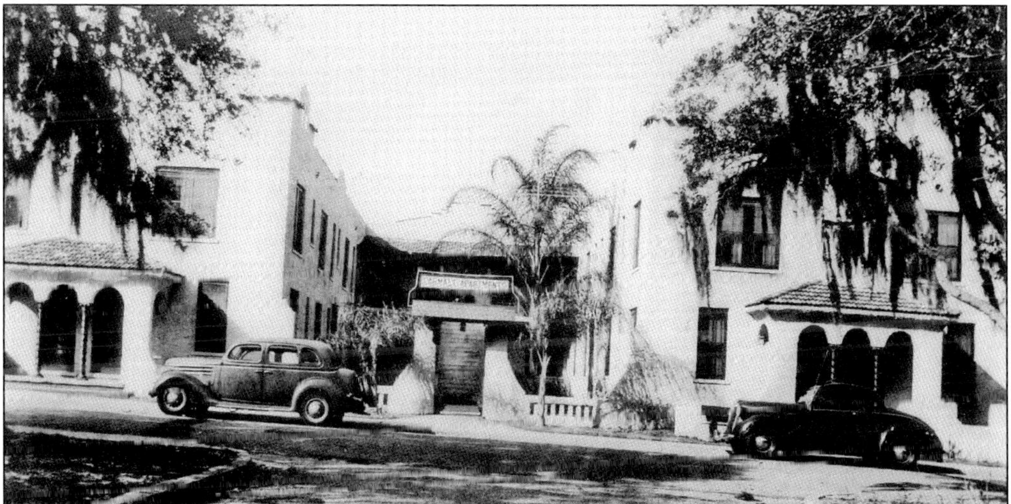

The Carmalt Apartments were built in the late 1920s, during the Florida land boom. Because of poor maintenance in the 1990s, the place was run down, but new owners repaired and upgraded it, changed the name to Cara Bella, and continued to rent the units as apartments.

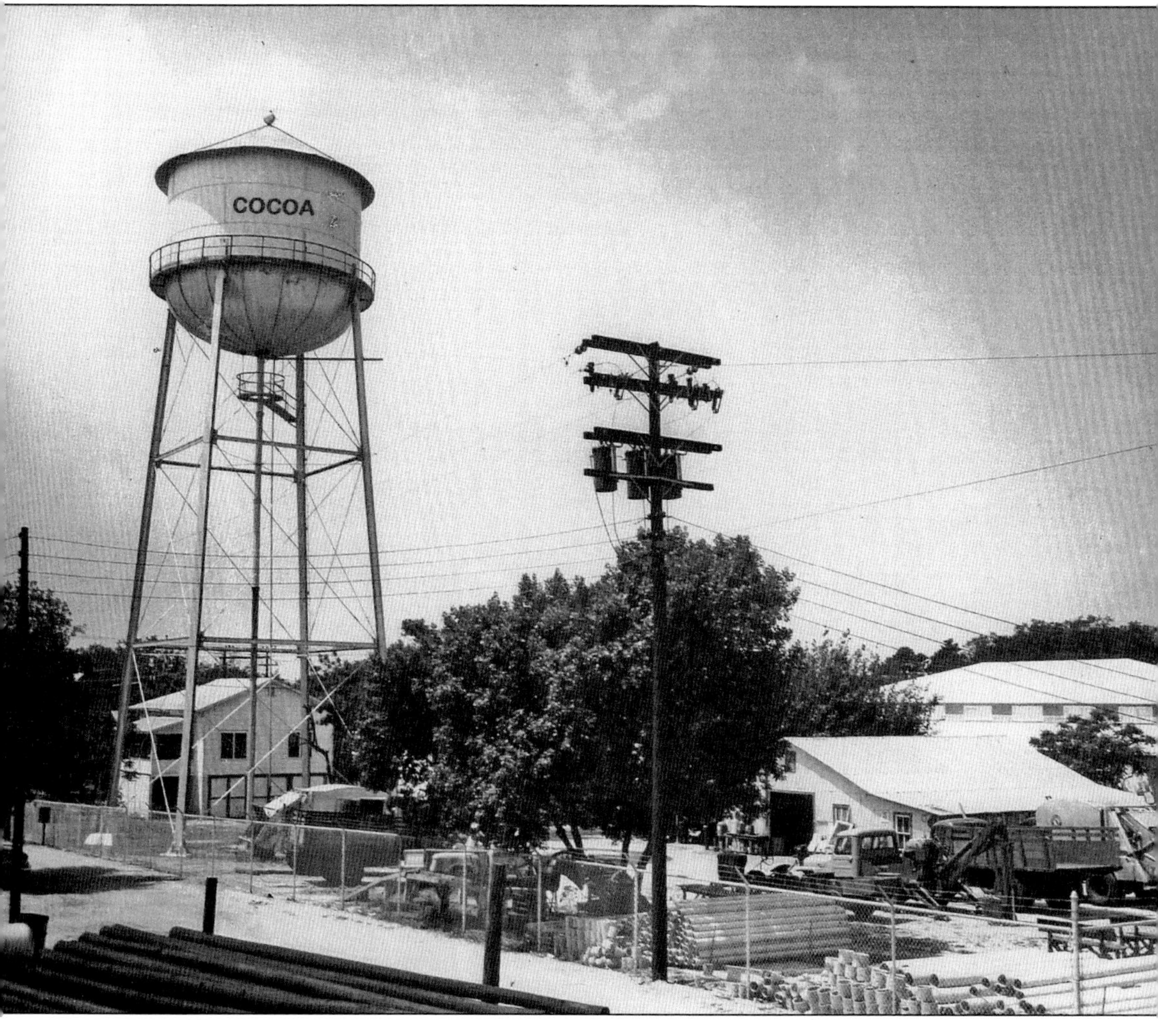

Pictured here are Cocoa's city water tank and city barn, located in the 200 block of Peachtree Street. By the 1960s, the many new residents working in the missile program were demanding more water than this small tank could provide. The present—and much larger—water tank was erected farther west on Peachtree Street.

Three

PEACHTREE STREET TO ROCKLEDGE

The area south of present-day Peachtree Street is now known as Cocoa Village. The first city dock was situated at the east end of Willard Street. That pier was the site where Cocoa received its name. Legend has it that the area was called Indian River City, but the U.S. Post Office had stated the name was too long for a postmark. Town leaders saw the Cocoa name on a drink box or sign and said, "Just call it Cocoa," and the name was adopted.

Businesses grew along Willard Street and Delannoy Avenue. As the town thrived, business buildings replaced houses along Brevard Avenue. The first bridge to Merritt Island, built in 1917 at the end of Harrison Street, was a two-lane wooden structure spanning from bank to bank. Today's bridges have causeways, however, and the banks on either side of the river have been filled in.

From Peachtree Street south, near the river, Willard, King, Harrison, Church, Maryland, Derby, and Oak Streets run east and west. The Cocoa city limits lie seven and a half blocks south, where the city of Rockledge begins.

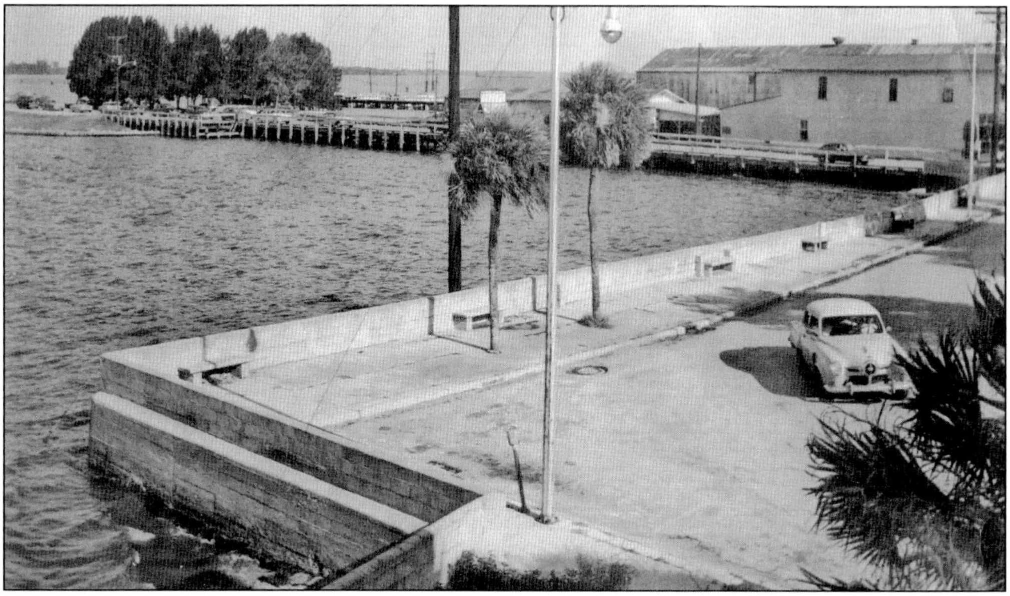

A bridge, present eastbound Highway 520, occupies the top of this view of Delannoy Avenue's north end. The river has been filled and is now the site of Sun Bank. The car in this photograph is a late-1940s or early-1950s Studebaker.

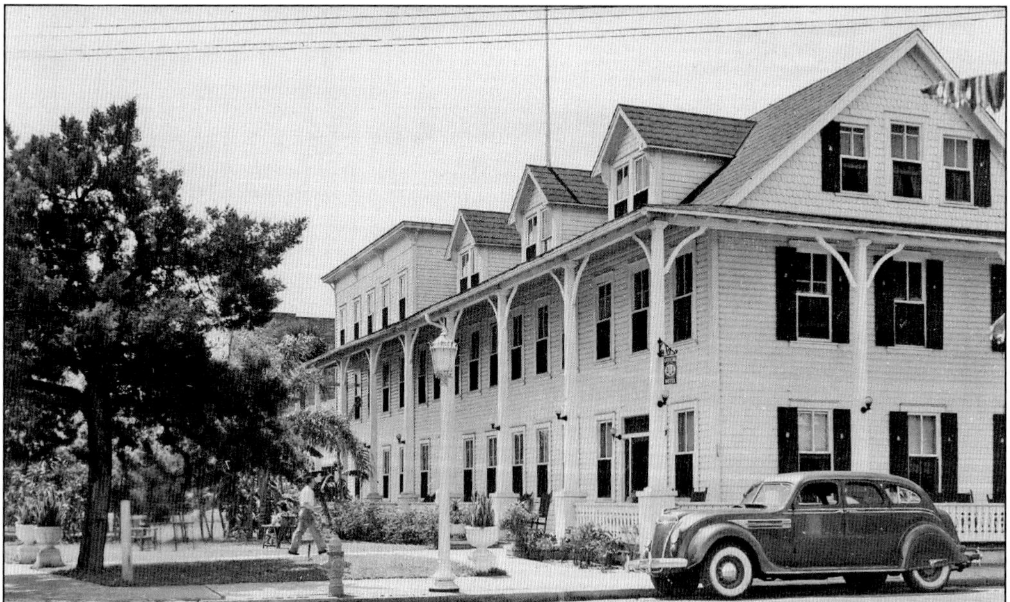

The Cocoa House, an early wooden hotel, stood at the southwest corner of Delannoy Avenue and Willard Street. The building was demolished by hand in the 1960s, and most of the material was used for other structures.

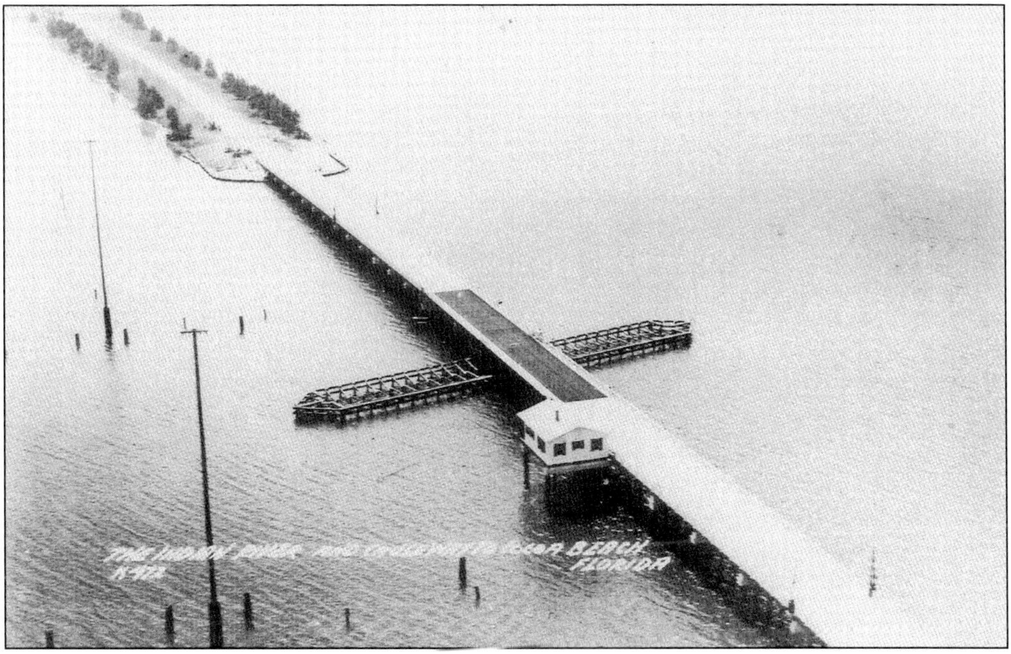

This view, looking southeast, shows the drawbridge over the Indian River at Cocoa. The bridge tender's house is at the lower center. The bridge tender was responsible for opening the draw span and allowing boats to pass 24 hours a day, seven days a week. Now the Highway 520 bridges are two separate spans with two lanes of traffic in each direction, and no tender is needed. The center portion of the old bridge has been demolished, and a portion on each side of the river has been left for fishing.

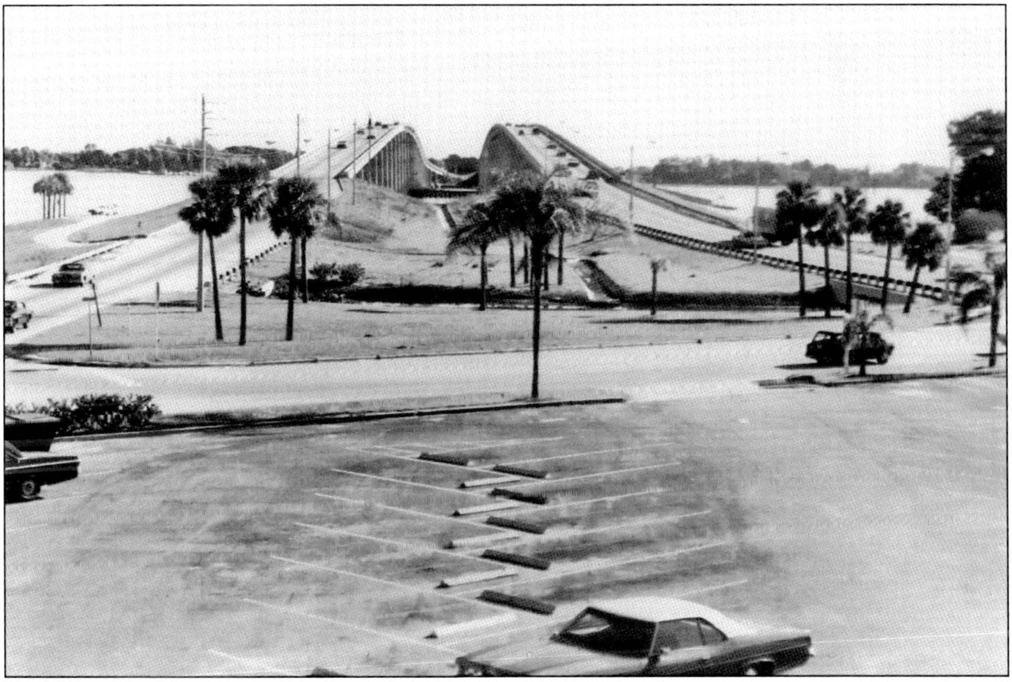

Looking east, this view of the Highway 520 bridges was taken from the Sun Bank parking lot.

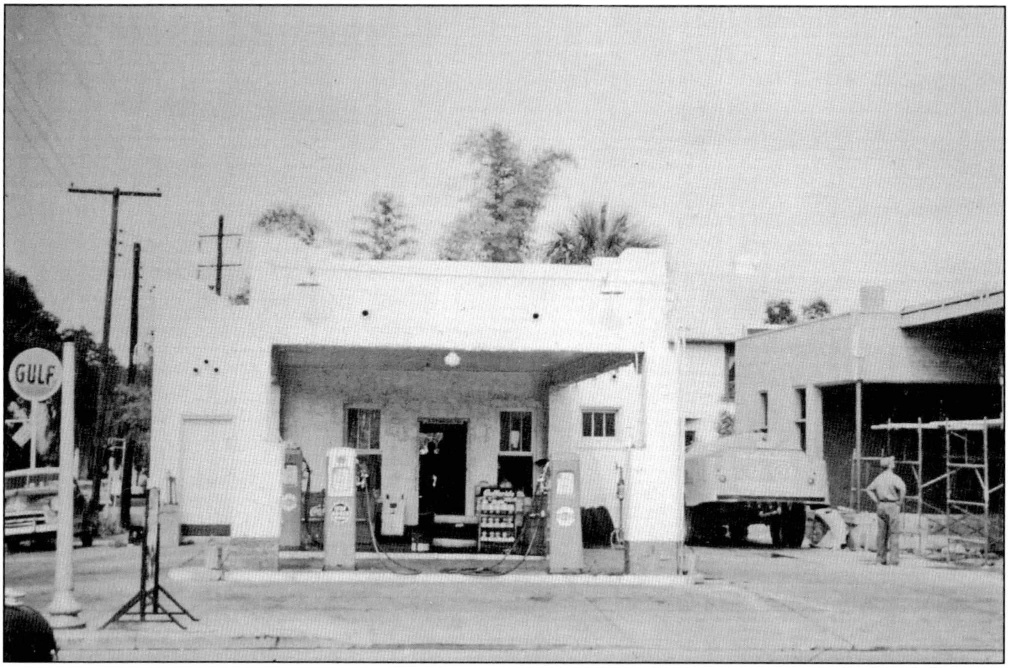

The Gulf Oil station at the southeast corner of Church Street and Brevard Avenue was run by Al Moody, then Jim Weinburg, and later Frank Schumacher. A new station is under construction at the right. This photograph was taken during the time of Jim Weinburg's management.

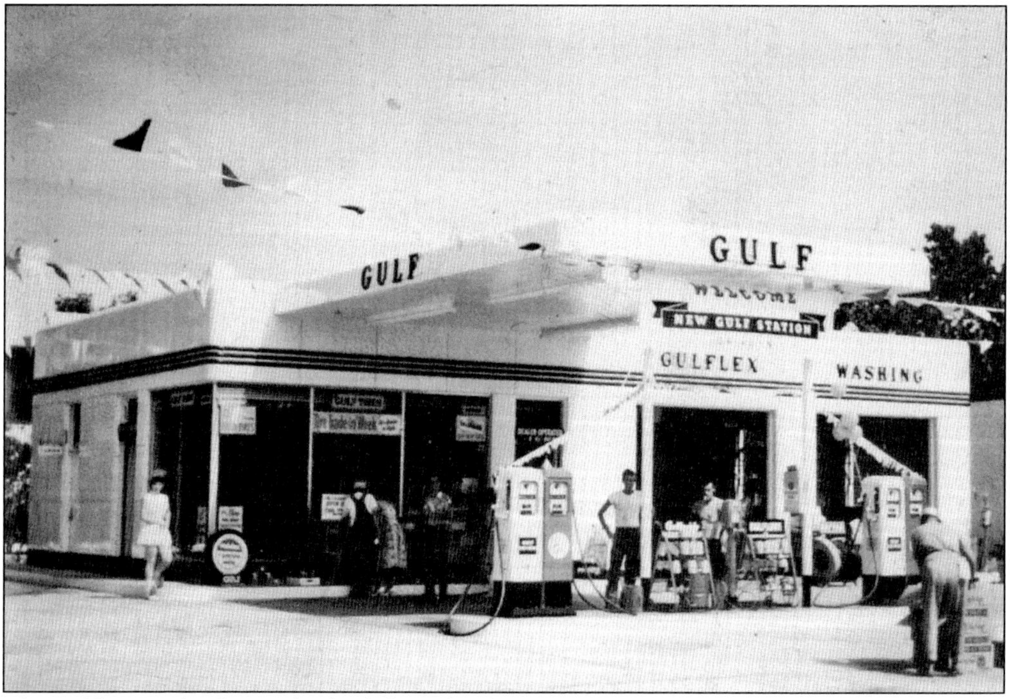

The Gulf station has been rebuilt while under the ownership of Jim Weinburg. Weinburg serviced the cars of most who worked in what is now Cocoa Village. The young man in the white T-shirt is Henry Kipp.

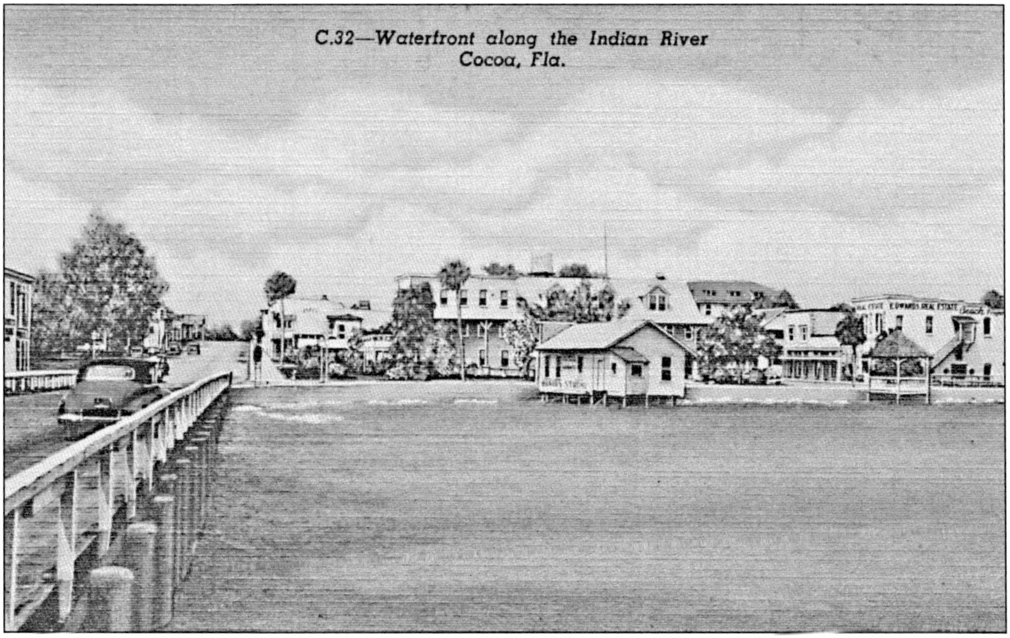

In this view, the bridge to Merritt Island appears on the left. The building over the water in the center is Blair's Photo Studio, and behind it is the Cocoa House, an early hotel. Gus Edward's office is the two-story building on the right.

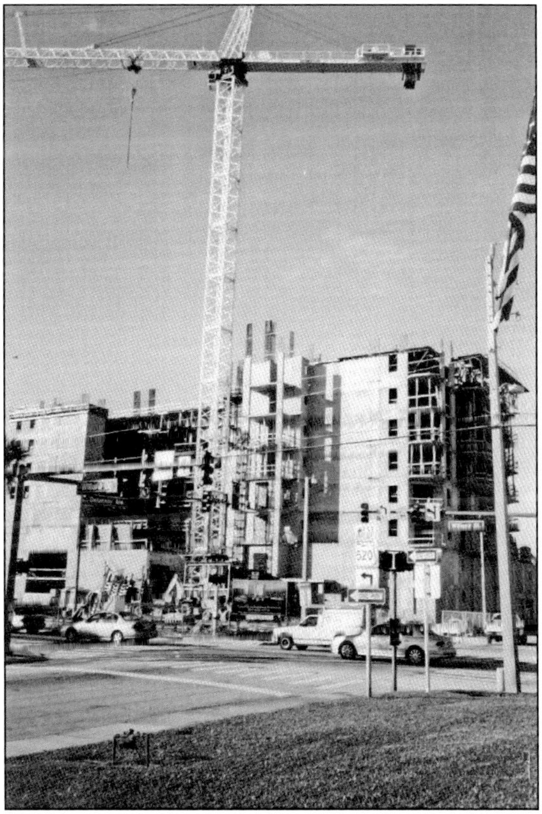

Looking northwest at the corner of Delannoy Avenue and Willard Street, this view shows the Whitley Bay Condominiums under construction. The overhead crane was the first used in Cocoa Village.

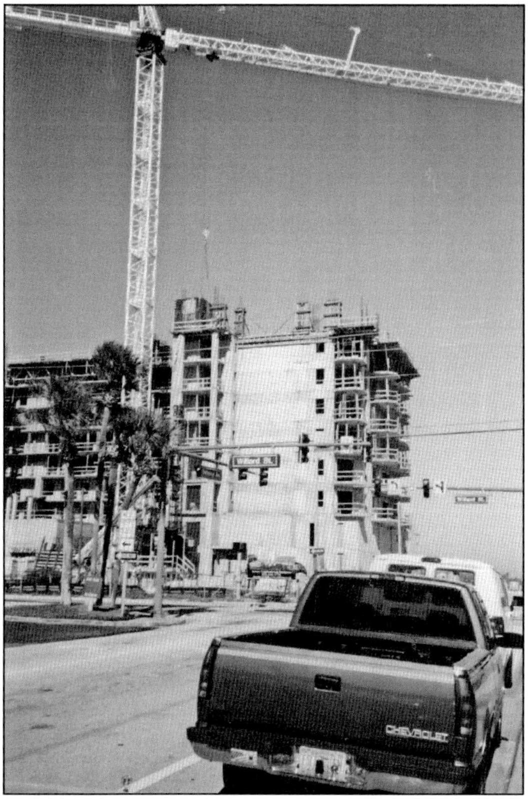

The Whitley Bay Condominiums are being built in this northward view of Delannoy Avenue and Willard Street. The river came up to a sea wall that was along the curb where the trucks are parked. Sun Bank currently stands on land that was created from dirt dredged from the Indian River. The first Cocoa city dock was located to the right at Willard Street.

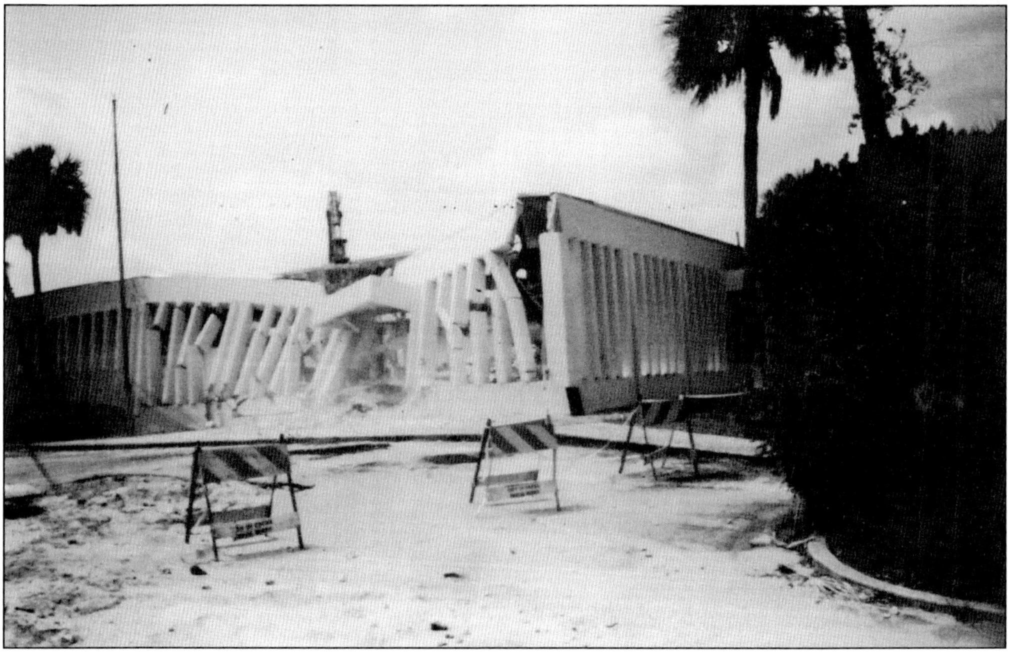

The abandoned post office building at 32 Orange Street in Cocoa is demolished in June 2007. A newer, full-service post office operates in north Cocoa, although a new substation is located immediately across the street from this site.

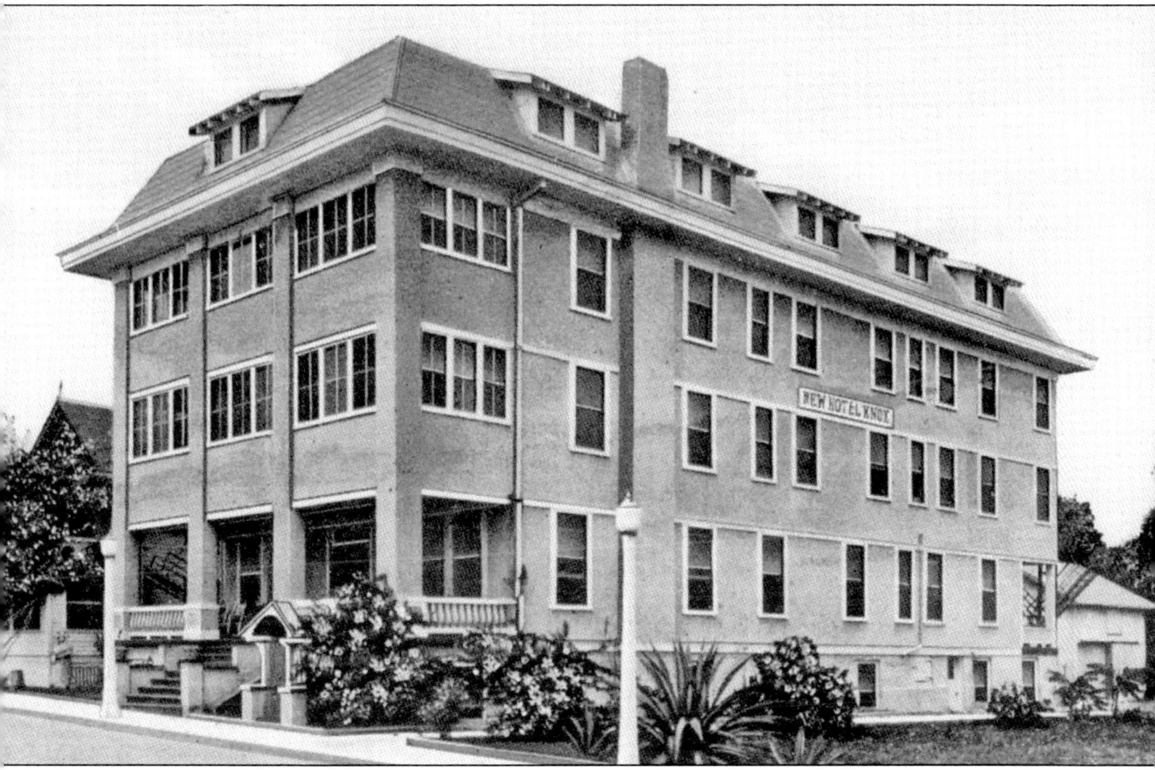

The Seminole Hotel was formerly known as the Knox Hotel. A new owner reportedly acquired the Knox and a hotel in Tallahassee at the same time. Wanting a new name for the Knox, he did the easy thing by bringing a sign from the Tallahassee establishment to Cocoa; thus, the Seminole Hotel.

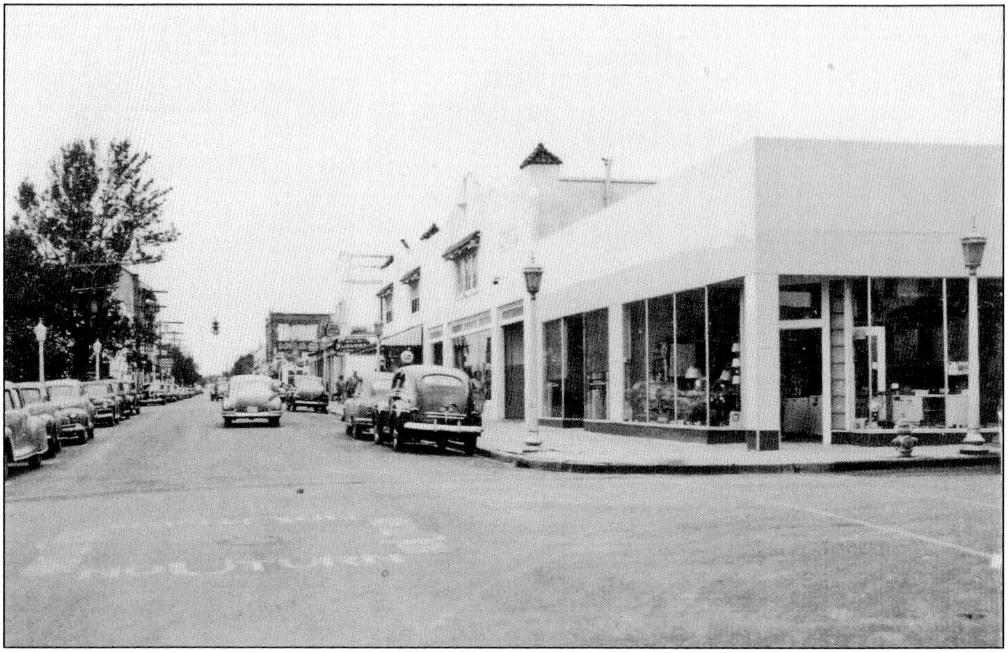

Looking south on Brevard Avenue at Willard Street, this view depicts the Florida Power and Light building on the right. At an earlier time and in an older building, S. S. Jones owned a store on this corner. Brevard Avenue has since been changed to a one-way street.

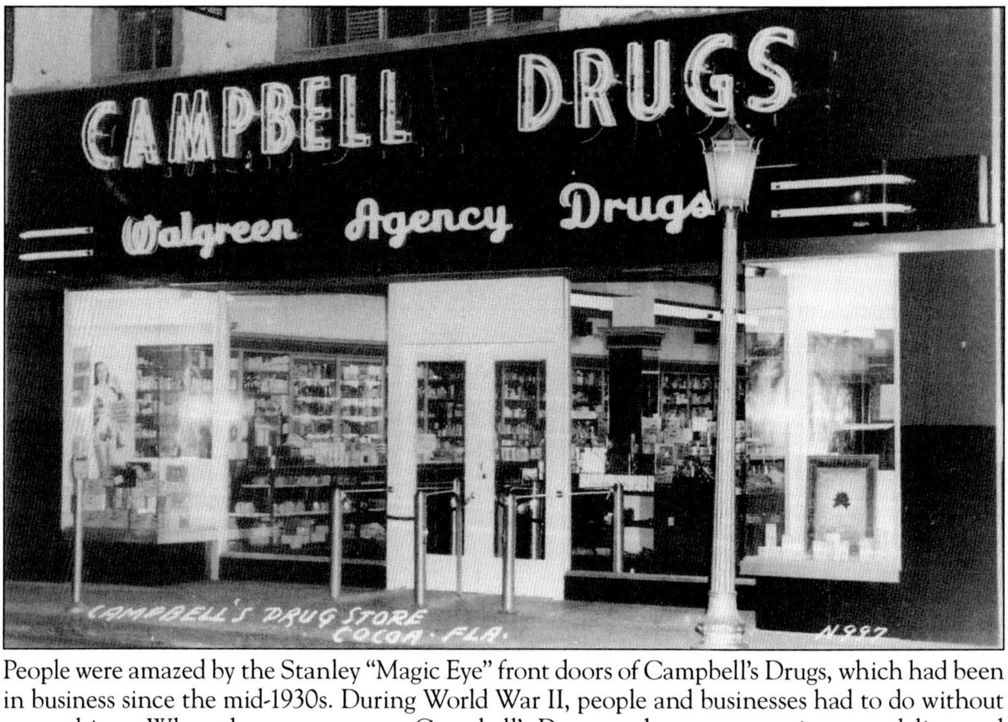

People were amazed by the Stanley "Magic Eye" front doors of Campbell's Drugs, which had been in business since the mid-1930s. During World War II, people and businesses had to do without many things. When the war was over, Campbell's Drugs underwent extensive remodeling and the installation of the first electric doors in Cocoa. March 4, 1948, was the grand opening for the remodeled store.

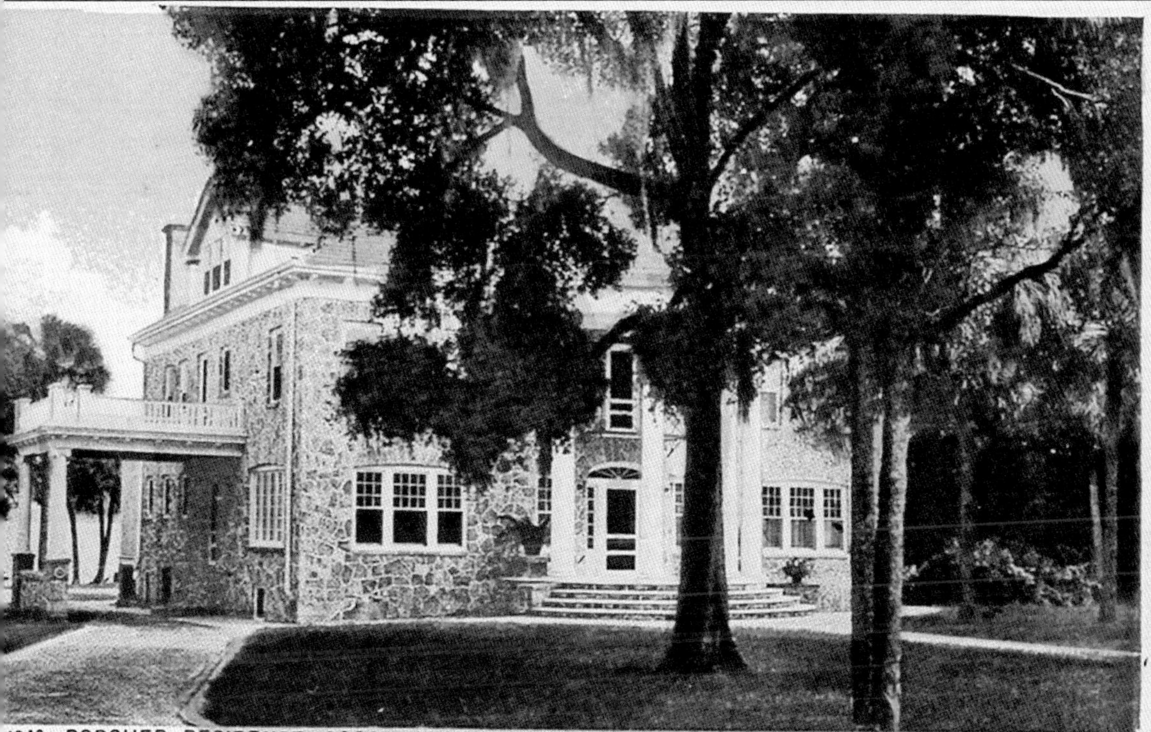

1346 PORCHER RESIDENCE, COCOA, FLA.

The Porcher House is now owned by the City of Cocoa. Cocoa Main Street keeps its office there, and other upstairs offices are leased. The first floor is rented for weddings and other social functions.

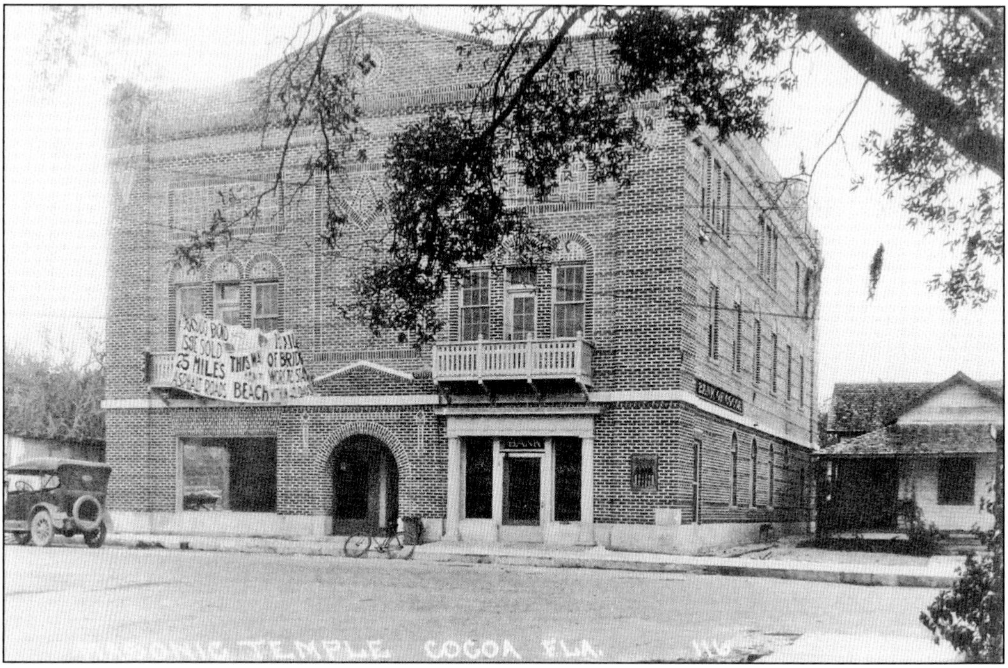

The Masonic Temple, built around 1925, is located at the northwest corner of Brevard Avenue and Stone Street. The banner over the street gives directions to Cocoa Beach. The bridge over the Banana River was newly completed and made it possible to drive to Cocoa Beach.

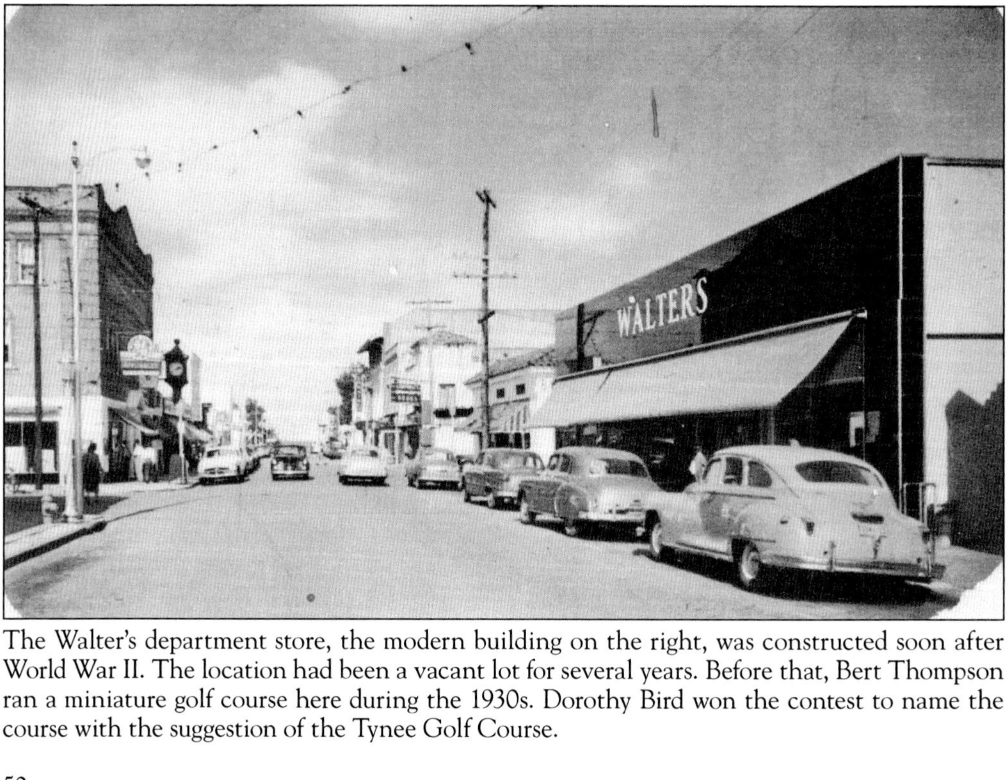

The Walter's department store, the modern building on the right, was constructed soon after World War II. The location had been a vacant lot for several years. Before that, Bert Thompson ran a miniature golf course here during the 1930s. Dorothy Bird won the contest to name the course with the suggestion of the Tynee Golf Course.

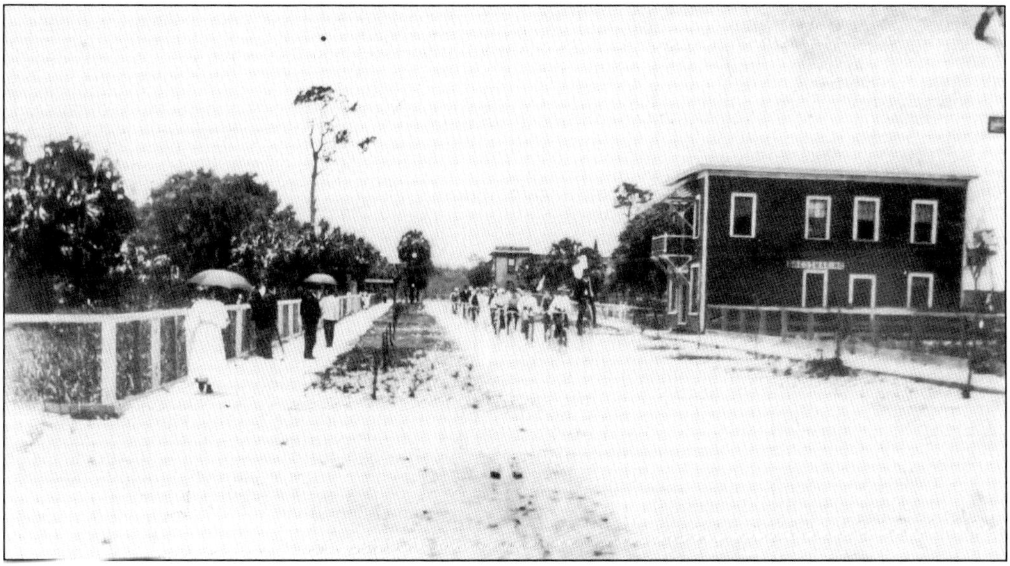

This view looks south on Delannoy Avenue from Harrison Street. The lot behind the fence on the left would later become Taylor Park. The building on the right was Julia Roberts O'Brien's dressmaking shop, where she gave classes in dressmaking. The structure has since been moved to the 500 block of Florida Avenue.

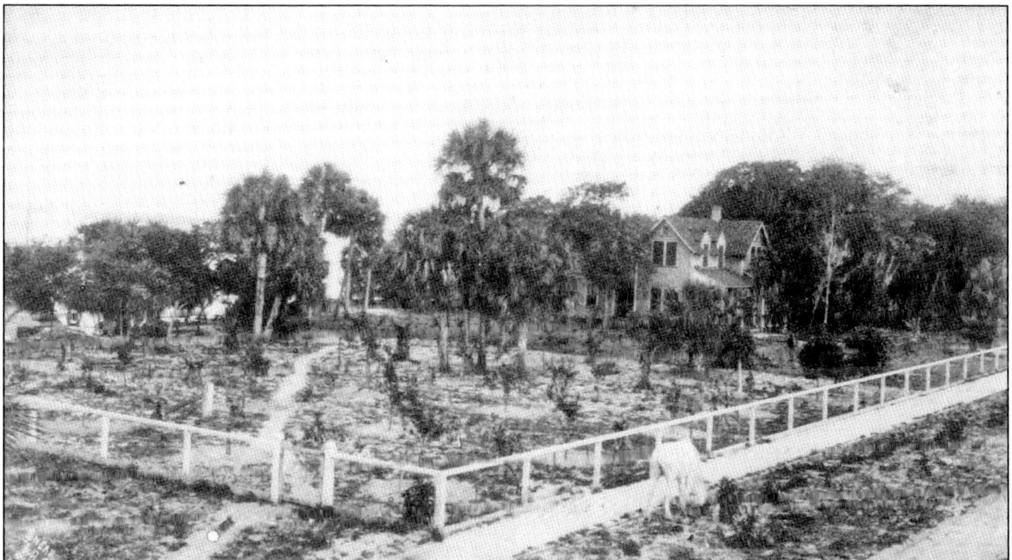

Taylor Park is the partially cleared land to the left center of this photograph. Albert A. Taylor's home, constructed about 1890, is visible to the right center. Harrison Street is to the left, and Delannoy Avenue is to the right. A goat or small cow grazes in the street.

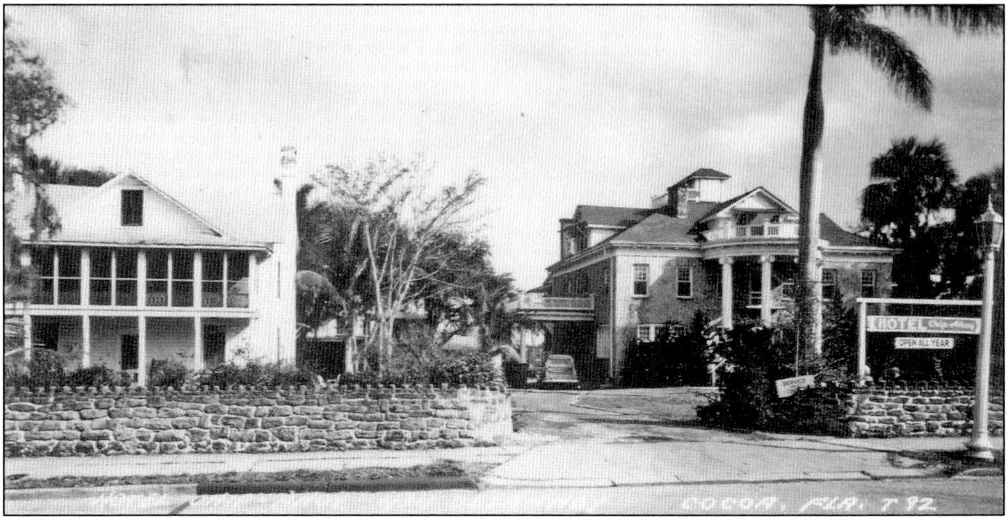

This photograph of the Porcher House was taken when it was being used as a hotel. The building on the left was the residence of L. S. Andrews Jr. and his wife, Myrtis, who was the daughter of the Porchers. The Porcher citrus packinghouse stood between these houses and extended over the river. Fruit to be packed was brought from Merritt Island by barge. The Porcher House has been used as the Cocoa City Hall; Chip Ahoy, a restaurant; and Aquarius Hall, a home for boys.

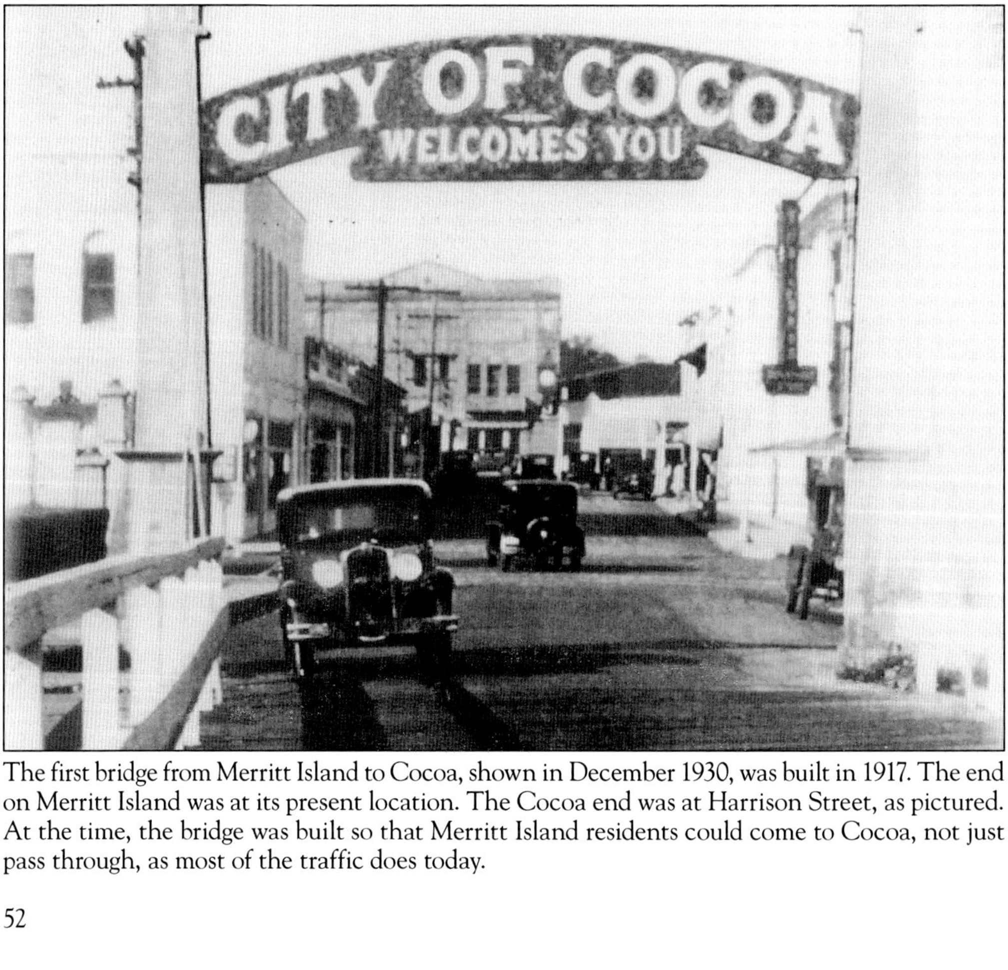

The first bridge from Merritt Island to Cocoa, shown in December 1930, was built in 1917. The end on Merritt Island was at its present location. The Cocoa end was at Harrison Street, as pictured. At the time, the bridge was built so that Merritt Island residents could come to Cocoa, not just pass through, as most of the traffic does today.

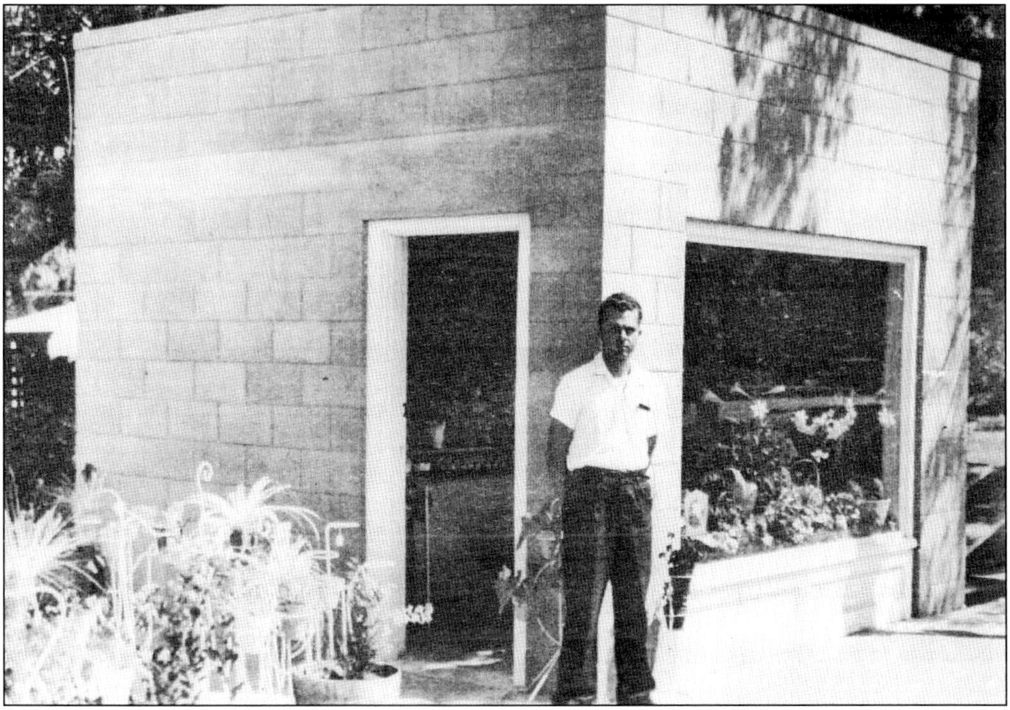

John England poses in front of Flower Dell Florist, located at 426 Brevard Avenue. England returned home after military service in World War II and constructed this building for his florist business. When the business prospered, he enlarged this building. He later moved into a larger, remodeled service station at 602 Brevard Avenue.

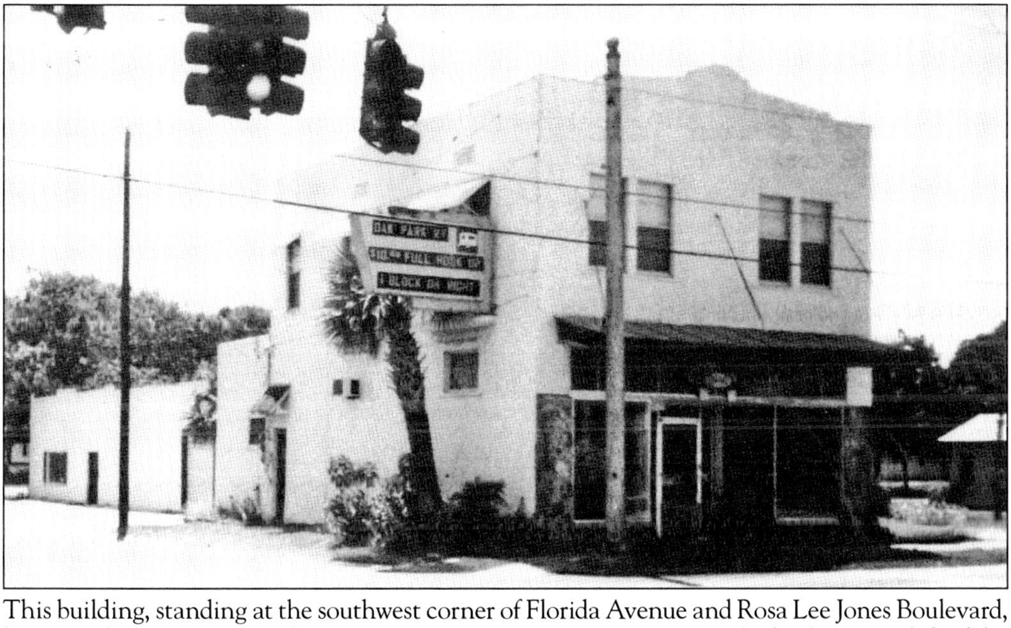

This building, standing at the southwest corner of Florida Avenue and Rosa Lee Jones Boulevard, has served many uses. The front portion was Kimrey's Grocery store. The back part, to left of the image, contained Luther Harrell's garage. The grocery store was later owned by Noah Butt and Curley L. Butler. Butler also managed the trailer park to the right.

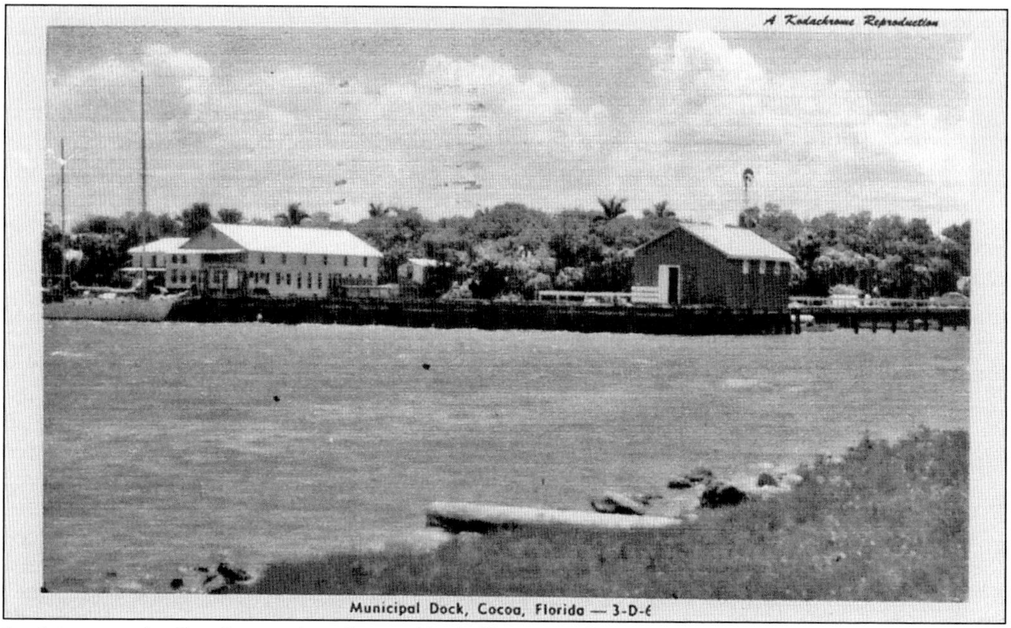

In this view, the Porcher packinghouse (far left) is seen from the river. The large building to the right stands on the city dock. The city dock is a portion of the first bridge to Merritt Island, at the east end of Harrison Street.

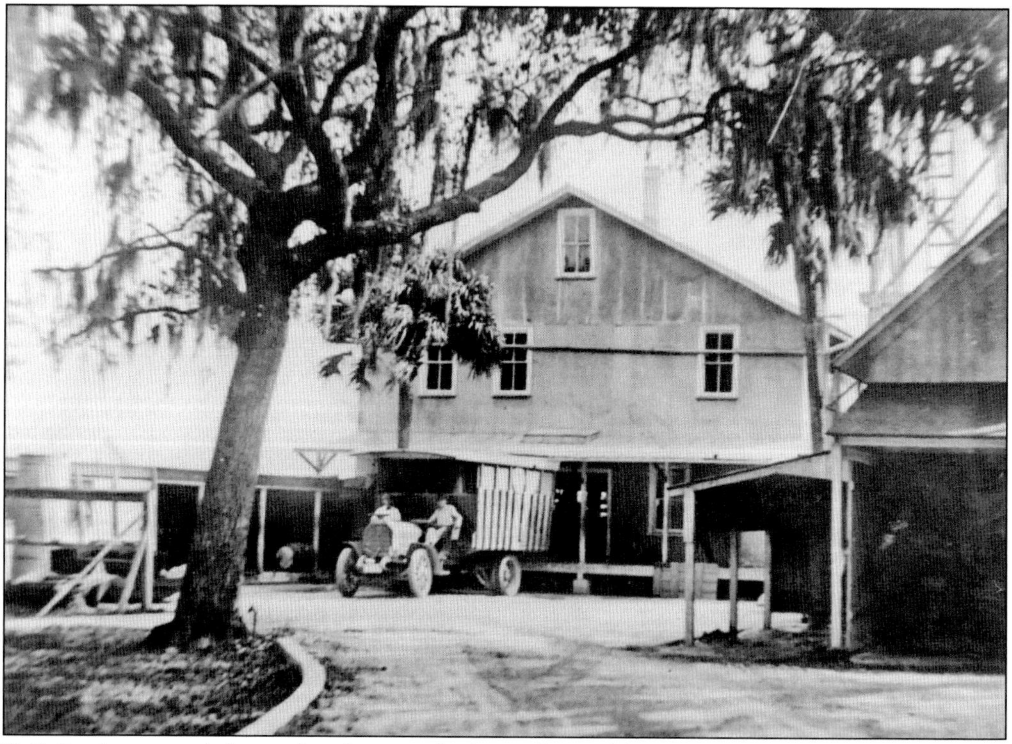

E. P. Porcher owned this packinghouse, which was located between the Porcher House and the present civic center. The back of the packinghouse extended over the water. Barges of citrus fruit were brought from groves on Merritt Island to be processed and shipped north for sale.

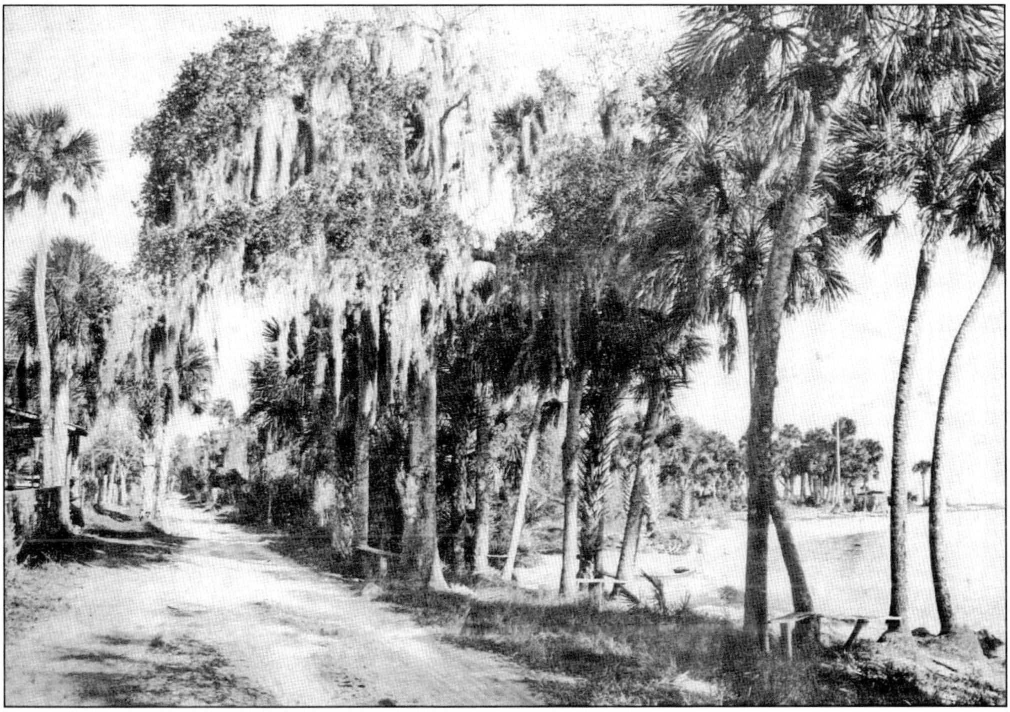

Riverside Drive was still a dirt road when May Day celebrations were held here on Oleander Point. People came from as far as New Smyrna and Fort Pierce to join the festivities. The Yacht Club was the first building on the site, followed by the Brevard Hotel and then the present-day Oleander Pointe Condominiums.

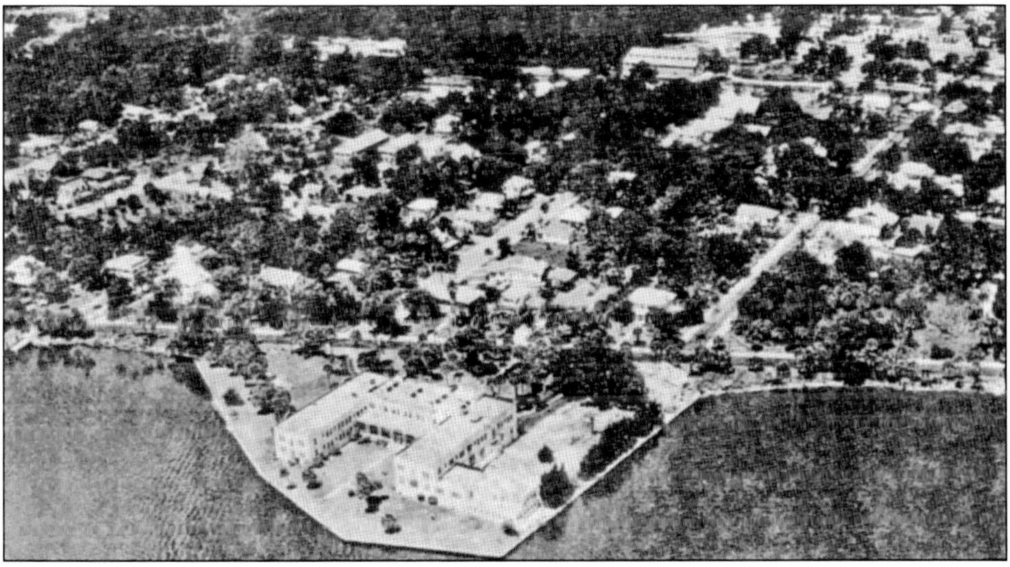

Oleander Point is shown from the air. Among the first known uses of this Cocoa promontory was as the site of the May Day celebration. Early settlers would arrive by boat to enjoy a picnic, games, races, and fellowship with other pioneers from the Indian River area. The Brevard Motor Hotel (pictured) was later constructed, and then razed in 1996. Presently three buildings of the Oleander Pointe Condominiums occupy the land.

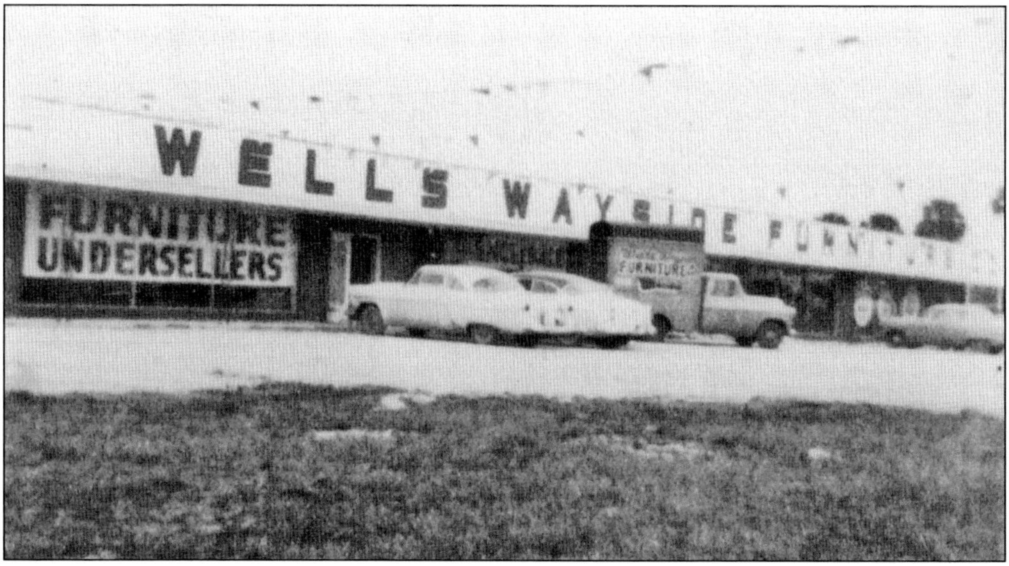

The Wells family moved here from North Carolina and built Wells Wayside Furniture, a large direct-furniture store, on Highway 520 west of Cocoa. It was a great addition to the area.

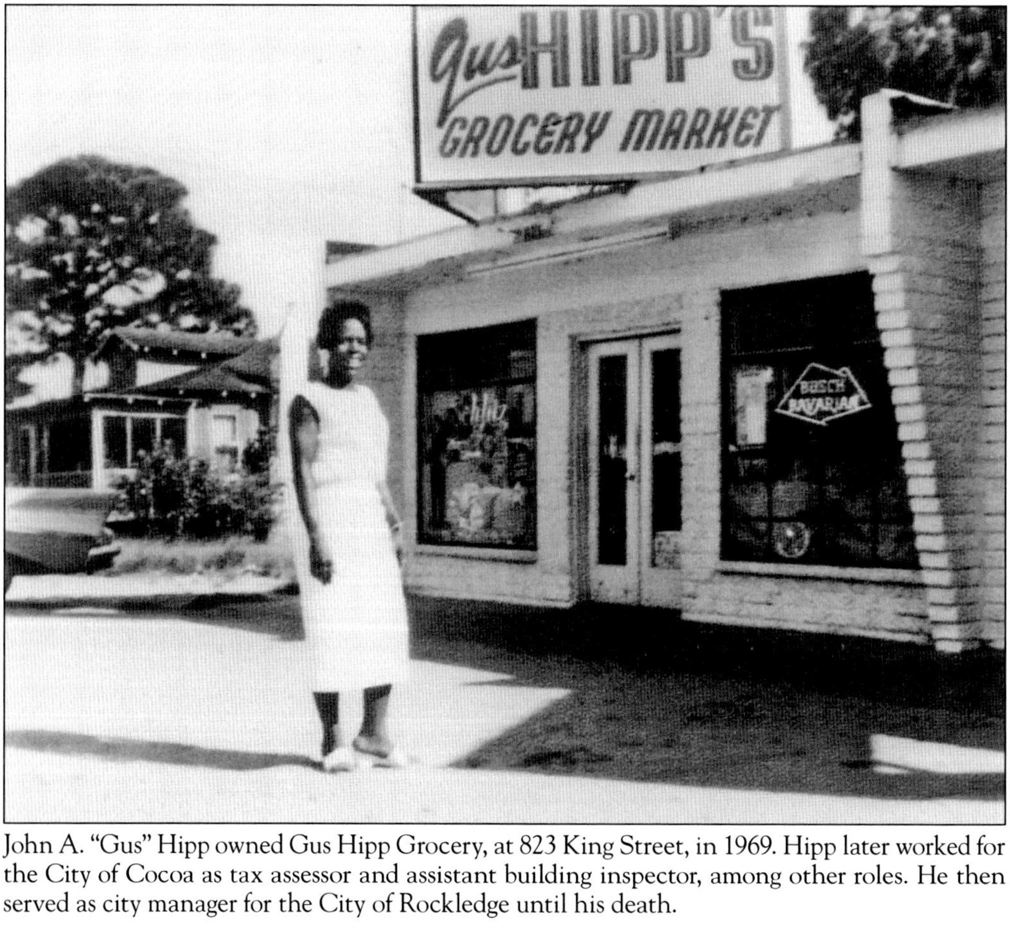

John A. "Gus" Hipp owned Gus Hipp Grocery, at 823 King Street, in 1969. Hipp later worked for the City of Cocoa as tax assessor and assistant building inspector, among other roles. He then served as city manager for the City of Rockledge until his death.

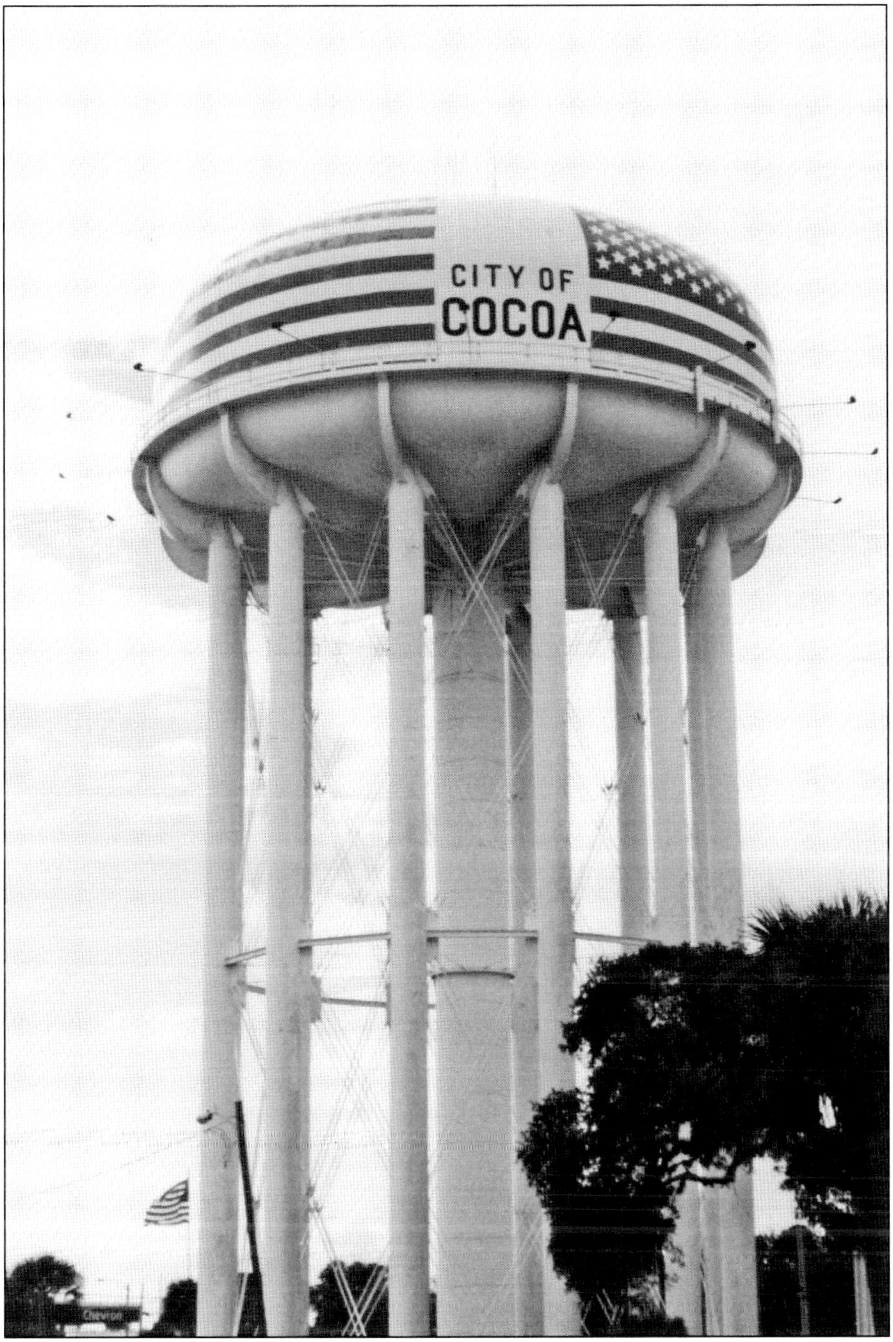

Cocoa and Rockledge joined the nation's bicentennial celebration by taking part in the county wide bicentennial committee headed by Bud Housner. Evidence of Cocoa's participation is the patriotic painting of the Cocoa water tower at the corner of Peachtree Street and North Coca Boulevard. The Royal Painting Company completed the $10,000 job at no cost to the city. Demetrious Dourakos, a native of Greece and president of the company, said he wanted to do the project, as Cocoa was now his hometown. Three American flags, the years 1776–1976, and "Welcome to Cocoa" were painted on the tower, which is visible to visitors as they enter the city.

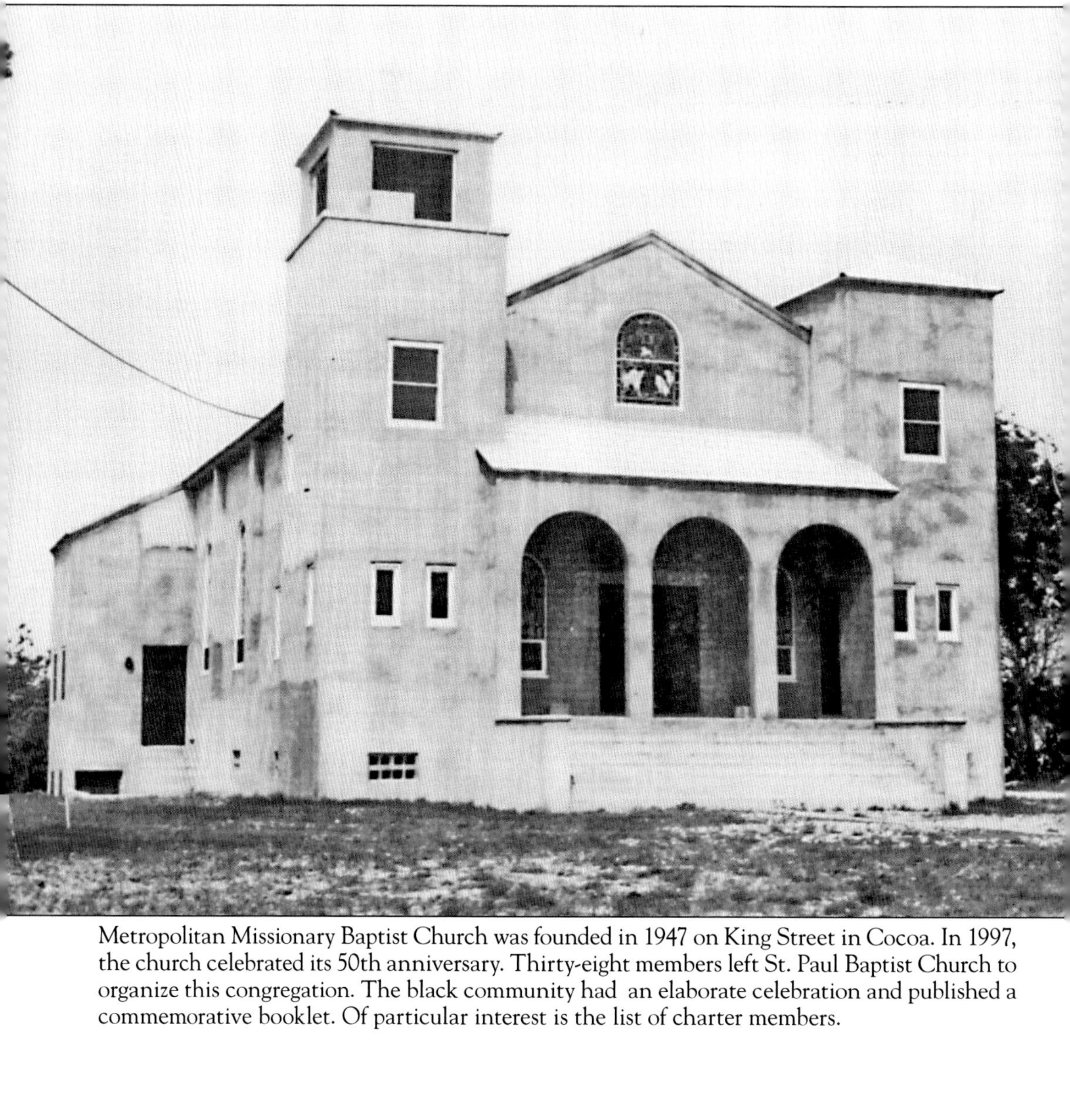

Metropolitan Missionary Baptist Church was founded in 1947 on King Street in Cocoa. In 1997, the church celebrated its 50th anniversary. Thirty-eight members left St. Paul Baptist Church to organize this congregation. The black community had an elaborate celebration and published a commemorative booklet. Of particular interest is the list of charter members.

HISTORY OF METROPOLITAN BAPTIST CHURCH

According to the records kept and the information obtained from some who were there in the beginning, the following facts were made available.

On November 6, 1947, thirty-eight members left St. Paul Baptist Church to organize another Church . The names of the members are as follows:

Walter Bulger
Katherine Bulger
Dessie Williams
Tilton Smith
Gus Williams
Georgia O. Slater
H. L. Jackson
Frank Cone
Clara M. Cone
Pinkcy Collins
James Collins
Amanda B. Jones
Ethel Jenkins
Lee Cotman
Ethel Cotman
Viola Howard
Lucille Osborne
Joe Osborne
Lizzie Miller
Cora Stepney
Minnie L. Ware
Ada Johnson
Timothy Johnson
Lula Furlow
Dave Leonnard
Flippie Leonnard
A. J. Lunday
Beaulah Cotman
Herman Cotman
Lillie Mae King
Willie Roy King
Johnnie Blutcher
Eloise Moton
Annie Ruth Collins
Walter Osborne
Gertrude Daniels
Sallie Long
Mary Brinkley

These Christians met at the home of Mrs. Georgia O. Slater. After devotion, a business meeting was held. Mr. Walter Bulger was made chairman of the group, Mrs. Georgia O. Slater, secretary and Mr. Gus Williams, Treasure.

A committee was appointed to find property that could be purchased for the erection of a church building. This committee consisted of the following persons: Brothers Walter Bulger, Frank Cone, Lee Cotman and Tilton Smith.

Two meetings were held at the home of Mrs. Slater, the third was at the home of Mr. and Mrs. John nad Amanda B. Jones.

The property committee reported finding a lot for $300 and recomended that the group purchase the lot. By motion it was adopted and the lot was purchased.

The group met at the home of Mr. and Mrs. Timothy and Ada Johnson,they offered her shop room that was vacant for a permanent meeting place. the offer was gratefully accepted by the group. Subsequently, chairs and furniture needed was purchased.

November 1947, the group met and after discussing their being organized into a Baptist Church, a committee was appointed to invite the following Churches:St.John,Miami; Macedonia, Miami; Mt. Olive, Ft Lauderdale;Mt. Olive, Ft Pierce; Bethel, Daytona Beach; Bethelem, Titusville and St. Mathews, Wabasso, for the purpose of organization.

Shown here are the Metropolitan Missionary Baptist Church records of organization. Included in their publication was a list of former church pastors.

March 1974, Rev. Harvey L. Riley, Pastor of the Friendship Baptist Church, Sharpes, accepted the call to serve as Pastor of Metropolitan. Under the prayful and dynamic leadership of Pastor Riley, Metropolitan grew in Christian love and Spiritual Awareness as a result of many hours in training through workshops, conventions and fellowship with other churches throughout the state. The membership grew continuously and the anual budget, grew progressively higher and exceeded it's goal; property on the north side of the church was purchased which at that time was valued at $80,000. Metropolitan; renovaed the main sanctuary and purchased several new pews and reupholstered the old ones; renovated the basement, making additional classrooms; tiked the floors and installed central heat and air conditioning.

On the fourth Sunday in October 1982, Rev. Harvey L. Riley terminated his Pastorship at Metropolitan. Metropolitan Baptist Church became a flock without a shepherd, and at this period, Rev. A. Houston was serving in an advisory capacity due to his declining golden years and religious endowment. The Deacons and Trustees recomended to the church that the Rev. Leonard Daggett serve as assistant to the Assistant Pastor, and the church sanctioned the recommendation. The Rev. A.E. Deveaux and the Rev. H. f. Brockington II were also recommended by the Daecons and Trustees to assist and work with Rev. Houston nad Rev. Daggett in what ever way they could.

Rev. Daggett began ministering unto the needs of the people. With his acceptance of the position and the smooth transition which he was able to make, the church kept moving. There were no missing kinks or breaks in service. Metropolitan took in a large number of membeers and paod off a second mortgage on the church which totaled $12,000.

August 1983, the church accepted Rev. Daggett's letter of resignation. the church asked Rev. Deveaux to serve as interim Pastor, Rev. Deveaux accepted and began the work of doing our father's business. His love for God and concern for others is still present today as he serves in his role of Assistant Pastor.

In January 1984, Dr. Eugene Burley was called to minister to the needs of the members of Metropolitan. During this time many converts came to be served.Dr. Burley continued to implement the plans of his predecessor. Under his administration was the initiation and organization of a ministry for the youth of the church. for those ages 3-12, he gave a special message .

In November 1984, the Rev. V. Benford Friar II, was called to the pastroate of Metropolitan Baptist Church. Metropolitan swiftly came to a greater realization of God and understood in our hearts and minds, that as Christians, we must be anout our father's business. Under this ministry the Church witnessed a spirit-filled tear. Through his leadership Metropolitan received; 116 converts/ 110 candidates for Baptism; initiated an orientation for new and veteran members; authorized a laymen's department; organized a weekly Bible Study; created inter-action sessions and implemented a leadership training class.

Shown here are the Metropolitan Missionary Baptist Church records of organization. Much of the history of the church is told through the record of the early pastors' bibliographies.

March 1974, Rev. Harvey L. Riley, Pastor of the Friendship Baptist Church, Sharpes, accepted the call to serve as Pastor of Metropolitan. Under the prayful and dynamic leadership of Pastor Riley, Metropolitan grew in Christian love and Spiritual Awareness as a result of many hours in training through workshops, conventions and fellowship with other churches throughout the state. The membership grew continuously and the anual budget, grew progressively higher and exceeded it's goal; property on the north side of the church was purchased which at that time was valued at $80,000. Metropolitan; renovaed the main sanctuary and purchased several new pews and reupholstered the old ones; renovated the basement, making additional classrooms; tiked the floors and installed central heat and air conditioning.

On the fourth Sunday in October 1982, Rev. Harvey L. Riley terminated his Pastorship at Metropolitan. Metropolitan Baptist Church became a flock without a shepherd, and at this period, Rev. A. Houston was serving in an advisory capacity due to his declining golden years and religious endowment. The Deacons and Trustees recomended to the church that the Rev. Leonard Daggett serve as assistant to the Assistant Pastor, and the church sanctioned the recommendation. The Rev. A.E. Deveaux and the Rev. H. f. Brockington II were also recommended by the Daecons and Trustees to assist and work with Rev. Houston nad Rev. Daggett in what ever way they could.

Rev. Daggett began ministering unto the needs of the people. With his acceptance of the position and the smooth transition which he was able to make, the church kept moving. There were no missing kinks or breaks in service. Metropolitan took in a large number of membeers and paod off a second mortgage on the church which totaled $12,000.

August 1983, the church accepted Rev. Daggett's letter of resignation. the church asked Rev. Deveaux to serve as interim Pastor, Rev. Deveaux accepted and began the work of doing our father's business. His love for God and concern for others is still present today as he serves in his role of Assistant Pastor.

In January 1984, Dr. Eugene Burley was called to minister to the needs of the members of Metropolitan. During this time many converts came to be served.Dr. Burley continued to implement the plans of his predecessor. Under his administration was the initiation and organization of a ministry for the youth of the church. for those ages 3-12, he gave a special message .

In November 1984, the Rev. V. Benford Friar II, was called to the pastroate of Metropolitan Baptist Church. Metropolitan swiftly came to a greater realization of God and understood in our hearts and minds, that as Christians, we must be anout our father's business. Under this ministry the Church witnessed a spirit-filled tear. Through his leadership Metropolitan received; 116 converts/ 110 candidates for Baptism; initiated an orientation for new and veteran members; authorized a laymen's department; organized a weekly Bible Study; created inter-action sessions and implemented a leadership training class.

Shown here are the Metropolitan Missionary Baptist Church records of organization. The service records of the succeeding pastors are continued here. The black community had the first-recorded minister in residence in the 1885 survey of Cocoa

On Novmeber 6, 1988, Rev. V. Benford Friar II's pastorate at Metropolitan Baptist Church was terminated.

On August 6, 1989, Dr. Floyd L. Bass Jr. accepted the call to Pastor the Metropolitan Baptist Church. He ministers not only to the Metropolitan family, but to the greater metropolis of Cocoa, Rockledge, Merritt Island and other adjacent communities. His theme and theory of ministry is based on the spiritual concept of " shared Responsibility" with emphasis on "reaching the lost, teaching the saved". Metropolitan has been richly blessed during Dr. Bass's tenure as pastor; 126 new disciples were added to the Lord's Church; a completed landscaping project; blessed to payoff the adjacent lot on King Street for $12,000, and completed a $16,000 building refurbishing program for the interior and exterior of the sanctuary.

Metropoliyan entered the 1990's with the introduction of a new structuring program and the Pastor's Vision, with a stronger determination to what God commanded us to do. Lost souls gave their life to Christ, willing souls re-dedicated their life to Him and Bible-based teaching was in full effect, old friendships were restored, marriage vows were renewed and souls were revived.

Metropolitan Missionary Baptist Church

50th

1947 1997

Anniversary

Cocoa, Florida

"Growing Together, Building In Faith"
'Not Equal Giving, But Equal Sacrifice"
Romans 12:3-8

Dr. F. L. Bass, Jr. — *Pastor*
Rev. A. E. Deveaux — *Asst. Pastor*

November 9, 1997

The Metropolitan Missionary Baptist Church has grown in membership and expanded with a new educational building on the property. The congregation has formed a partnership with the congregation of the Rockledge Presbyterian Church, which has a predominately white membership. Both churches have benefited by interacting with each other.

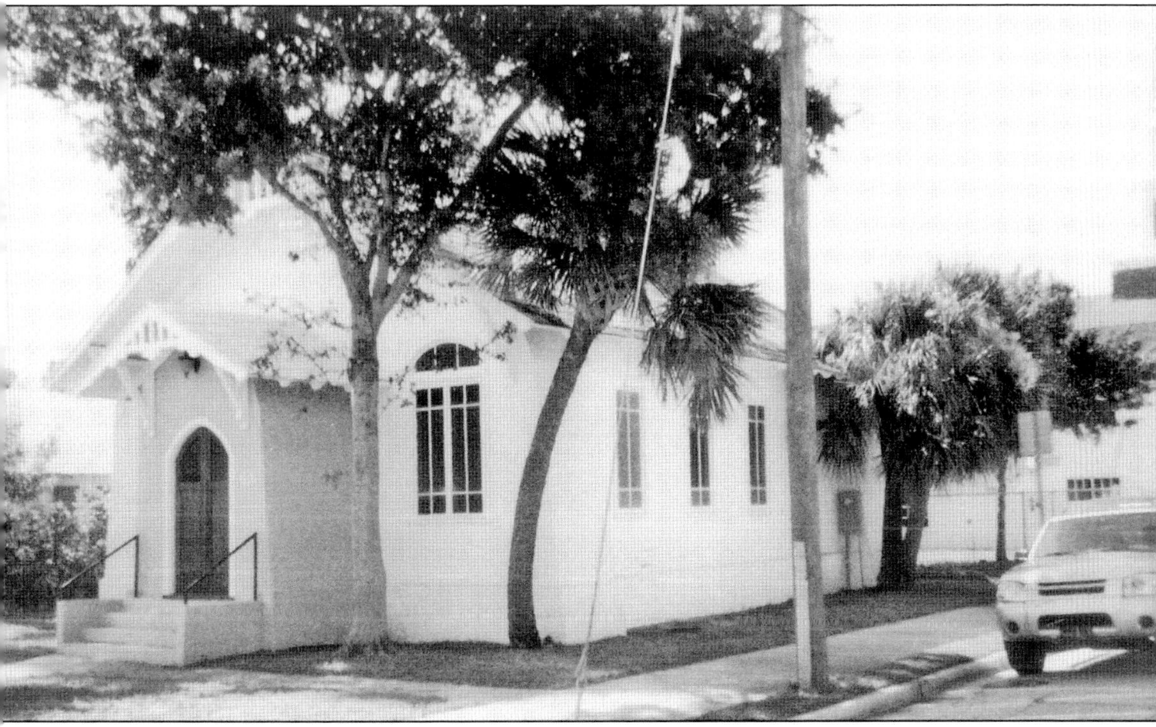

The historic Derby Street Chapel is located at the southeast corner of Derby Street and Brevard Avenue in Cocoa.

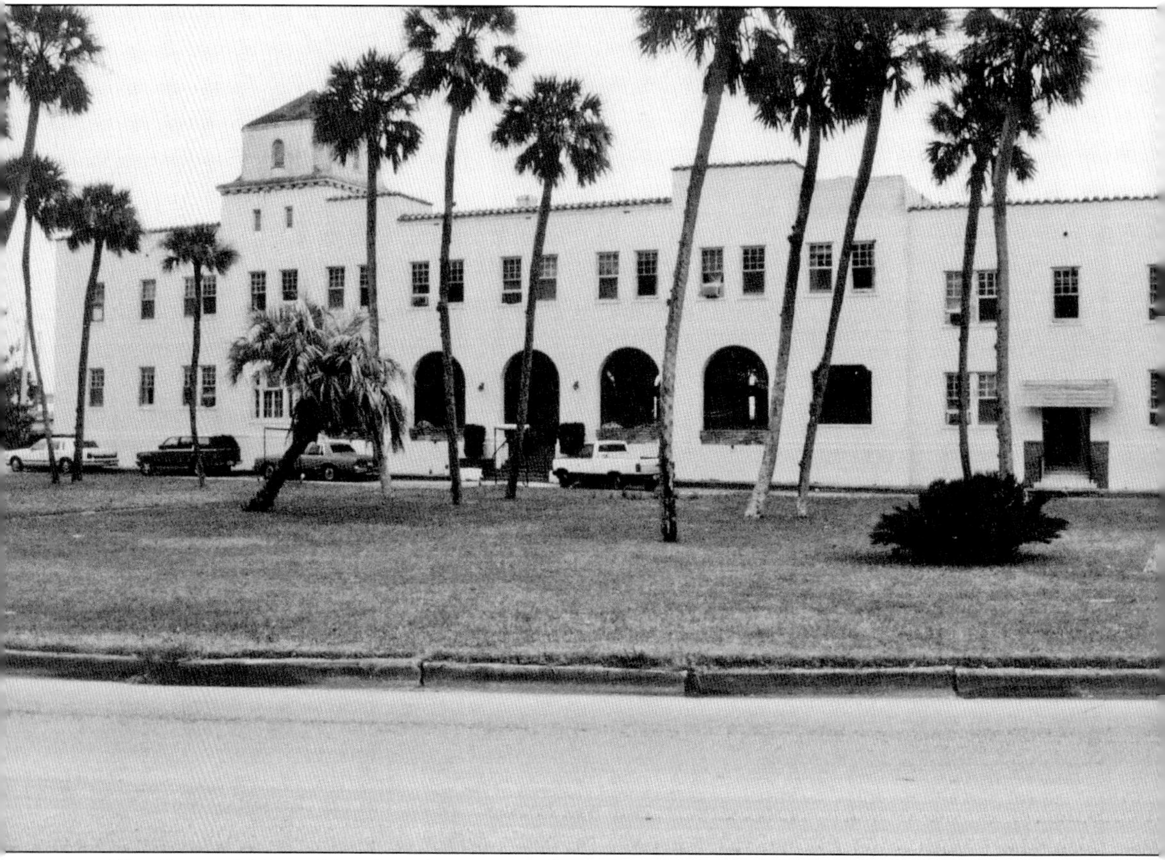

The Brevard Motor Hotel made news in the mid-1980s, when it was rumored that it would be razed and replaced by a condominium known as Oleander Pointe. Oleander Point (the geographic location) had long been a Cocoa landmark as the site for the annual May Day celebration, the residence of Sarah DeLannoy Wade, and the home of the Cocoa-Rockledge Yacht Club. The 53-room Brevard Motor Hotel, nicknamed "the Grand Old Lady," was built on four acres directly on the Indian River and opened on March 10, 1924. Its demise at the hands of bulldozers began in March 1996.

List Of Those Who Have Received Tires Published By Board

The supplemental list of local residents qualifying under the tire rationing rules and regulations who have received tires during the past month up to and including March 13th, as furnished by the local tire rationing board, was as follows:

Floyd C. Gast, truck; George Edwards, passenger; Joe Cowart, obsolete; Gardner Gingras, truck; Arthur N. Lloyd, truck; Ard Groves, truck; Postal Telegraph Co., passenger; Arthur N. Lloyd, truck; J. V. D'Albora Co., truck; J. J. Atkinson, truck; William Garafolo, truck; George Timmerman, truck; James O. Cole, truck; H. L. Syfrett, obsolete; Fla. Indian River Fruit Co., obsolete; James Atkinson, truck; J. V. D'Albora Co., truck; Fla. Indian River Fruit Co., obsolete; George Lundberg, passenger; Southern Bell Tel. Co., truck; M. S. Whaley, truck; J. A. Whittington, obsolete; Brevard Sch. Board, truck; Dr. W. C. Page; passenger; Board of Public Instruction, truck; George Edwards, passenger; J. V. D'Albora, truck; H. C. Cresson, truck; Einer Arveson, passenger; Floyd Gast, truck; Robert Honaker, truck.

During World War II, tires were among the many items that required approval of the ration board.

Southern Bell Telephone and Telegraph Co.

Incorporated

COCOA, FLA.

S. E. GLASS, Manager, Cocoa, Fla.

T. J. ROEBUCK, Group Mgr., Daytona Beach, Fla. J. A. MOONEYHAM, Dist. Mgr., Orlando, Fla.

VERNON BAIRD, Florida Mgr., Jacksonville, Fla.

Employes of this Company are forbidden to accept either oral or written telephone messages to be transmitted by an employe of this Company over the lines of this Company.

In case of trouble with your telephone call REPAIR SERVICE.

(By arrangement with the Postal Telegraph-Cable Company and the Western Union Telegraph Company, any telephone subscriber of this exchange may have charges for messages received or sent by Postal Telegraph-Cable Company or Western Union Telegraph Company charged to his telephone and collected with his telephone bill.)

Corrected through DECEMBER 5, 1931

Abney & Abney general mdse City Point 345-J
Acme Fruit Co packing hse Oleander 80
Aikens L B r Barton av 166-W
Alderman F A r 530 W Peachtree 227-W
Alford W H Mrs r Georgianna .... Call L D
Allen Jack C ofc S Dixie hgwy 9124
Allen L P r Rockledge 256-W
Allen Realty Co 146 Brevard av 51
Allen T S r Rockledge 115-J
Amer Fruit Growers Inc ofc 71
Anderson L L Dr r Valencia 206-J
ANDERSON LESLIE L DR
Dent Aviles bl 49
Andrews L S r 3 Riverside dr 260-J
Andrews L S Jr r 34 Michell 129-W

B

Barnett Natl Bank of Cocoa 15 Harrison 5
Bass D C r Merritt Fla 185-W
Bass Emma Mrs r 505 Brevard av 322-W
Beach C H r Rockledge 303-W
Beaty F P r 112 Highland Park av 111
Bennett H E Store Brevard av 74-J
BLACK CAT DRY CLEANER CO
11 Oleander 92
Blakeslee D A r S Rockledge 145-W
Bodifield Chas T Mrs r Sunrise 356-R
Booth A E r Highland av 210-W
Bovard O B City Point Fla 345-M
Braun P Mrs r Courtenay Fla .... Call L D
Brock G R r Valencia dr 248-W
Brodmann R W r Rockledge 118
BROWN ELECTRIC CO
307 Delannoy av 39
Brown F L r 19 Parkway 314-J
Bruen Geo H r .... Call L D
Buck A A r Indianola 149-J
Buick Automobile Agency 223 King 29
Bus Station of
COLONIAL STAGES SOUTH INC
210 Williard 161
Buxton W W r Rockledge 270-J

C

Canaveral Pier & Fish Co Harrison 18
CANDY SHOP THE
205 Brevard av 9115
Cannon H W r 44
Cannon H W Jr r 175-J
Carlton B F r Indianola 164-W
Chalker J N r Rockledge 127-W
Childs A F r 225 Riverside dr 115-W
Childs Grace Mrs r 15 Palmetto av 327-J
City—See Cocoa City of
Cleveland Charlie r Merritt Fla 185-R
Cocoa Beauty Parlor Bellair Arcade 101-J
Cocoa City of
City Hall 350
Chief of Police r Sou Bell Tel bl 280-J
Fire Department 100
Police Department 45
Toll Bridge 95
Water Works 90
Cocoa Feed Co Magnolia av 56
Cocoa Fishery Delannoy 261-W
COCOA GARAGE CORP
Ofc 146 Brevard av 51
Cocoa High School principal's ofc 64
COCOA HOME LAUNDRY
King 177
Cocoa House ofc 101 Delanoy av 4
Cocoa Merritt Island Citrus Assn 19
Cocoa Millwork Co ofc 801 Brevard av 63
Cocoa Tribune ofc 407 Delannoy av 60
Cogswell H M r Barton av 190-J
Coleman H H r Rockledge 200
COLONIAL STAGES SOUTH INC
210 Williard 161
Colton Alfred S r Sharpes Fla .... Call L D
Copeland C R r Broadview Manor 330-W
Cox Geo O r Carleton ter 197-J
Crisman E M r Rockledge av 224
Crisman's Cadillac-LaSalle Service Orange av 223
Culler L M Mrs r 219 Oak 323-J

D

D'Albora John V r 12 Oak 133
Daniel L T Dr r 407 Palmetto av 76
Davidson Geo S r Broadview Manor 315-W
Davidson-Malone hdw 314 Delannoy av 1
Davis Manning J r N River dr 348-W
Day William M r Rockledge 125-M
DeBerry John R r Valencia rd 196
Dixon A L r City Point 348-J
Drinkwater A C r City Point 2004
Dunaway H M 126 Peachtree 83-J
Dunham J N r Valencia dr 186

E

EAST COAST LBR & SUPPLY CO
Ofc 221 Willard 7
Eastwick A M r Rockledge 235-W
Elks Club Dixie Hghy 9108
Ewing Henry W r Carleton ter 156-W

Seen here is the Cocoa telephone directory of connected numbers as of December 5, 1931. This 1931 telephone directory covered the Cocoa area from Sharpes to the north and Bonaventure to the south.

6 Fai—Par COCOA

PALMS DRY CLEANERS A Complete Modern Plant

F

Fairchild D M Mrs Merritt Fla 179-R
Fairview Land Co 291-J
Faulk W H r Rockledge 263-J
Fay Carl H contractor 136
Fay Carl H Mrs r Carleton ter 87-J
Fay L E r 106
FIELD J E
Groceries 304 Brevard av 21
Field J E r Indianola 164-R
Field R A r Rockledge 167-W
Fire Department Cocoa 100
Fire Department Rockledge 141
Fiske A C r S Riverside dr 42
Fleming W O r 7 Riverside dr 260-W
Fleming & Snow attys Central Arcade 229
F E C Ry passenger depot Poinsetta dr 22
Freight Ofc 28
FLORIDA POWER & LIGHT CO
401 Brevard av 50
Ice Plant Factory 122
Forest Ave Service Station Forest av 9112

G

Gable P K r River dr 360-M
Gast H F r S Rockledge 127-M
Geiger R L r Rockledge 262-W
Geiger R L Fertilizer Co Oak 93
Georgia-Florida Motor Lines Inc
(See Colonial Stages South Inc)
Gibbons D J r Merritt Fla 157-M
Gingras Geo r Rockledge 154-W
Glass S E r River dr 9080
Grimes E E Mrs r 413 Palmetto av 103
Grosse Otto R r Merritt Fla 159-W
Guice R R r Broadview Manor 315-J
Gulf Refining Co North 202

H

Hall Chester L r S River dr Rockledge 250-R
Heaton Wm r 42 Mulberry 360-J
Heilman H J Rockledge 262-R
Hendry Ewart Dr r City Point 198-J
Heule Holsey r Carleton ter 330-J
Hibbs C H Jr r 823 Florida av 194-J
Hibbs C H Sr Mrs r 644 Brevard av 174-W
Highfill L R r 54 Mulberry 359-J
Hill C L Dr r Indianola Fla 149-W
Hill L B r Olive 116
HILL MOTOR CO
308 Delannoy av 48
Hindle Wm r 10 South 13
Holderman C H Mrs r 61 Mulberry 326-J
Holmes R B r 235 Palmetto av 284-J
Hooper J W Fertilizer Bus King ..... 108 J
Hooper James W r Carleton ter 349-R
Howard B H r 209 S River dr 124-W
Humphrys F G r Indianola 179-W

I

Indian River Garage ofc 223 King 29
★INDIAN RIVER HOTEL Rockledge 230
Indian River Sub Exchange 8

J

Jackson James J atty Bellair bl 204
Res Riverside dr 33-J
Jaeger A B r Grimes 112
Jarvis Julia E groc 54 Parkway 78
Jenkins Chas R Jr Sharps Fla ..... Call L D
Johnson E C r 703 Palmetto av 210-R
Johnson E P r Valencia rd 120
Joiner C J r 5 Florida av 220
Jones Brick r King 121
Jones Virginia N Mrs r 326-W

K

KEMPFERS MARKET
301 Brevard av 52
Kenaston Thos C Dr ofc 416 Brevard av 213
Res 28 Mitchell 335-W
If no answer call 81
Kennedy A J r 114 Oak 325-J
Kershaw P L r 517 Palmetto av 357-J
Kiser R M ofc Rockledge 267
Kling C B r Rockledge 219
★KNOX HOTEL 210 Willard 161
Knox James C r Valencia rd 248-J

L

L & L FREIGHT LINES INC
122 Delannoy av 6
Langbein L J r Merritt Fla 157-R
Lapham Jelly Co Main 138-J
LaRoche D J r Courtenay ..... Call L D
LaRoche Edwards r Courtenay ..... Call L D
LaRoche R B r Courtenay ..... Call L D
LaVogue Beauty Shop 405 Delannoy av 119-J
Lawrence H W r Georgianna ..... Call L D
Liggett's Drug Store 315 Delannoy av 68
Lilly J W r 544 Delannoy av 9029
Lincoln Alice C Mrs r 227 Palmetto 296-J
Lockett D T r Indianola ..... Call L D
Loring Ralph N r 127 Grimes 210-M
Ludicke Ernest J r Carleton ter 240-R

M

MacFarland F H r 309-J
MacMillan J F ins Brevard av 188
MacMillan J F r Carleton Terrace 320-J
Malone Rogers W r Broadview Manor 315-W
Marston L C r 817 Palmetto av 151-J
Maxwell W V r Brevard Apts 211-W
McGinnis Almeda C Miss r Palmetto av 312-J
McGlaun Albert r Carleton ter 233-J
McKeown Arthur H r Rockledge 170-J
McLeod C E Mrs r Merritt Prk 147-R
Melton Wm r Courtenay ..... Call L D
Merritt Island Garage Merritt Fla 185-J
Mitchell J F r 307 Palmetto av 335-J
Moody A T Mrs r 617 Brevard av 252-W
Murrell R L r Rockledge av 271-R

N

Nelson Feed Store Willard 27
Nevins Fruit Co Forest av 245

O

Oaks Hotel Barton av 9109

P

Packard R M r 809 Palmetto av 356-W
PACKARD'S TRANSFER CO
Office 122 Delannoy av 6
Page W C Dr r Merritt 159-J
Page W C ofc 317 Delannoy av 31
Palm Dry Cleaning Co 203 Brevard av 16
Palmer C M r Rockledge 125-R
Parks & Van Nest Packing House Forest av 130-J
Parrish H U r 106 Riverside dr 246

Seen here is the Cocoa telephone directory of connected numbers as of December 5, 1931. Some calls to Sharpes, Georgiana (south Merritt Island), Courtenay (north Merritt Island), and Bonaventure were long-distance calls.

Cleaners---Dyers---Alterations Tel. 16
SHOE REPAIRERS

Paterson John r 133 Peachtree..............129-J
Paterson W G r 215 Riverside dr...........124-J
Peckenpaugh E P r Sweet...................354-R
Perry Walter D r Rockledge................239-W
Pinkerton S M r Sharpes...................2002
Pluckebaum Geo J r Old Dixie Hghwy.........127-J
Police Department Cocoa...................45
Police Department Rockledge...............303-W
Poole Wm H r 19 South.....................176-J
Porcher A G r.............................255
Porcher E P ofc...........................253
Porcher E P r 434 Delannoy av.............254
Porcher E P Grove Courtenay.............Call L D
Post Office U S Govt......................10
Postal Telegraph Co 116 Harrison........Call Postal
Provost C D r 837 N Palmetto av...........43
Provost Office Equipment Co Harrison av...75
Pruitt Vulc Works Willard.................9104
Pursell H E Carleton ter..................98-W

Q

Quinby W H Mrs r Rockledge................145-J

R

Railway Express Agency Inc Oak............300
Ranck Earle E r Rockledge.................114-W
RED STAR PHARMACY
305 Delannoy..............................9111
Reed Charles E r 106 Sweet Rockledge.......354-J
Reed J E r Indianola......................149-R
Rembert R M r Rockledge...................270-R
Rhoads A S r Carleton Ter.................349-M
Ribsam N J r City Point...................198-W
Richards C E Mrs r Indianola..............179-M
Ringo M A r Carleton ter..................240-W
Roberts C V r S Riverside dr..............351-J
Rockledge City of
City Marshall.............................303-W
Fire Department...........................141
Rockledge Woman's Exchange Barton av......91-W
Ronald T G r 11 Riverside dr..............257-W
Rothmund Jennie Mrs r Rockledge...........170-W
RUBIN BROS
Store.....................................41
Rubin I r.................................33-W
Rummell Richard W r Valencia dr...........247-J

S

Sams J Devoe r Courtenay................Call L D
Sanders Lilla V Miss r 226 Willard........242-W
Schlernitzauer Bob Dr ofc S Riverside dr..23
Res S Riverside dr........................271-M
Schnabel Carl A Mrs r Riverside dr........346-J
Scott George J Georgianna...............Call L D
Scurry B C Dr r...........................173-J
Seagroatt H G Mrs r Carleton Ter..........244-W
Seely D N r City Point....................345-R
Shanahan Chas E r Valencia rd.............166-J
heffield Sarah Mrs r N River dr...........346-W
Shell Service Station S Magnolia av.......9106
Shelton V E r.............................354-W
Shelton's Pharmacy 305 Brevard av.........81
Shepard John D atty Harrison..............30
Shepard John D r Rockledge................259-W
Shiver Louis Mrs r Poinsetta dr...........338-W
Ske'ly G W r S Riverside dr...............271-W
Skinner Alfred F r 829 N River dr.........89
Skinner Alfred P r Valencia rd............184
Smith Chas D r City Point.................198-M
Smith C Sweet r Carleton Ter..............337-W
Smith's Grocery Store Sharpes Fla.......Call L D
SMITH'S MOTOR CO
Ofc 109 Brevard av........................3
Snow Russell r Broadview Manor............283-J
Snyder L V r..............................175-W
SOU BELL TEL & TEL CO INC
For reporting trouble with your telephone
call....................................Repair Service
For subscribers not listed call.........Information
Business Office...........................9000
Standard Oil Company ofc..................54
Standard Oil Co Forrest av................9118
Standard Service Station Magnolia av......9116
Stark E E Mrs r S River dr................270-M
Sterling's Garage Bonaventure...........Call L D
Stewarts Garage Fla av....................9119
Swan W H & Co dry goods 307 Brevard av....237

T

T R Indian River Orange Co Williard.......77
Tarter C R r City Point...................345-W
Taylor E Wright atty Delannoy av..........134
Thompson Bert r Barton av.................169-W
Thompson H A r 107 Oak....................266-J
Tobacco Dealers Co ofc 103 Brevard av.....110
Tomasello P Jr Brevard av.................35
Tompkins E J r Rockledge..................20
Townsend W O r Carleton Ter...............98-J
Trafford A R r 109 Indian River dr........73
TRAFFORD & FIELD
Realtors..................................66
TRAFFORD & FIELD INS CO
Harrison..................................188
Travis Alma K Mrs r 128 N Palmetto av.....53-J
TRAVIS INSURANCE CO
Ofc.......................................58
TRAVIS S F & CO
Hdw 300 Delanoy av........................2
Tucker Edna Mrs SBT&T Co Delannoy av......9040
Res Delannoy av...........................9084
Tucker W A r..............................280-J
Turner Clara E Mrs r 29 Highland av.......210-J

U

United Realty Co 409 Brevard av...........58

V

Von Toble A F Rev r W Orange av...........190-W

W

WALLER JAS B DR
Ofc Aviles bl.............................47
Res Orange av.............................169-J
Walton Fred r Sunrise.....................356-J
Watkins Market Brevard av.................9122
Watt Chas C r 227 Riverside dr............307-J
Weathers Billiard Parlor 201 Brevard av...9123
Wells W G r Carleton ter..................240-J
Western Union Tel Co....................Western Union
Whaley M S r Rockledge....................125-J
Wheeler R N r Carleton ter................98-R
Whisonent Van groc 323 Magnolia...........173-W
White C M Rev r 216 Oak...................174-J
White Chas B Dr r Highland Ct Apts........123-W
Whitworth J B r Rockledge.................235-R
William's Service Sta 221 Forrest av......9120
Williams Myra Gray Miss r Rockledge.......313-J
Wilson & Toomer Fertilizer Co Warehouse...201
Wolary Carl L r 30 Highland av............216-J
Woodruff H R r............................291-J

Seen here is the Cocoa telephone directory of connected numbers as of December 5, 1931. To use telephones in the directory, callers picked up the receiver, and an operator asked, "Number, please?" Then the caller told the operator the desired number. Outlying area telephones had a crank on the side used to ring the operator.

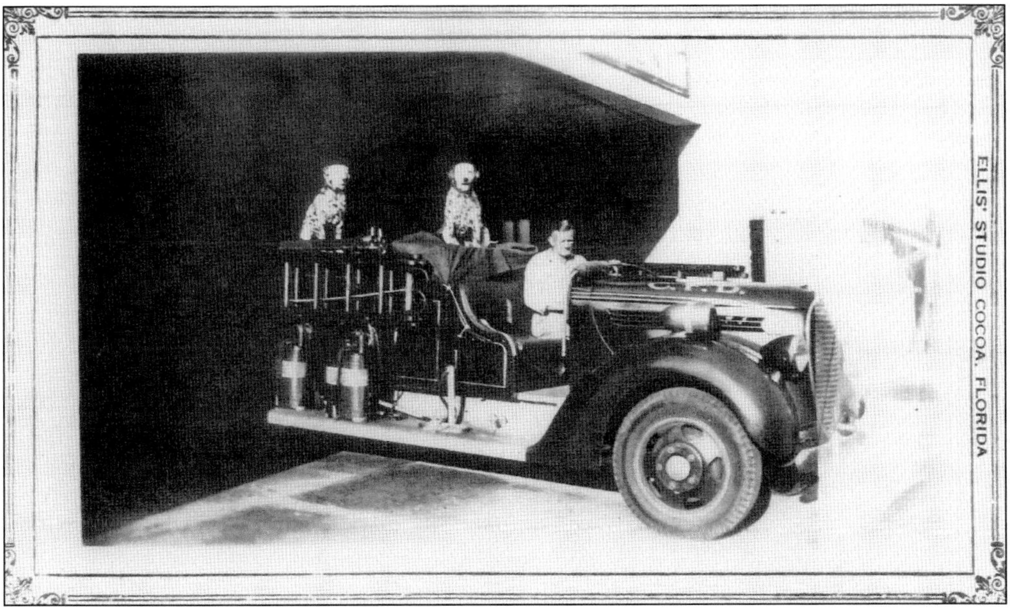

Brick Jones, assistant fire chief for the City of Cocoa, drives Cocoa's new 1935 Ford fire truck. The fire station was located at 224 King Street, and the city jail inhabited the rear of the building. The Jones family lived on the second floor. This building is no longer in existence.

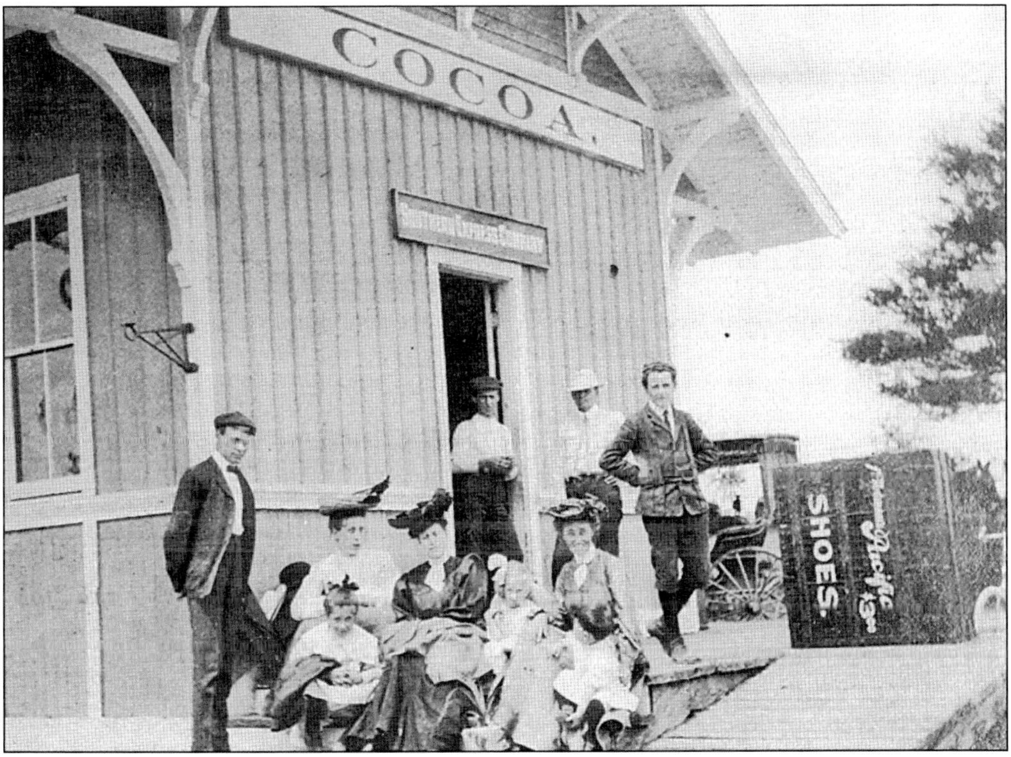

This photograph, taken by Charles A. Vuille, shows an early railroad depot in Cocoa. This depot was located near the intersection of Forrest Avenue and Peachtree Street. (Courtesy Vuille and Sayers families.)

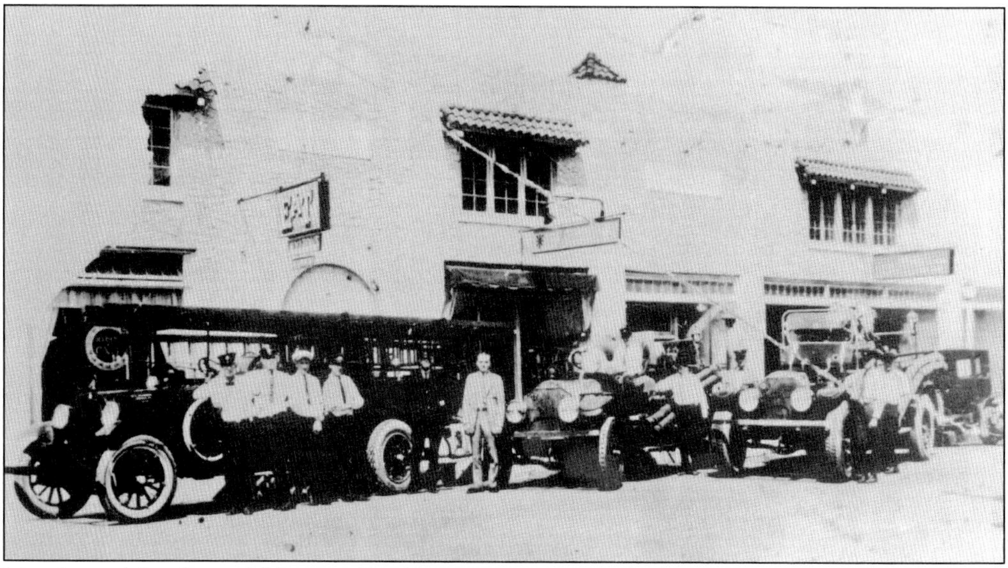

Members of the Cocoa Volunteer Fire Department pose with the mayor of Cocoa around 1923. Pictured from left to right are R. M. Kiser, Cary Kiser, Joe Cowart, Harrison Daniel, police chief Herbert Ray, Mayor Louis Andrews, driver Brick Jones, Earl Lamar, Charlie Hibbs, two unidentified men, and James Footman. The portion of the building behind the car was Smith and Wooten's Ford dealership.

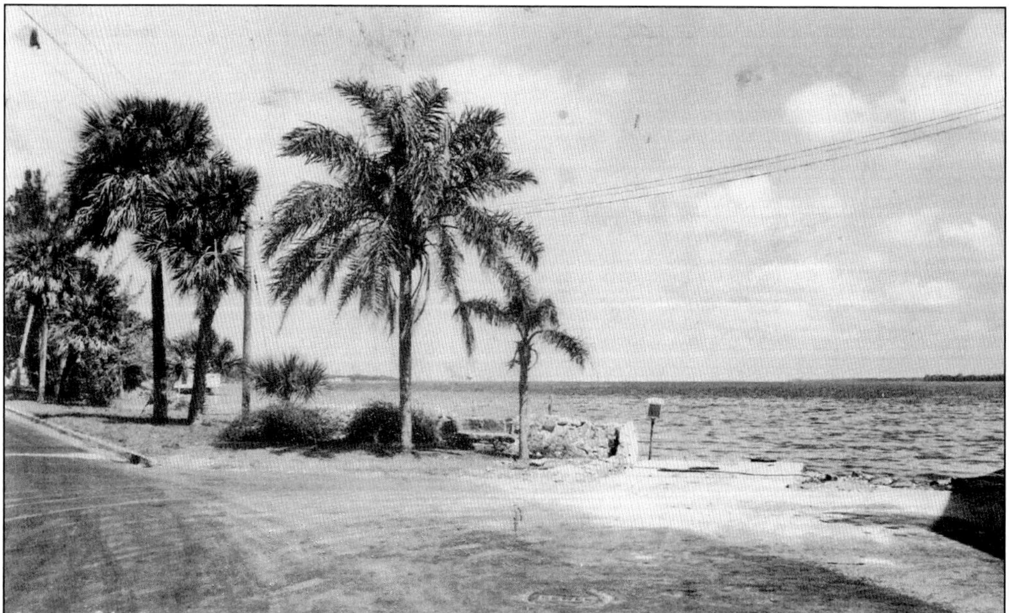

This view of the Indian River depicts the north end of Brevard Avenue and the intersection of Indian River Drive, formerly known as Palmetto.

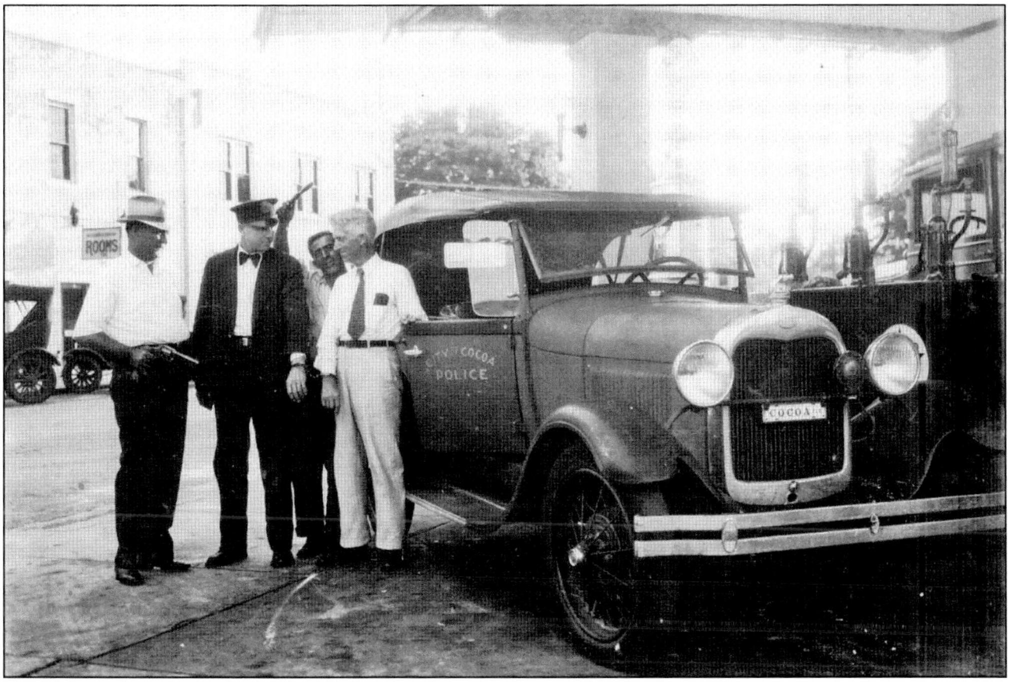

A Cocoa police car is parked at Keehner's Gulf Service Station, at the northwest corner of Brevard Avenue and Oleander Street. Shown from left to right are Brevard County deputy Link Silsby, night policeman Henry K. Evans, unidentified, and Lou Fenner.

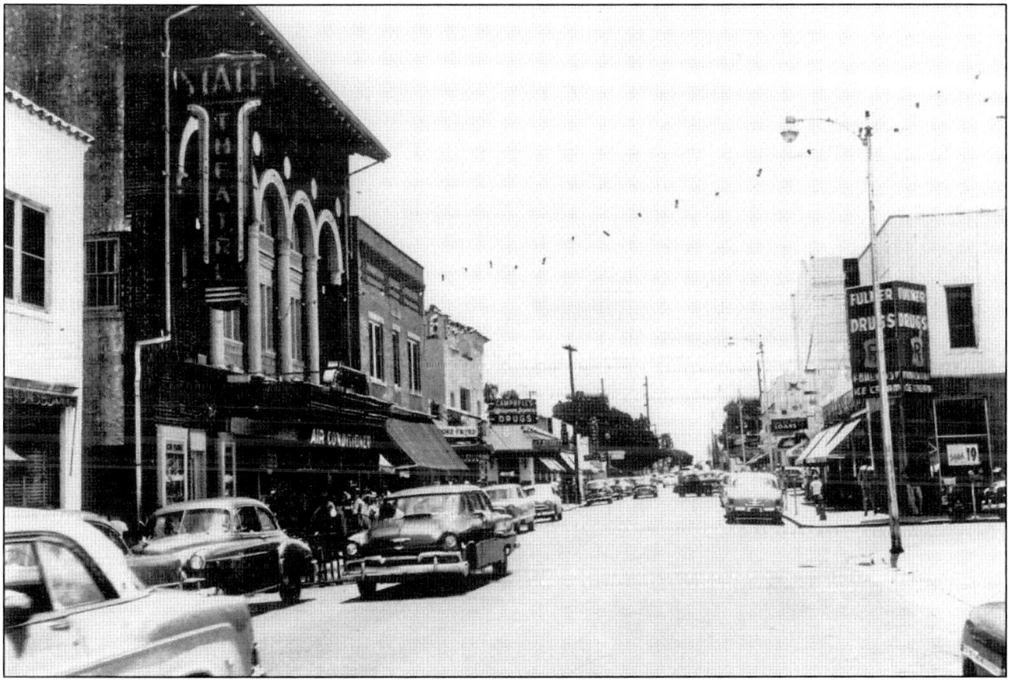

Brevard Avenue is pictured in this c. 1950 southward view. The Cocoa Village Playhouse and Campbell's Drug Store and Fountain are on the left, while Fulmer Drugs, also with a soda fountain, is on the right. These were great places for teenagers to hang out.

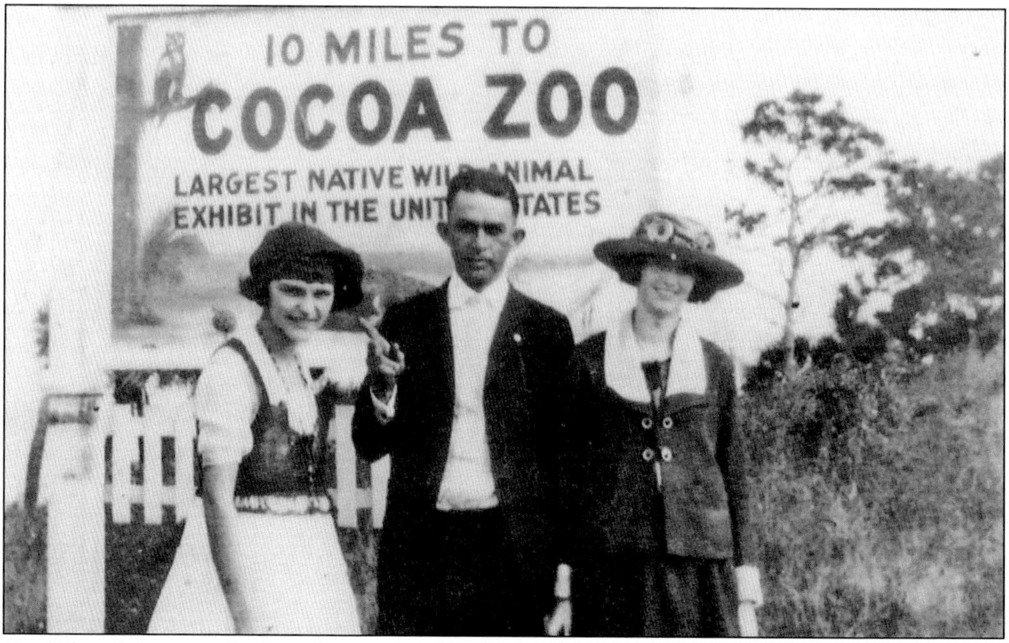

Gus Edwards is reputed to have been invited to the area by S. F. Travis. Edwards was an entrepreneur of the first order. He had practiced law in Georgia, spent time in Texas, and later, during World War II, served in an official government agency. After arriving in Cocoa in 1918, he, along with various associates, developed Cocoa Beach in the 1920s. Always promoting new ventures, Edwards decided to bring a few of the armadillos that he had become familiar with in Texas to Cocoa. They would become the nucleus of the Cocoa Zoo. Eventually the zoo went broke, and someone released the armadillos. Seen here from left to right are Eva Taylor, David Taylor, and Babe ?, potential customers from North Brevard.

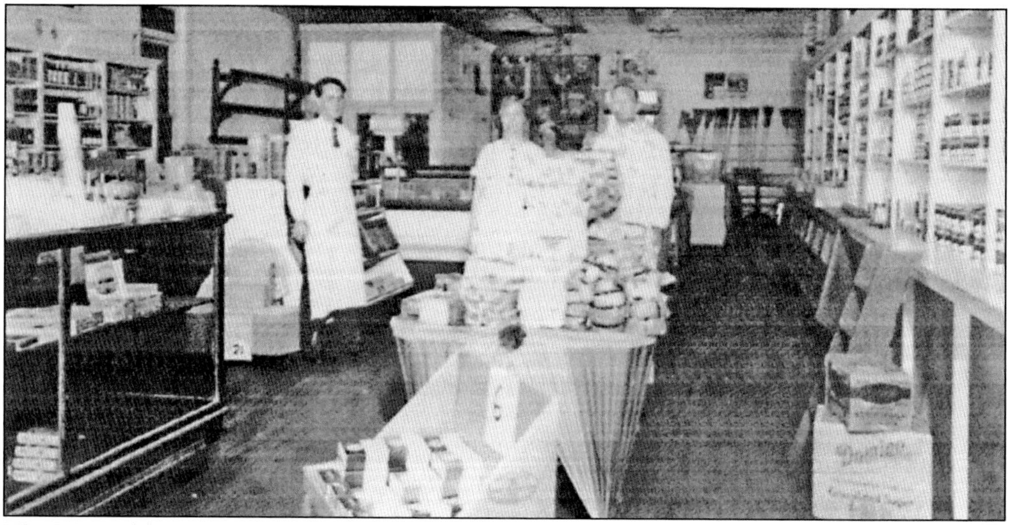

The J. E. Field Grocery store, the interior of which is seen here, was located at 304–306 Brevard Avenue. It is the building south and adjacent to today's Village Playhouse. Field had an earlier store at Indianola. When the bridge from Merritt Island to Cocoa was completed in 1917, allowing easier crossings of the Indian River, Field moved his business to Cocoa. Edward Field (left), Joe Field (center), and Joe's wife, Louise Field, are pictured.

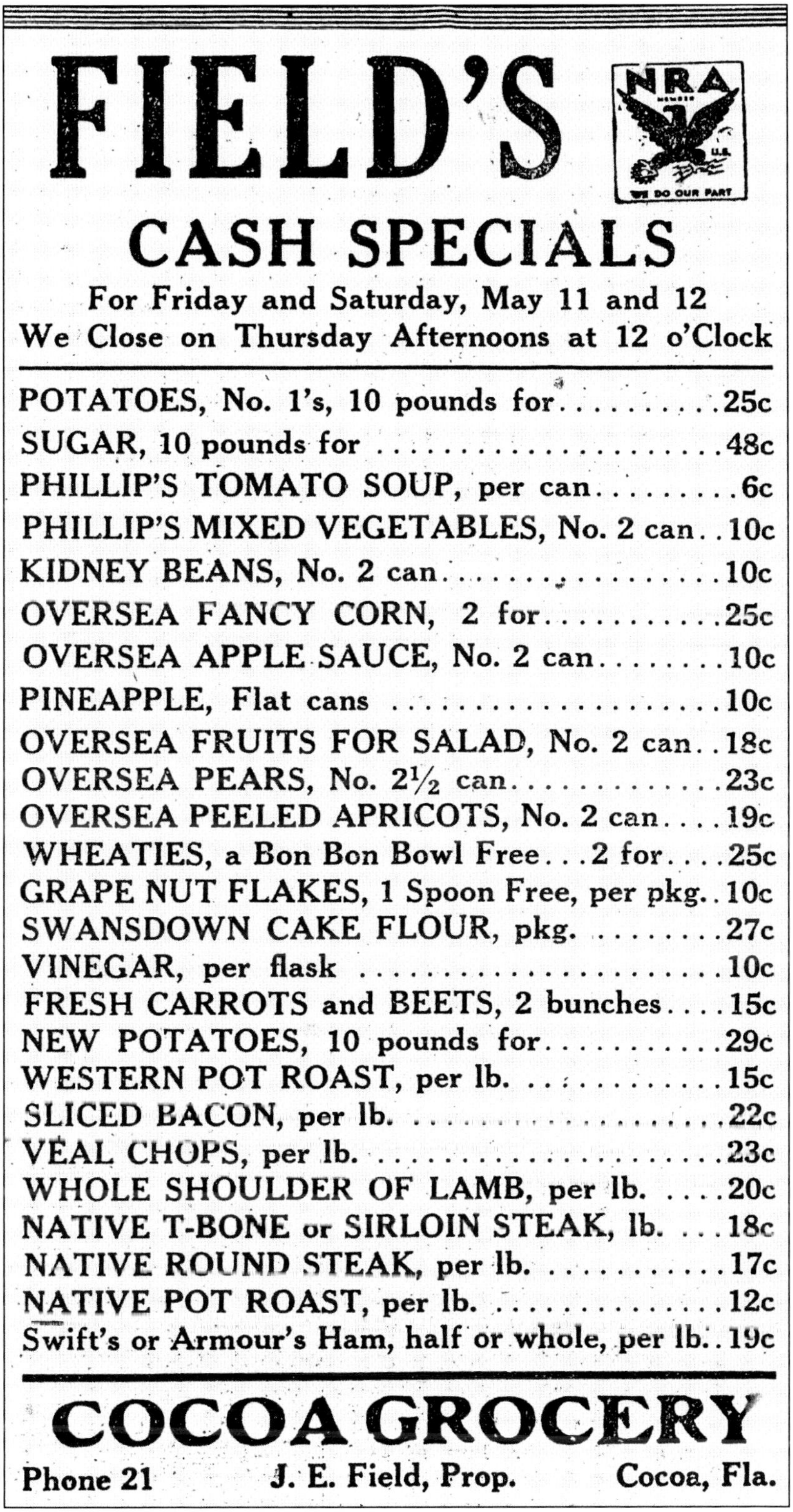

FIELD'S

NRA MEMBER U.S. WE DO OUR PART

CASH SPECIALS

For Friday and Saturday, May 11 and 12
We Close on Thursday Afternoons at 12 o'Clock

POTATOES, No. 1's, 10 pounds for 25c
SUGAR, 10 pounds for 48c
PHILLIP'S TOMATO SOUP, per can 6c
PHILLIP'S MIXED VEGETABLES, No. 2 can .. 10c
KIDNEY BEANS, No. 2 can 10c
OVERSEA FANCY CORN, 2 for 25c
OVERSEA APPLE SAUCE, No. 2 can 10c
PINEAPPLE, Flat cans 10c
OVERSEA FRUITS FOR SALAD, No. 2 can .. 18c
OVERSEA PEARS, No. 2½ can 23c
OVERSEA PEELED APRICOTS, No. 2 can 19c
WHEATIES, a Bon Bon Bowl Free ... 2 for 25c
GRAPE NUT FLAKES, 1 Spoon Free, per pkg .. 10c
SWANSDOWN CAKE FLOUR, pkg. 27c
VINEGAR, per flask 10c
FRESH CARROTS and BEETS, 2 bunches 15c
NEW POTATOES, 10 pounds for 29c
WESTERN POT ROAST, per lb. 15c
SLICED BACON, per lb. 22c
VEAL CHOPS, per lb. 23c
WHOLE SHOULDER OF LAMB, per lb. 20c
NATIVE T-BONE or SIRLOIN STEAK, lb. ... 18c
NATIVE ROUND STEAK, per lb. 17c
NATIVE POT ROAST, per lb. 12c
Swift's or Armour's Ham, half or whole, per lb. . 19c

COCOA GROCERY

Phone 21 J. E. Field, Prop. Cocoa, Fla.

This advertisement ran in the *Cocoa Tribune* on October 18, 1934, during the Depression following the stock market crash of 1929. These prices are hard for today's generation to believe. The emblem in the upper right corner signifies the National Recovery Act.

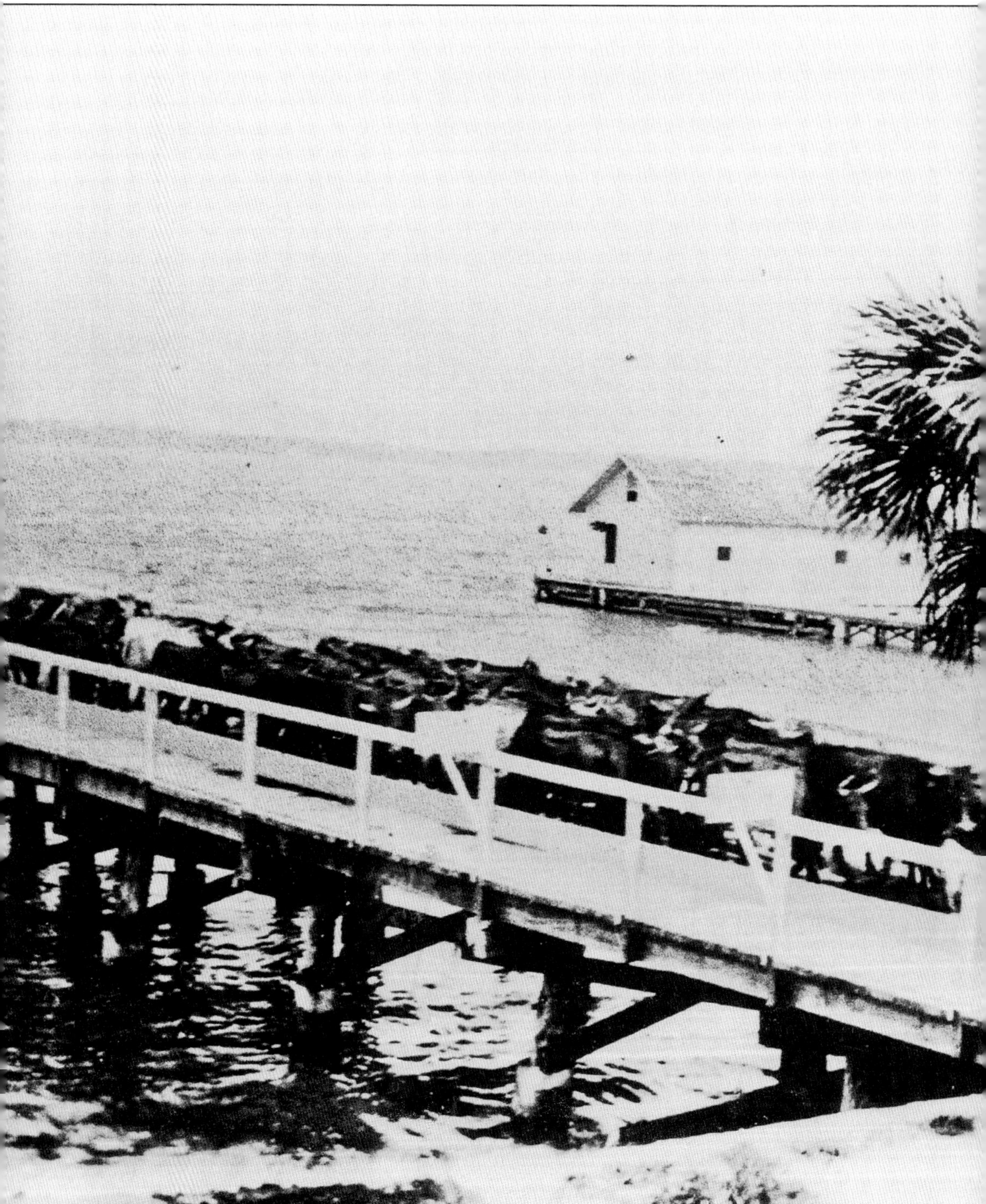

Cattle are driven from Merritt Island over the newly completed bridge to Cocoa. Open-range cattle roamed freely on Merritt Island until a fence law was passed requiring the animals to be

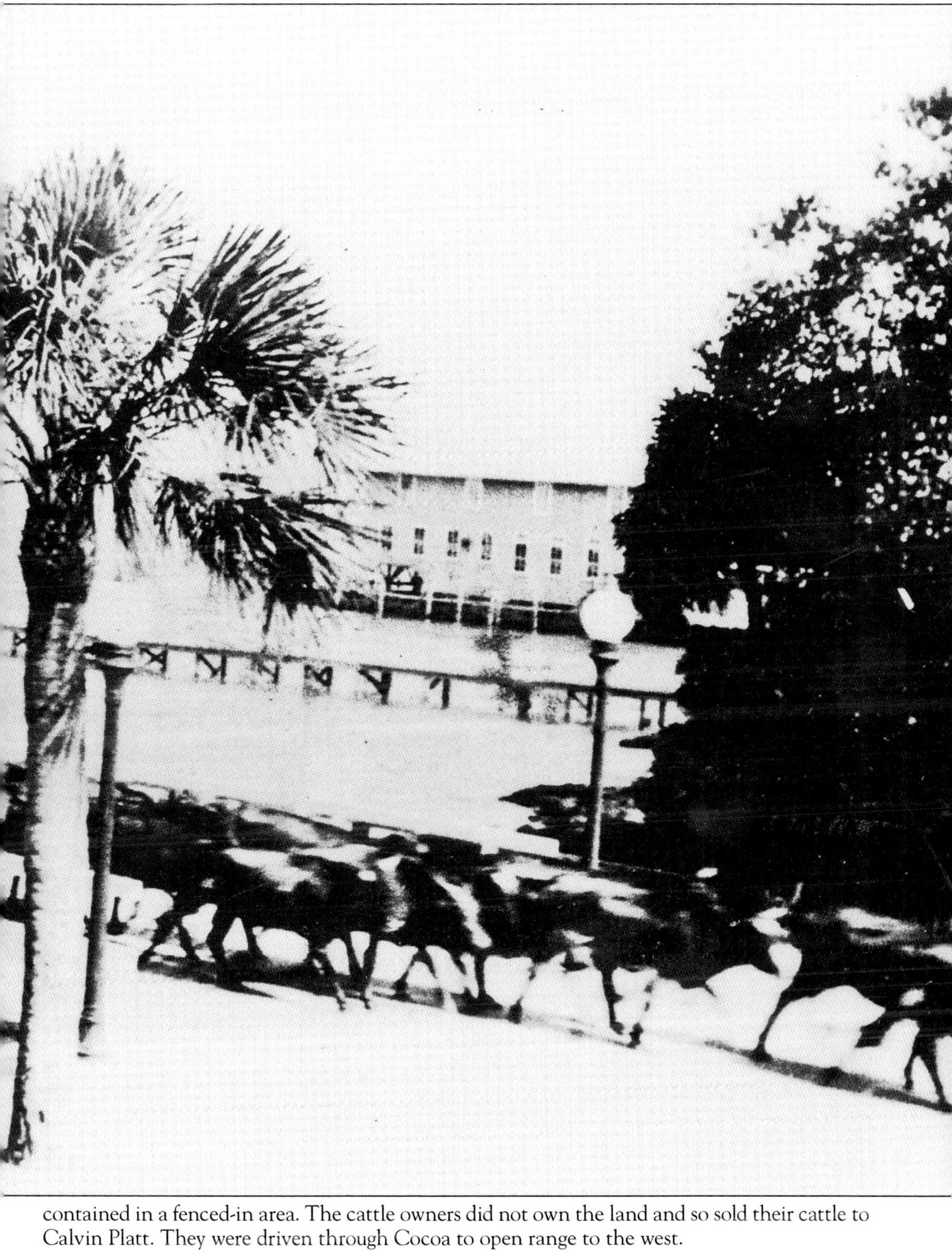

contained in a fenced-in area. The cattle owners did not own the land and so sold their cattle to Calvin Platt. They were driven through Cocoa to open range to the west.

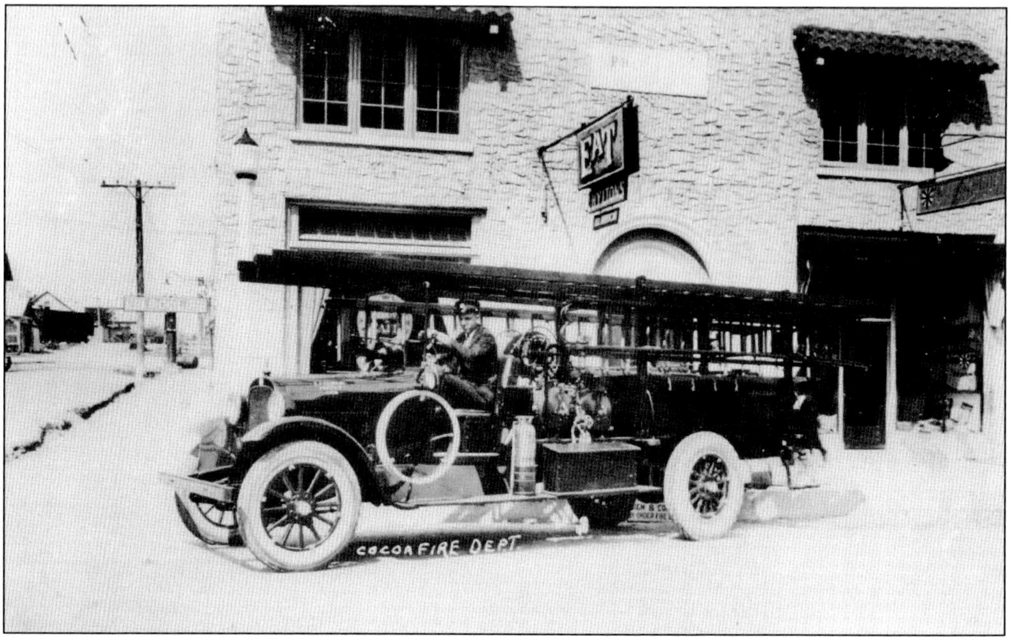

A calamitous fire destroyed a large part of downtown Cocoa in the 1890s, but rebuilding began immediately. By the early 1920s, a modernized fire department was in place. Here Robert Copeland mans the wheel of the newly purchased fire engine. Many proud residents signed up to be part of the volunteer fire department.

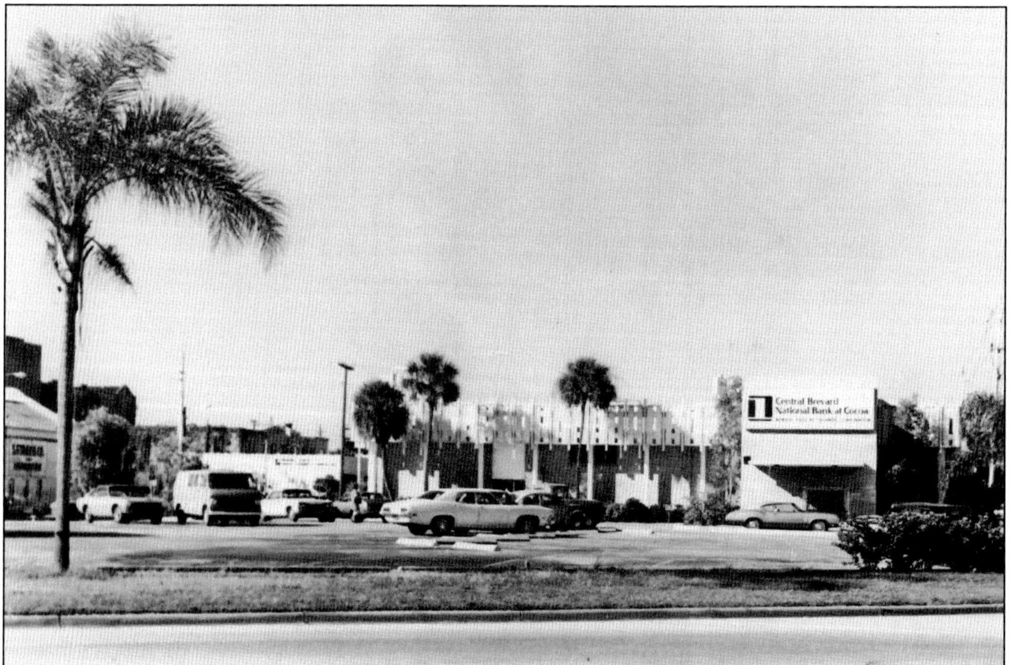

This view looks west at Central Brevard National Bank, built in 1956–1957, where a portion of the Indian River was filled in by dredging, thus creating land. Barnett National Bank had been Cocoa's only bank since the 1929 stock market crash until this institution was built.

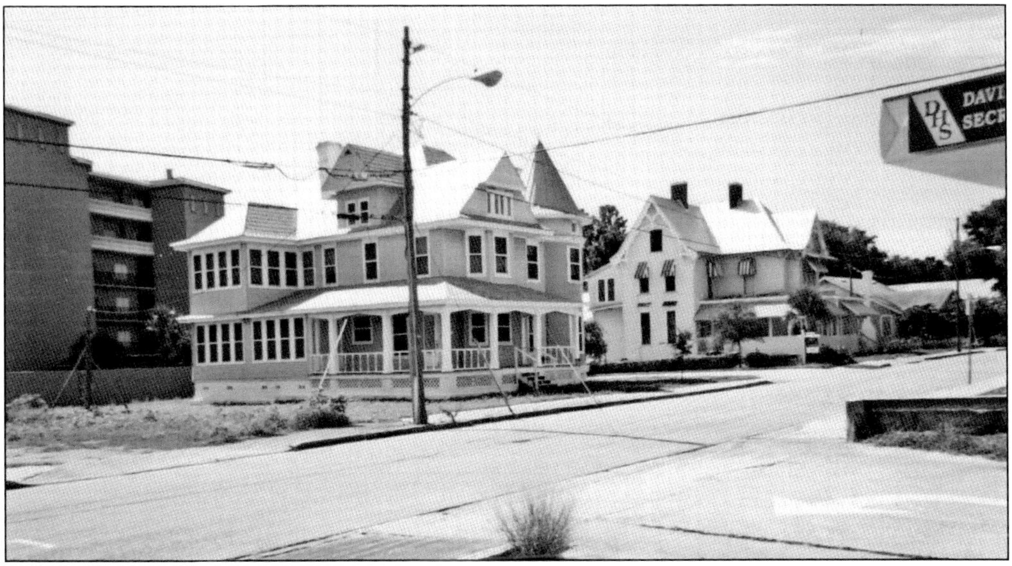

A couple of "mobile" homes sit today on Delannoy Avenue, both moved from their original settings. The late-19th-century Shepard Home (in the forefront) was brought by barge up the Indian River from Rockledge to join the Parrish Home, built in the 1880s as a hunting lodge. The Parrish Home was also originally a riverfront residence, but around the start of the 21st century was turned around and brought to rest in its present location. Between the houses is a driveway leading to the Riverside Landing Condominium, which now occupies the original Parrish Home site.

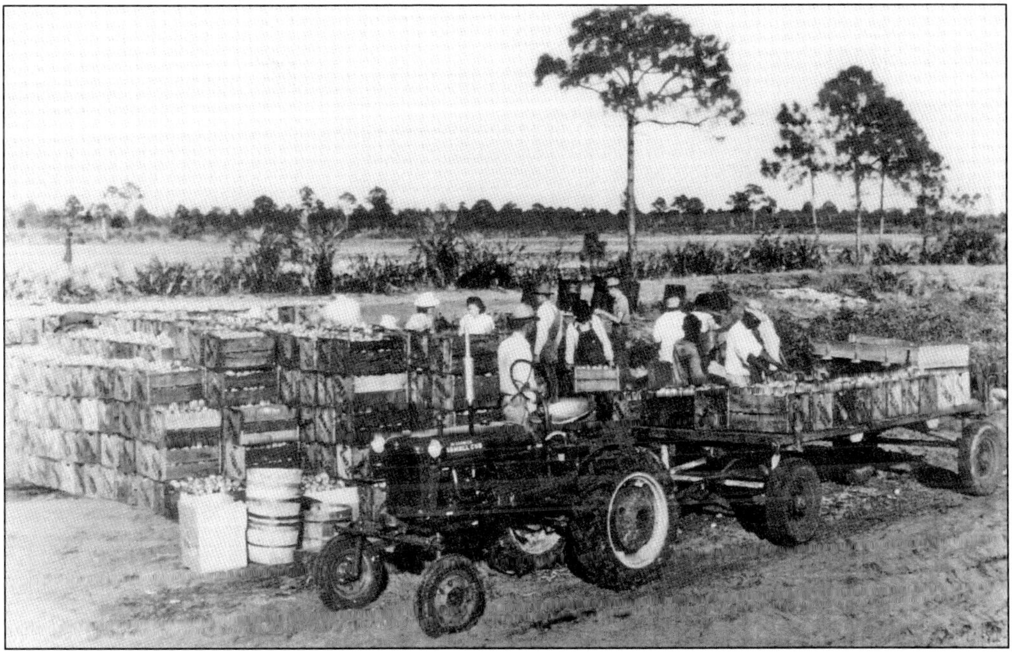

Tomatoes are harvested on Jimmy Atkinson's farm west of Cocoa. Farming was one of the area's foremost activities from the beginning settlement. This photograph was taken shortly after World War II. People believed that new land was best for growing tomatoes; after one or two crops, the land would not produce a quality crop.

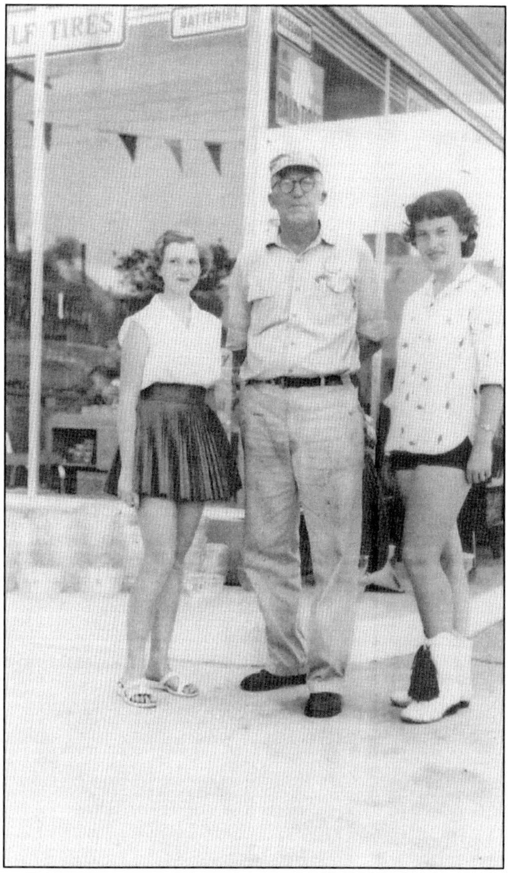

Opening festivities occur at Weinburg's Gulf service station, at the corner of Brevard Avenue and Church Street. Peggy Burcham (left), Jim Weinburg (center), and Faye Ackroyd are pictured. Al Moody had owned the old station, and Weinburg worked for him before buying the business. Frank Schumacker worked for Weinburg and eventually purchased the station, running the business until it closed.

This *c.* 1946 view looks north on Delannoy Avenue from Harrison Street. To the back of the stores on the right was the Indian River. The building at the far end of the street (Blair's Studio) was entirely constructed over the water. Travis Hardware, the tall building on the right, has been in business for more than 100 years.

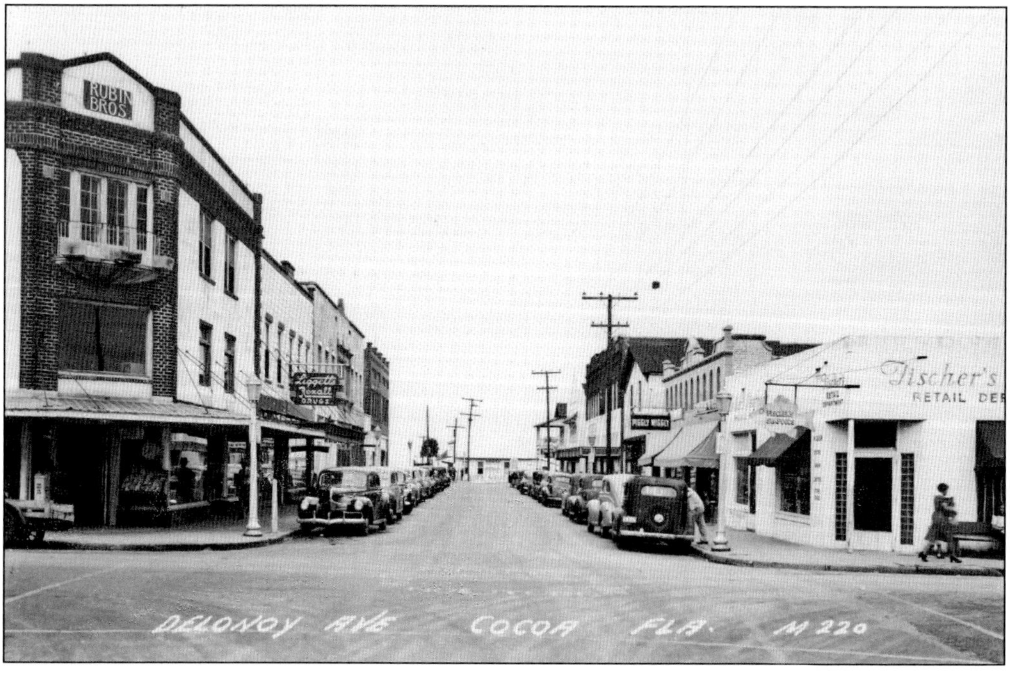

Four

Rockledge to Pineda

In the early days of Rockledge, people went south by traveling upstream on the St. Johns River. The St. Johns is navigable as far south as Sanford on Lake Monroe. Smaller, shallow draft steamers brought passengers south from Enterprise on the north shore of Lake Monroe to Lake Poinsett, then east through Lake Florence up Rockledge Creek to a landing. At this point, mules and wagons took over. Small settlements such as Pineda and Bonaventure were established. These places did not have stores to supply all the needs of the settlers, so Cocoa—a town with doctors, drugstores, and trades of the day—became more and more important.

Brevard's first state senator introduced a bill into the Florida legislature to incorporate Rockledge as a city. On August 6, 1887, after little debate, Rockledge became Brevard's first incorporated city.

Cocoa became an incorporated city on October 1, 1895. Its south boundary and the north boundary of Rockledge met, making the towns adjacent. For many years, Rockledge served as a bedroom community for Cocoa, but now with business and industrial sections, it has in fact grown larger than its sister city.

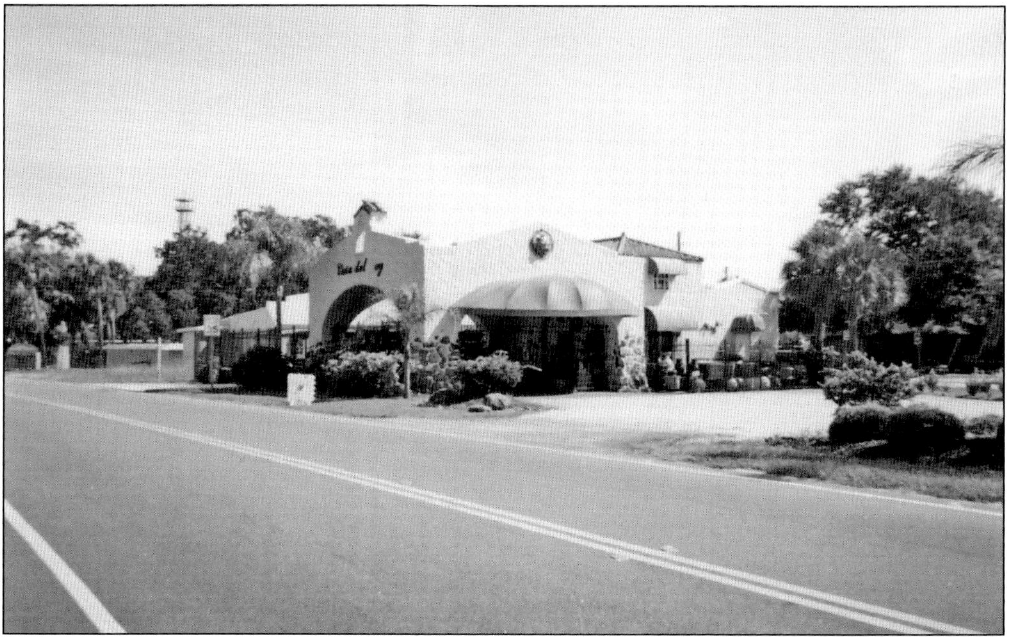

Dyal's Service Station stood on Florida Avenue, which was then U.S. Highway 1, the main north-south route through Cocoa and Rockledge. The station was open 24 hours a day and provided a great hangout spot for teenagers during World War II.

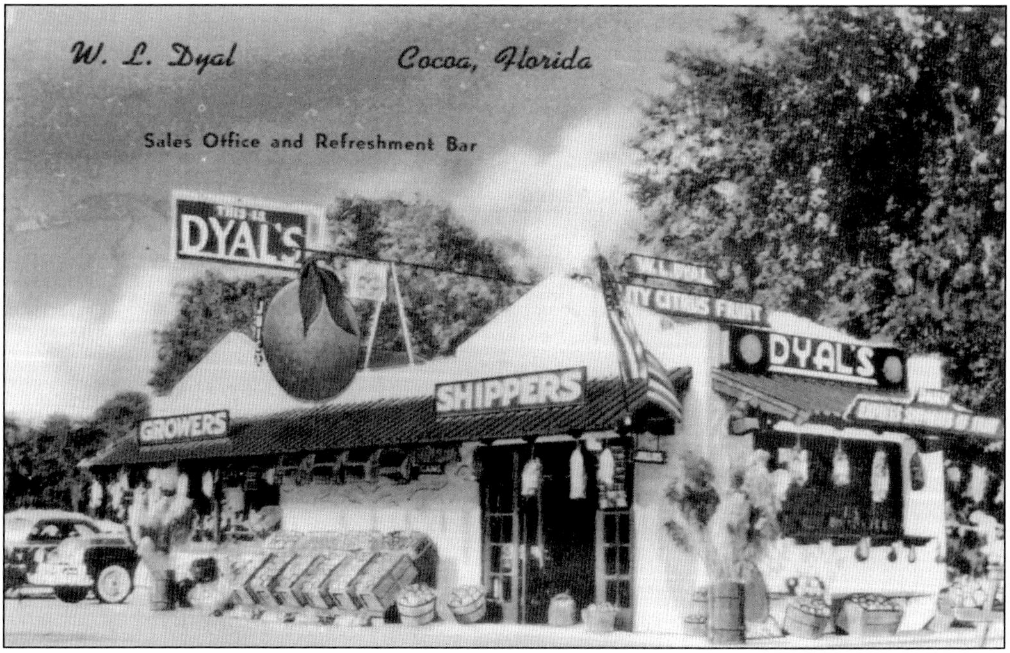

Located adjacent to the service station was Dyal's Fruit Stand, at the intersection of Brevard and Florida Avenues. When U.S. Highway 1 was relocated west of Florida Avenue, this building became the Triangle Bar, serving the coldest draft beer in the area.

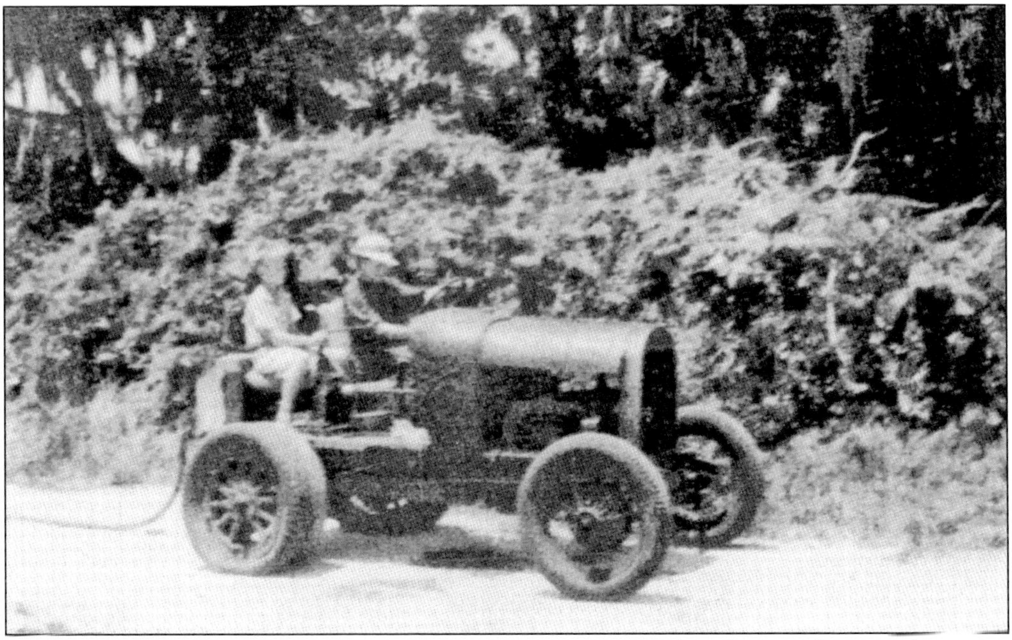

Emma Mae Rambo and her nephew Marcellus Rambo Benson ride on Emma's homemade tractor. In the 1930s, many people would cut cars down to bare essentials and change the rear wheel–drive mechanism to one from a truck to increase the pulling power. This "tractor" consisted of a motor and front end from a Model A Ford and a rear end from an unidentified truck.

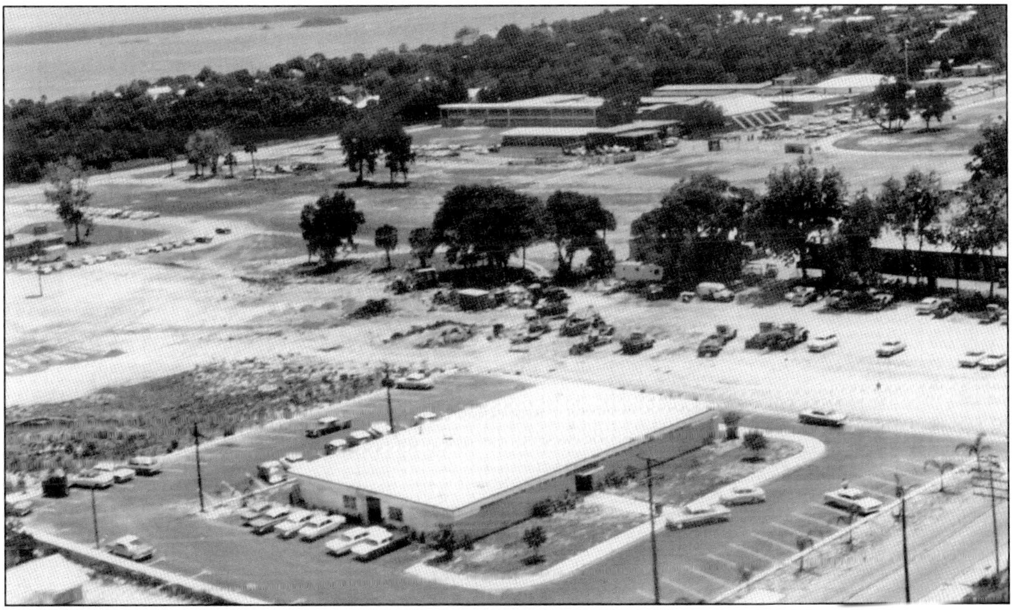

This overview depicts the Brevard County Branch Courthouse in Rockledge, which stands on the old U.S. 1 (now Florida Avenue). Courtrooms were located here, and the county clerk also handled local services. In the background is the former Cocoa High School, which really was in Rockledge at that time. The round building is the auditorium, and the structure with the flying buttresses is the gymnasium. In 1970, Cocoa High got its own home on Rosetine Street in Cocoa, and this campus became Rockledge High School.

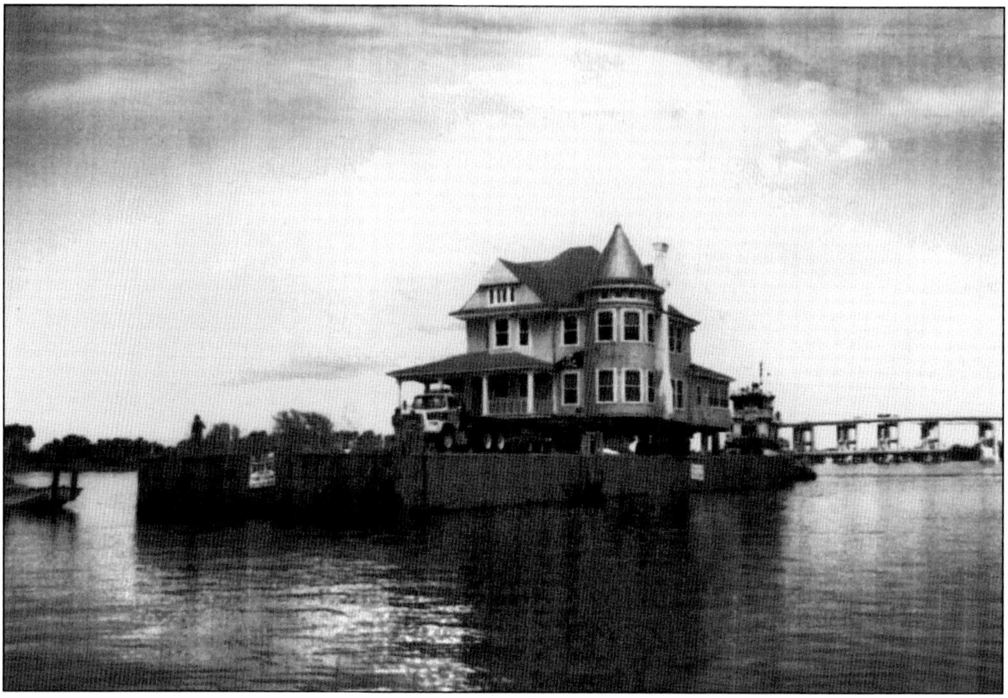

This late-19th-century Queen Anne–style home, originally at 621 Rockledge Drive in Rockledge, was purchased in 2004 and scheduled for demolition to allow for a high-price housing development. The residence belonged to the John D. Shepard family. Henry Parrish III heard about the impending demolition and bought the house. He had it loaded on a barge in the Indian River and floated it to its new site on Delannoy Avenue in Cocoa. It is situated next to the Parrish Home, which was rotated and settled on Delannoy Avenue, leaving the riverfront in Cocoa as the location for the Riverside Landing Condominium.

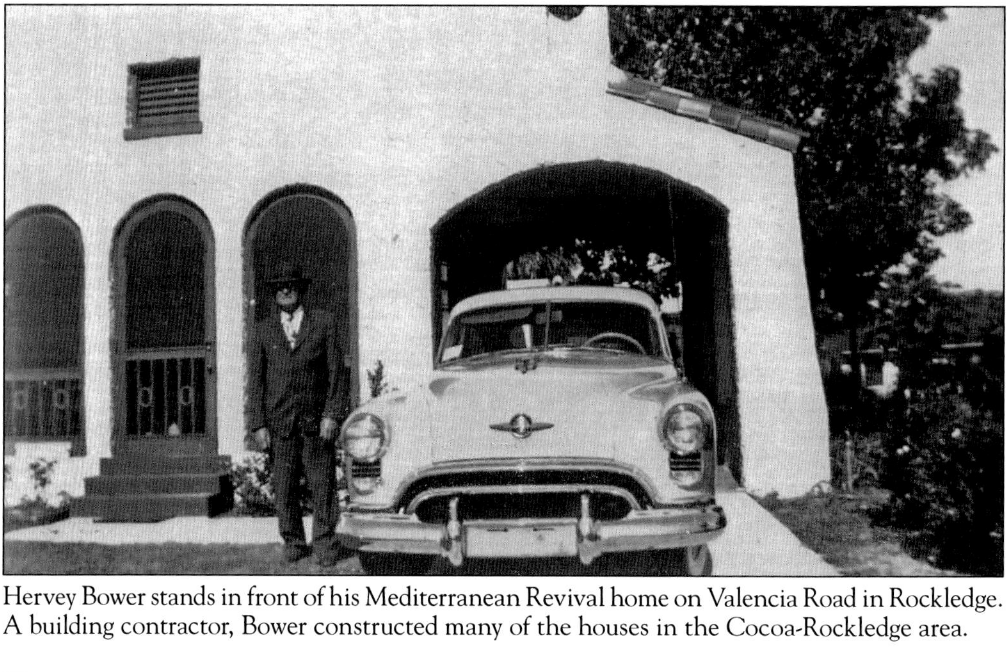

Hervey Bower stands in front of his Mediterranean Revival home on Valencia Road in Rockledge. A building contractor, Bower constructed many of the houses in the Cocoa-Rockledge area.

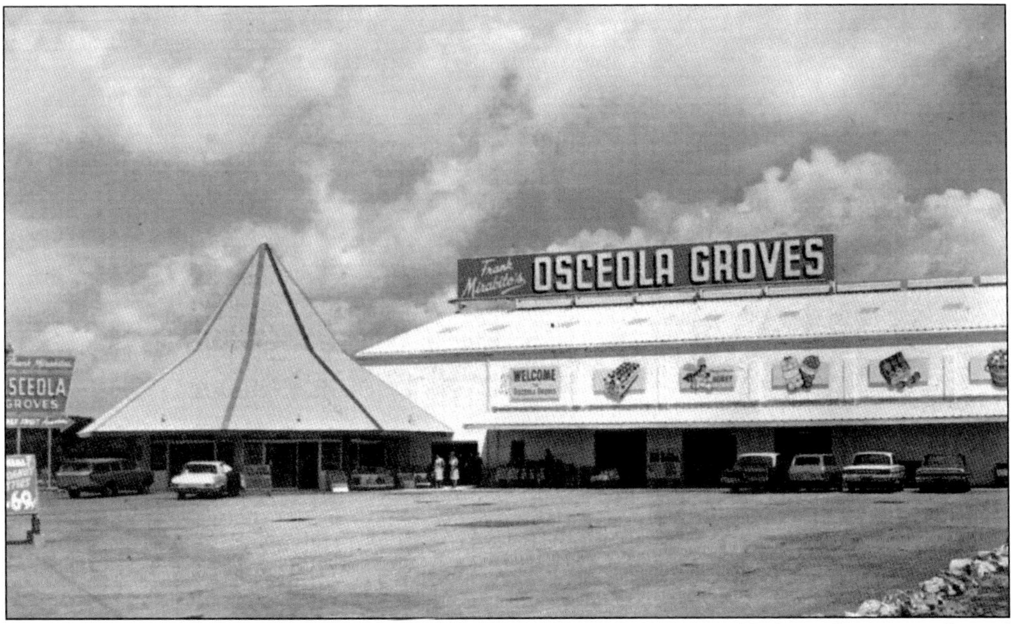

Frank Mirabito owned Osceola Groves, situated on U.S. 1 in south Rockledge. The teepee-shaped part of the building was added after Mirabito closed the fruit business. The building currently houses the Blind Place, a Venetian blind store.

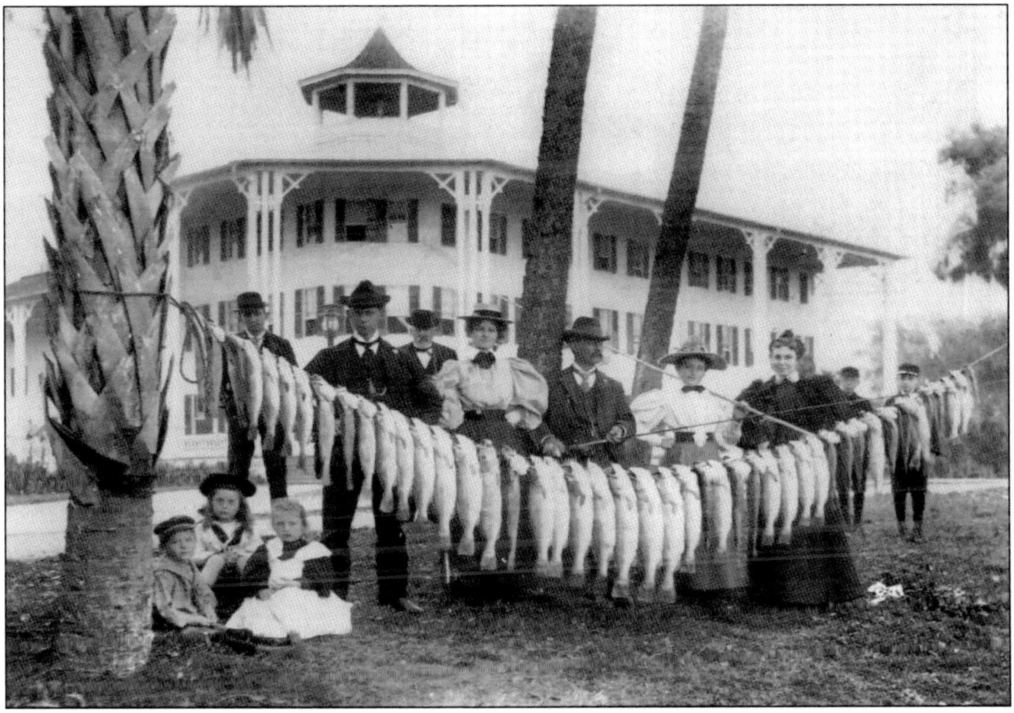

This photograph was taken at the Plaza Hotel in Rockledge on February 27, 1896. Guests of the hotel are admiring a fine catch of spotted weakfish, also known as saltwater trout. Old-timers say that in these days a fisherman had to go behind a tree to bait his hook, or else a fish would get the bait.

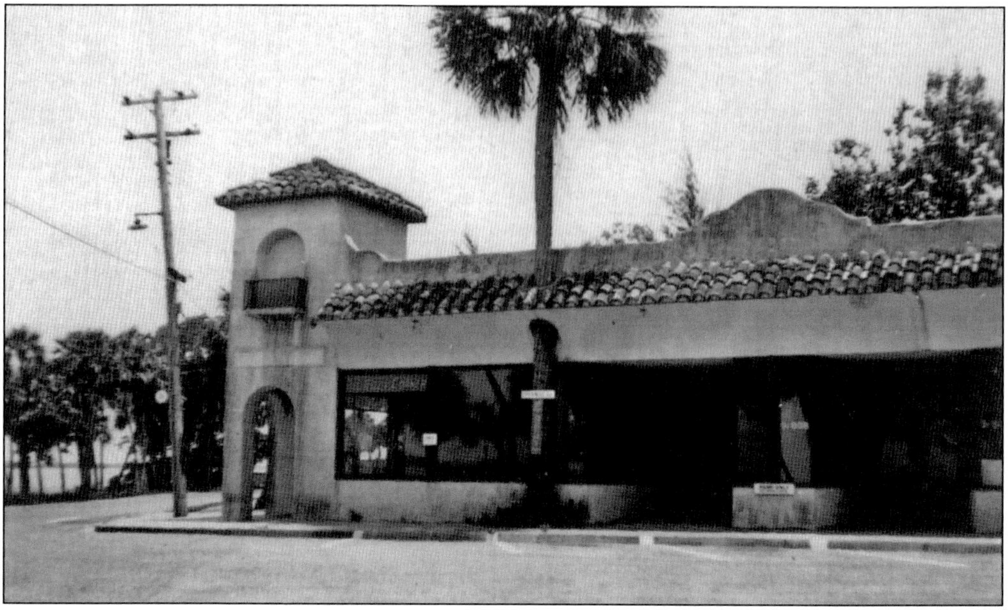

If you ever lived in or visited Rockledge, you would be familiar with this well-known corner building. It has served as a post office, a dance studio, dental offices, and many other things. The Little Store accommodated one's needs for many years when a trip to a larger grocery store was not practical.

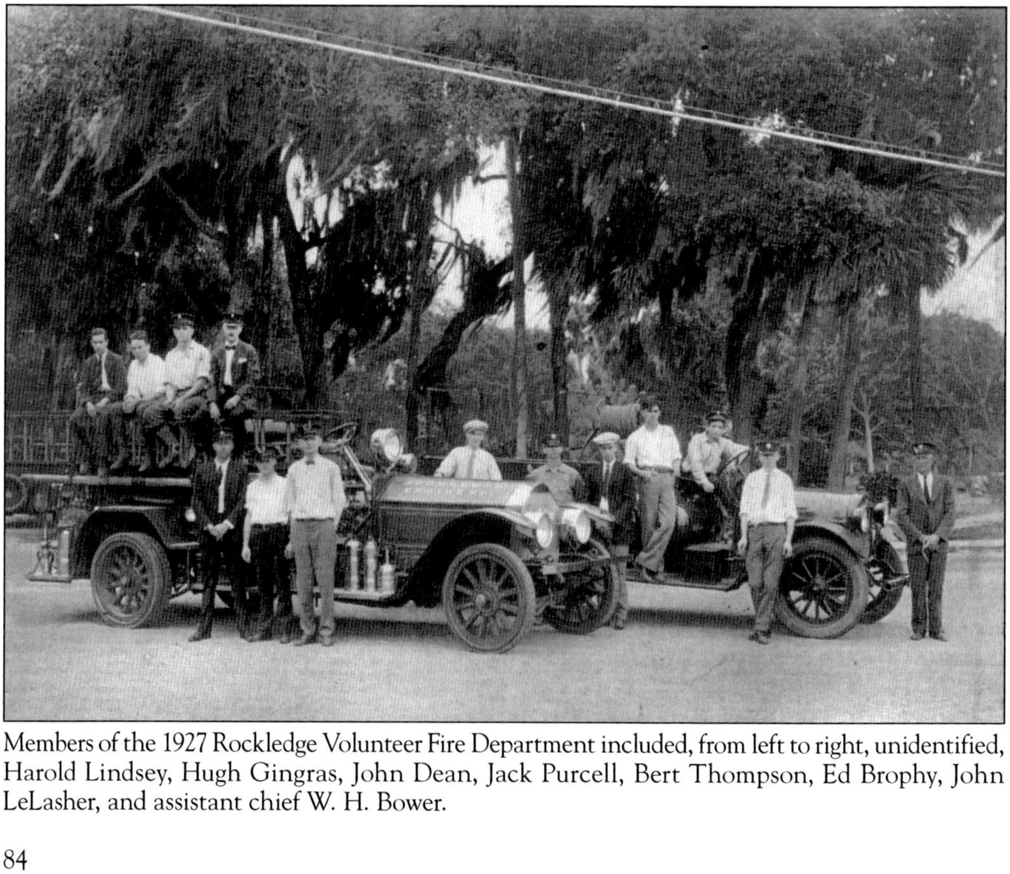

Members of the 1927 Rockledge Volunteer Fire Department included, from left to right, unidentified, Harold Lindsey, Hugh Gingras, John Dean, Jack Purcell, Bert Thompson, Ed Brophy, John LeLasher, and assistant chief W. H. Bower.

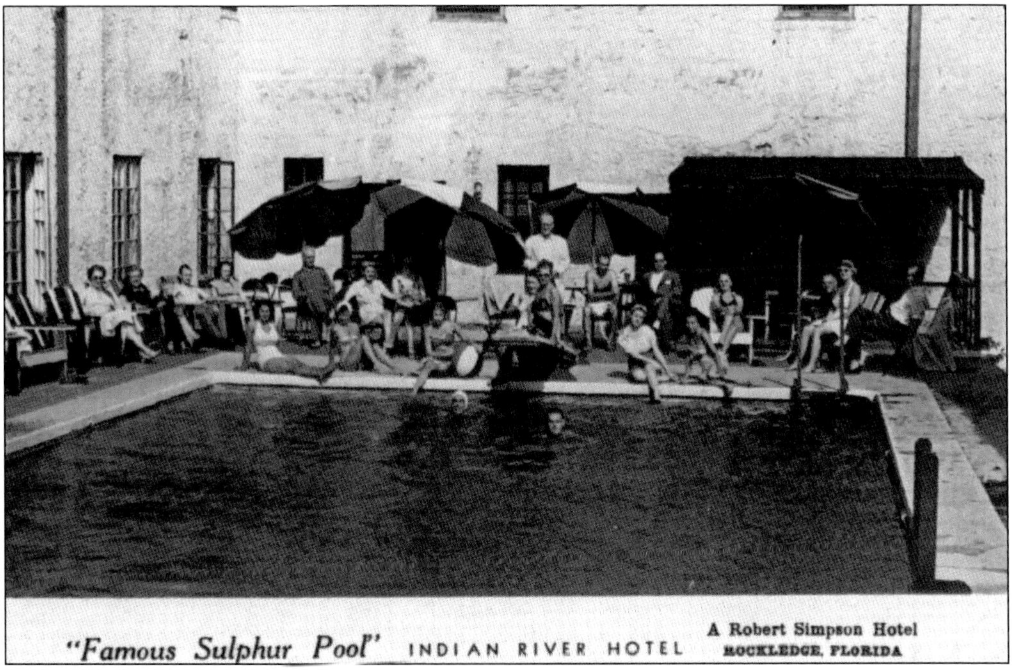

Guests of the Indian River Hotel enjoy the sunshine at the pool. During the summer months, when hotel guests were few in number, many local children learned to swim here. The charge was 10¢, or if one did not have the money, he could help clean the pool on the day it was closed. Gertrude Ederle practiced in this pool for her historic swimming of the English Channel.

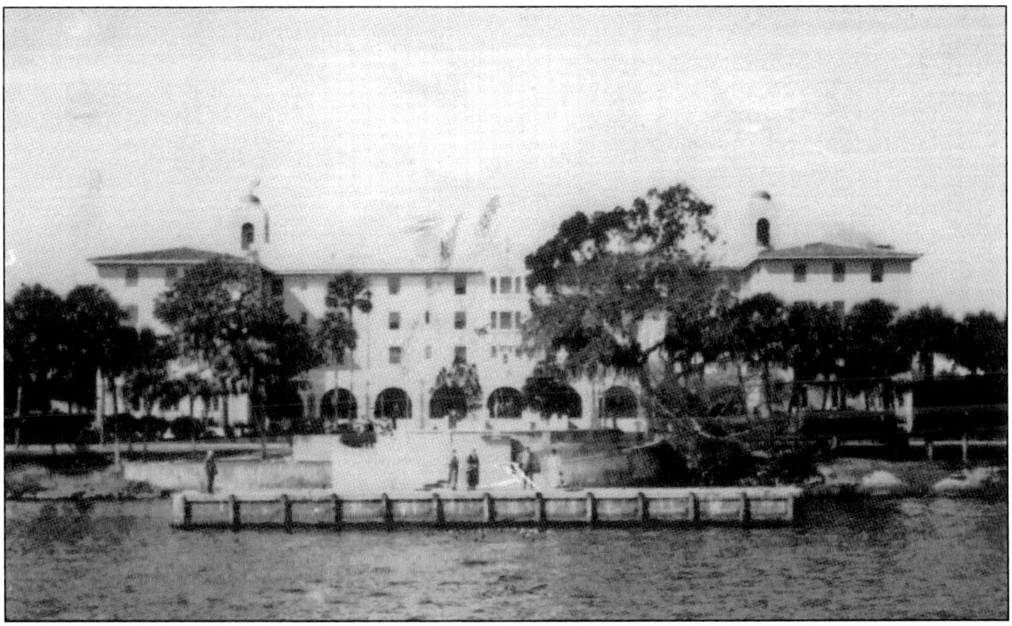

This view depicts the last Indian River Hotel in Rockledge. There were three different hotels on this location: the first burned, and the second was demolished to make way for the building shown. Many guests saw this scene when arriving by boat.

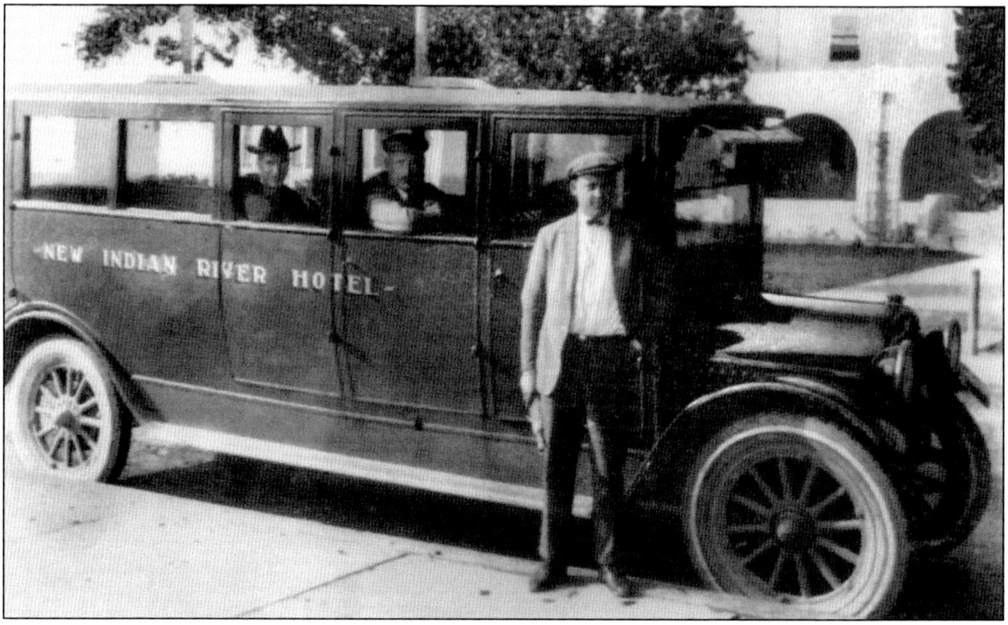

The Indian River Hotel limousine was used to transport guests to and from the train depot, on excursions to Cocoa Beach, and to other events.

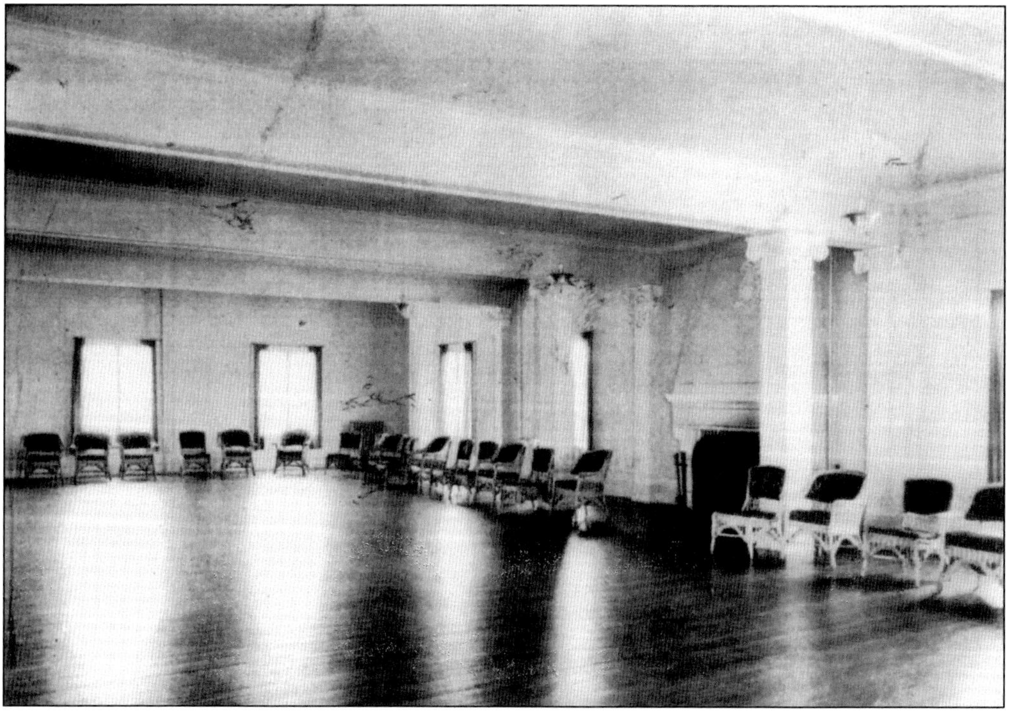
Pictured here is the ballroom at the final Indian River Hotel. This ballroom was the site of many junior-senior proms, Orange Jubilee Balls, unforgettable New Year's Eve parties, and other events.

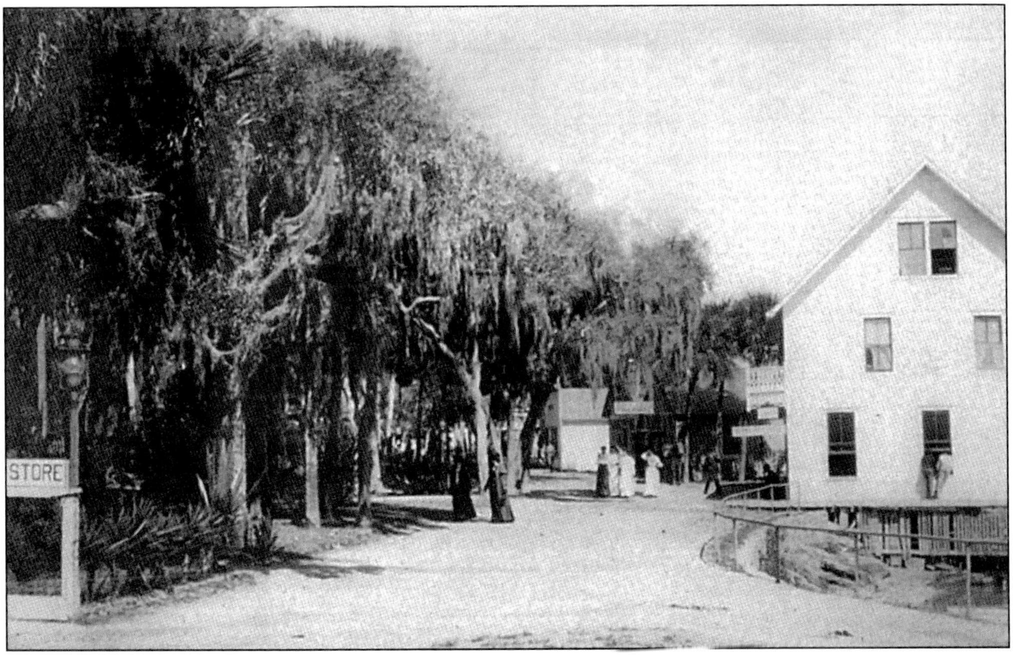

Hatch's Store, owned by Alabama native Andrew Leland "A. L." Hatch, was built partially over the Indian River in Rockledge. Hatch bought two steamers that ran the St. Johns River and set up a merchandise business from Rockledge to Sanford. He was appointed treasurer of the Brevard County Board of Public Instruction in 1875. (Courtesy Vuille and Sayers families.)

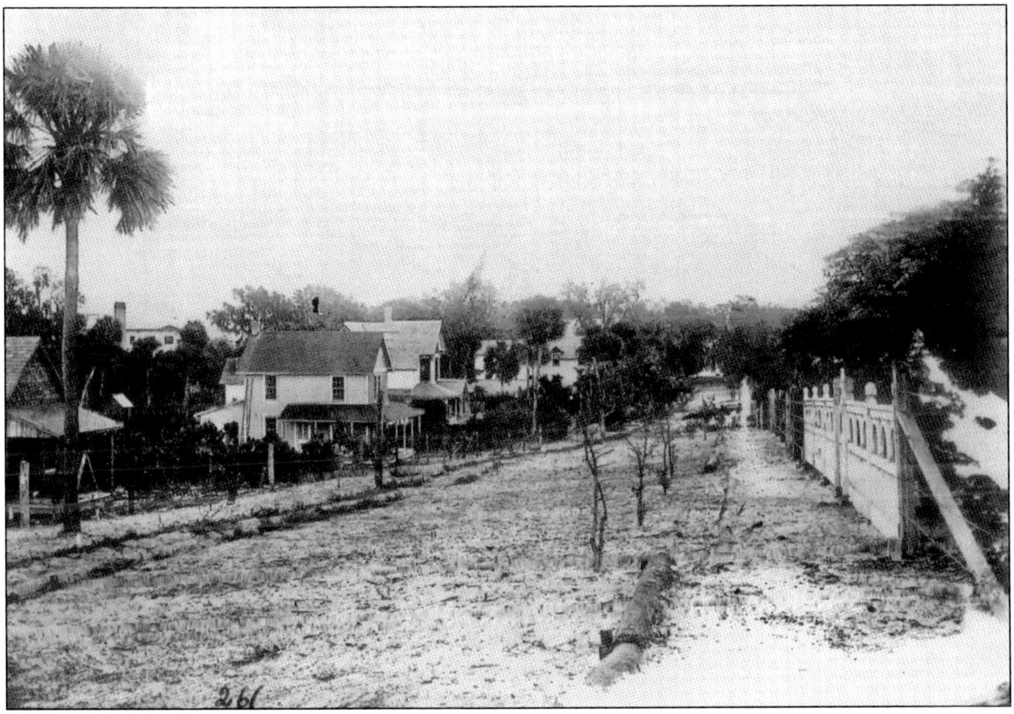

This view looks east on Barton Avenue. Some of these houses remain. The top of one of the hotels can be seen to the left, under the palm tree.

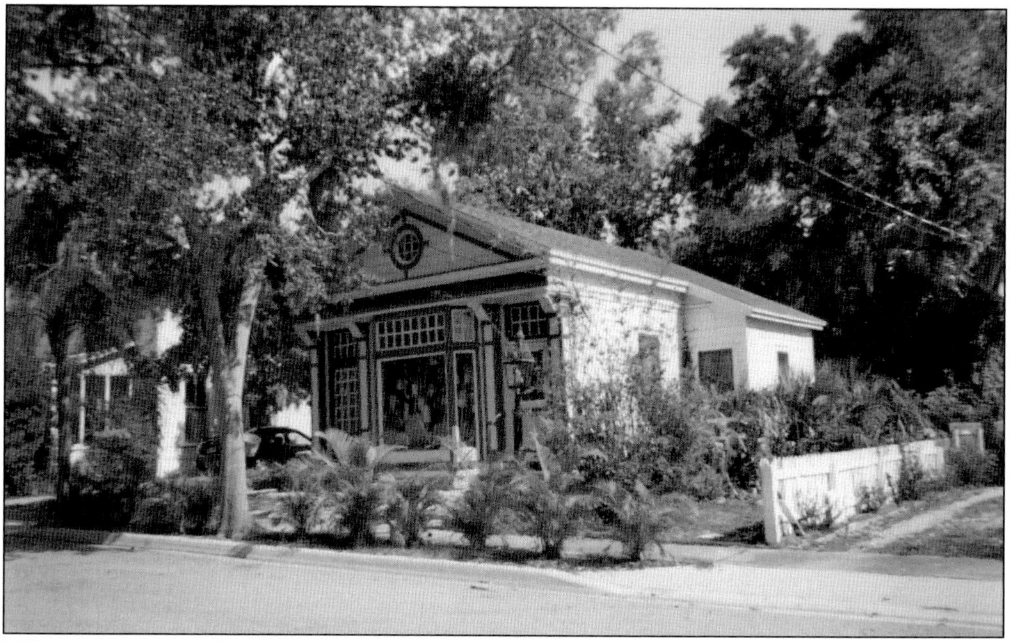

When May C. Quinby's parents died, she moved into the back of her Barton Avenue business. The Women's Exchange served as a trading place for the handwork done by the women of the community. Upon Quinby's death, Al and Bernice Stefurak turned the building into a full-fledged antique shop, which survives today under different management. Quinby, known as Rockledge's "Blue Lady," traveled around in an electric car.

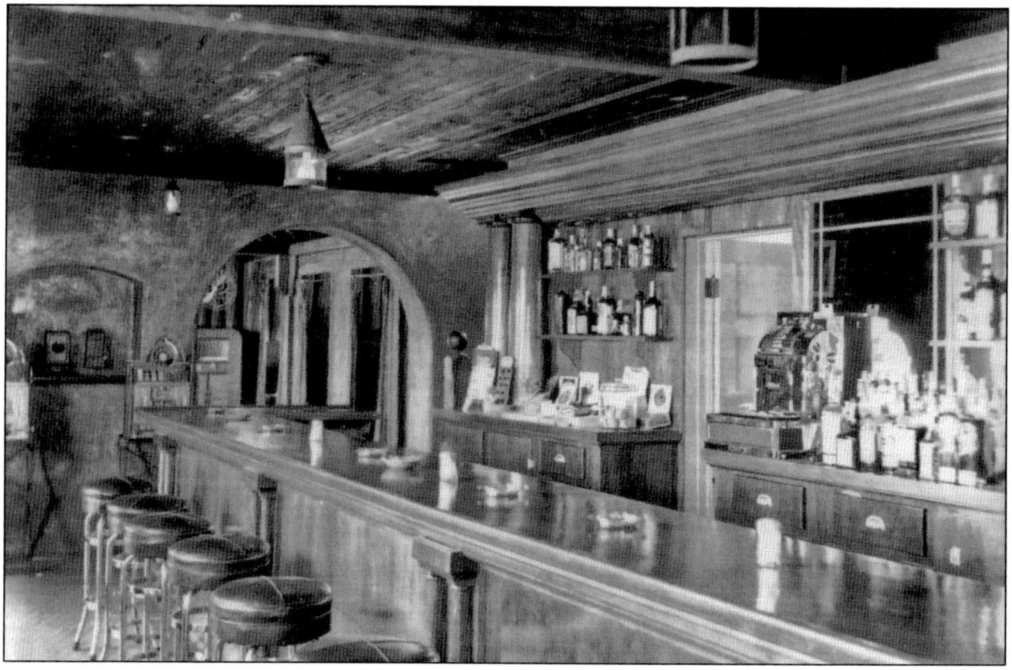

Jack's Tavern, now known as Ashley's, was opened after Prohibition by Jack Allen. It had several names before becoming Ashley's several years ago. Note the slot machines on the left, past the end of the bar. Another claim to fame: it was featured on television as being haunted.

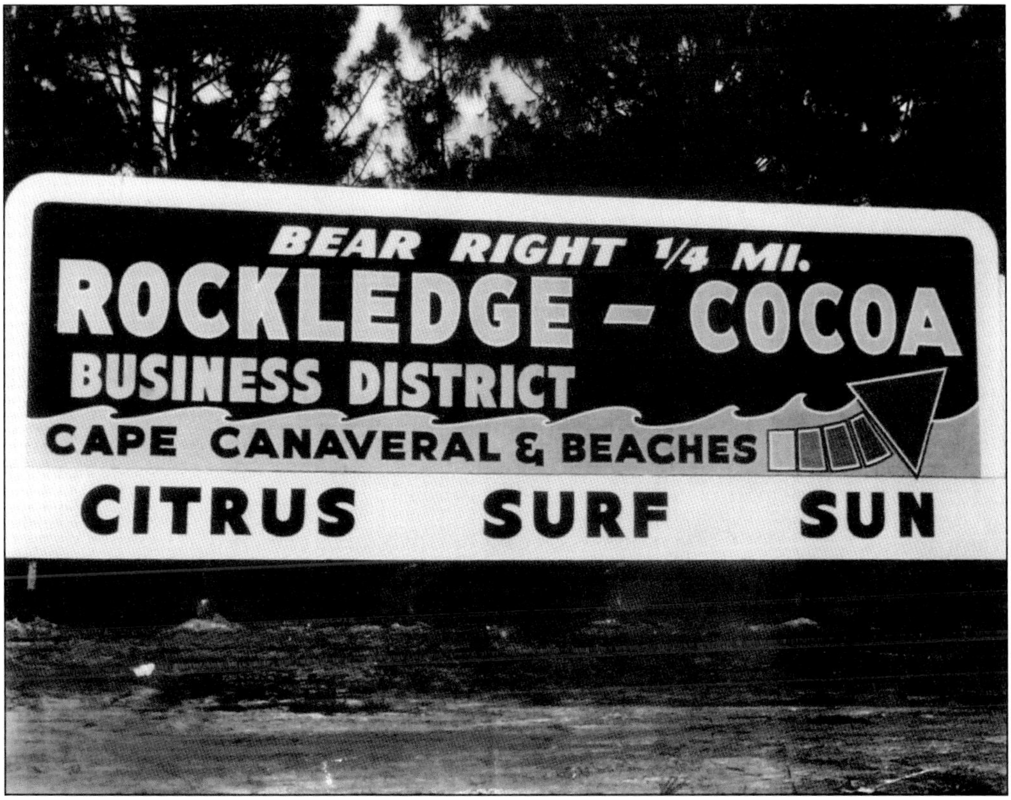

This sign was situated along U.S. Highway 1 in the south part of Rockledge. It directed traffic to what was the early business district of Cocoa and Rockledge. Rockledge has since grown and has business districts south and west of this direction.

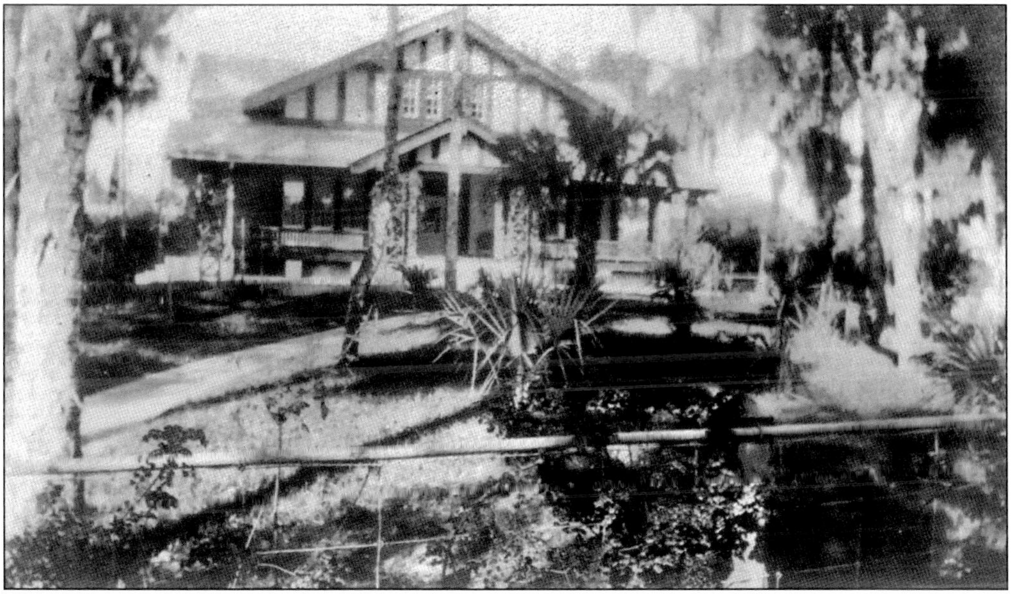

Bonnie Bank, at 1201 Rockledge Drive, is the current home of Dora Ann Thompson. The house was built by William H. Quinby, the father of May Quinby.

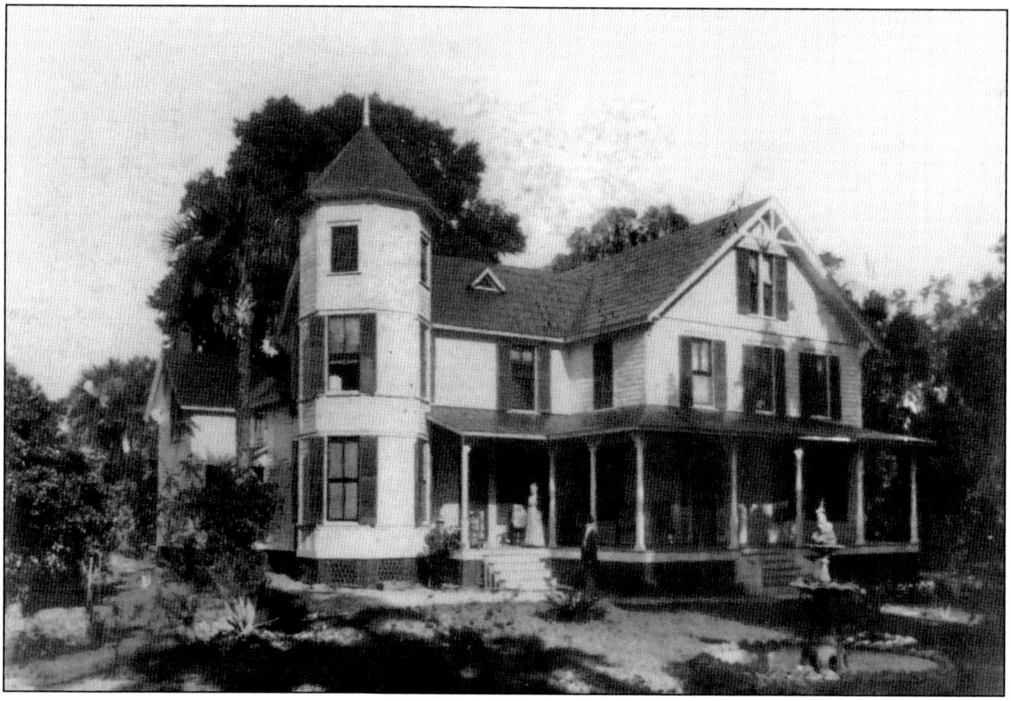

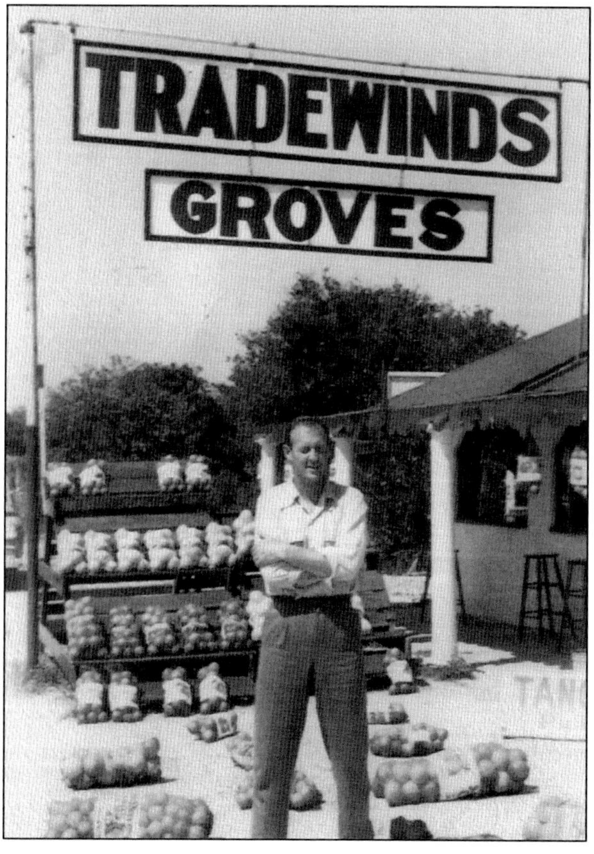

Designed and built by pioneer Hiram Smith Williams in the late 1800s, this house was one of the first in Rockledge, located on the riverfront. In the 1980s, it was purchased by Brevard County Parks and Beaches Board.

Tommy Ronald poses in front of a citrus stand along U.S. 1 in Rockledge. Many such stands were located along U.S. 1 before Interstate 95 was constructed. One of the tricks was to park the stand owner's car out front, open the trunk, and place bags of fruit in the trunk. This helped to get other cars to stop.

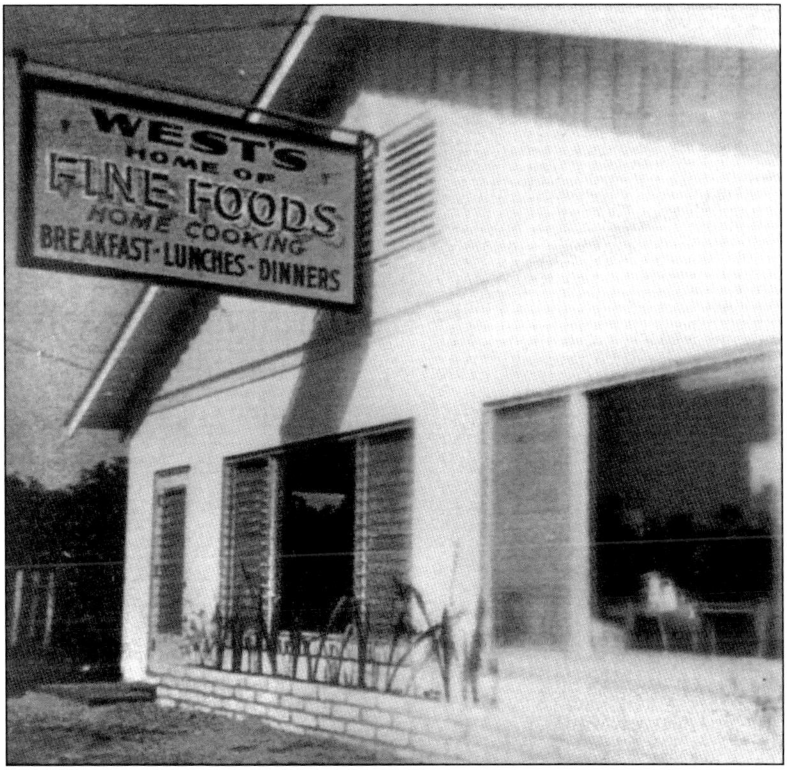

West's Restaurant stood along south U.S. 1 north of Barnes Boulevard, across the road from Harvey Groves, in the 1950s. The completion of Interstate 95 took its toll on small businesses along this route.

This stock certificate was issued during the height of the Florida land boom, which eventually fizzled before the stock market crash of 1929.

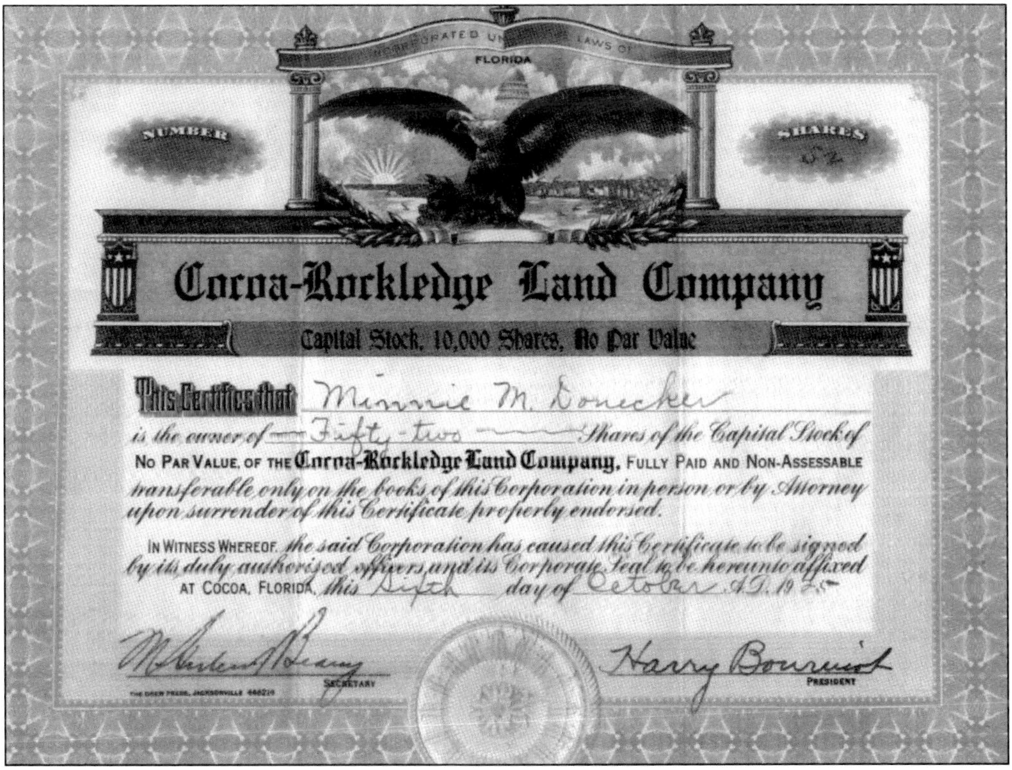
FLORIDA

NUMBER

SHARES 52

Cocoa-Rockledge Land Company

Capital Stock, 10,000 Shares, No Par Value

This Certifies that Minnie M. Donecker is the owner of Fifty-two Shares of the Capital Stock of No Par Value, of the Cocoa-Rockledge Land Company, Fully Paid and Non-Assessable transferable only on the books of this Corporation in person or by Attorney upon surrender of this Certificate properly endorsed.

In Witness Whereof, the said Corporation has caused this Certificate to be signed by its duly authorised officers and its Corporate Seal to be hereunto affixed at Cocoa, Florida, this Fifth day of October A.D. 1925

Secretary

Harry Bourniot
President

BONAVENTURE

Adjoining Rockledge on the south, on the F. E. C. Ry. and on the Dixie Highway.

*Addely A lab
*Addely Henry lab
Appley John (Eliz) fruit grower
Averill A L fruit grower
Baer Gordon (Gladys) r Geo Matthews
Bailey Wm
Benn Earl r Ralph Benn
Benn Ralph (Evelyn) sign pntr
*Bland Tunk (Mary) lab
*Campbell Steven lab
Carey DuPree W mech r P B Dealing
Cox I M (Carrie) fruit grower
Dealing Paul B (Emma; Rockledge Garage & Boat Shop)
Deese Chas A
Frey John florist
Gordon James T
Griggs Hubert E student r J B Griggs
Griggs Jos B (Nannie) fruit grower
Griggs Orvis B student r J B Griggs
Harvey Roy (Blanche) r Ralph Benn
Hunter Walter (Mattie) lab
Kline Orland W (Esther M) fill sta
Luch C K fruit grower
Matthews Geo fruit grower
Matthews Henry
Mertins Ferdinand r Wm Mertins
Mertins Gertrude r Wm Mertins
Mertins Wm
Miller Saml
Miller Wm L (Dora)
O'Conner Wm (Eliz) linemn r P B Dealing
Pearson John H (Hallie) fruit grower
Pond Jos (Wilma) lab
Ramsey David (Mary)
Rockledge Garage & Boat Shop (Paul B Dealing)
Simmons Dairy
Stackhouse G B fruit grower
Stevens R W (Mabel)
Stewart Claude fruit grower
Stewart Mary r Claude Stewart
Turner Grace fill sta and genl mdse
Webster Chas r F L Webster
Webster Fred L (Fanny) fruit grower
White Robt J mgr Trussler Bakery r Grace Turner

Seen here is a listing of Bonaventure residents from a 1926–1927 directory.

PINEDA

Located 9 miles south of Cocoa on the F E C Ry and on the Dixie Highway

Beaulne Norbert (Ella R; Pineda Tourist Camp)
Britton Jas bkpr r Arthur West
Bunce Clarence L (Vivian) bldg contr
*Coverton Heck (Ollie) lab
Green Herbert (Nellie) formn
Green Max lab r Herbert Green
Harris Chas E (Juanita) well driller
Harris Harlan E (Mary E) well driller
Harris Jos E (Lillian) truck farmer
Harris Ola r J E Harris
Harris Walter E G (Hattie) real est
Hendricks Edna Mrs r J E Harris
Howe Carl H mech r W H J Howe
Howe Walter H J (Sarah; Pineda Garage)
Hyden Georgia Mrs (Pineda Restaurant)
*King Florence (wid J W)
*King Manus lab r Florence King
Pineda Garage (W H J Howe)
Pineda Restaurant (Mrs Georgia Hyden)
Pineda Tourist Camp (Beaulne Norbert) Pineda
*Ross Elias (Clara) lab
Sawyer C H r C E Harris
Thomas Lawrence (Lorraine) carp
*Upton Henry (Bertha) lab
Watson Millicent Mrs clk Pineda Restaurant r Mrs Georgia Hyden
West Arthur formn
WEST CHAS W (Nellie), Cement Products Mfrs, Office Eau Gallie, Fla

These people resided in Pineda, according to a 1926–1927 directory.

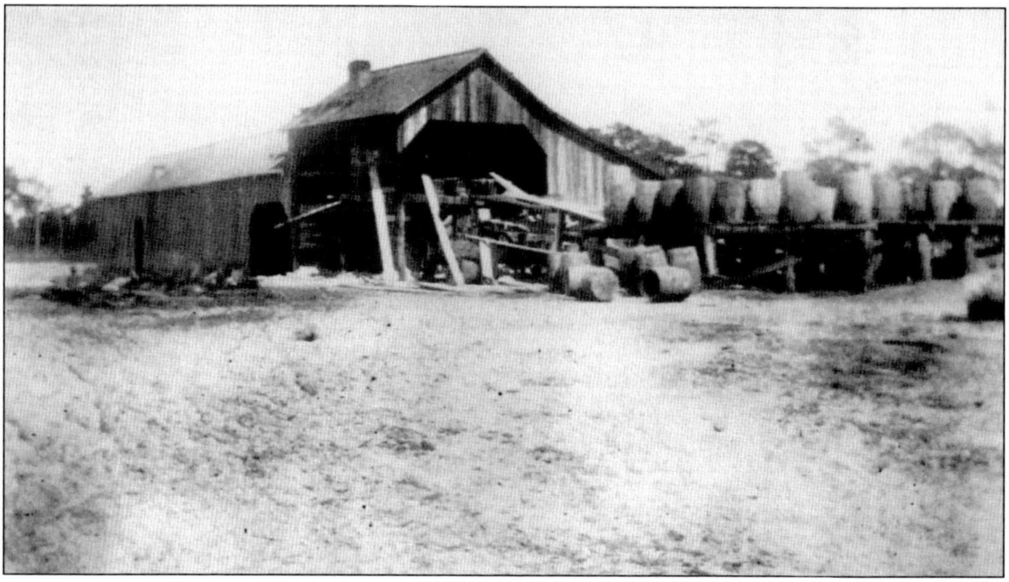

A turpentine still, pictured in March 1917, was located west of the Florida East Coast Railroad at Pineda. This operation lasted until the 1930s, and prisoners were rented from the state as employees.

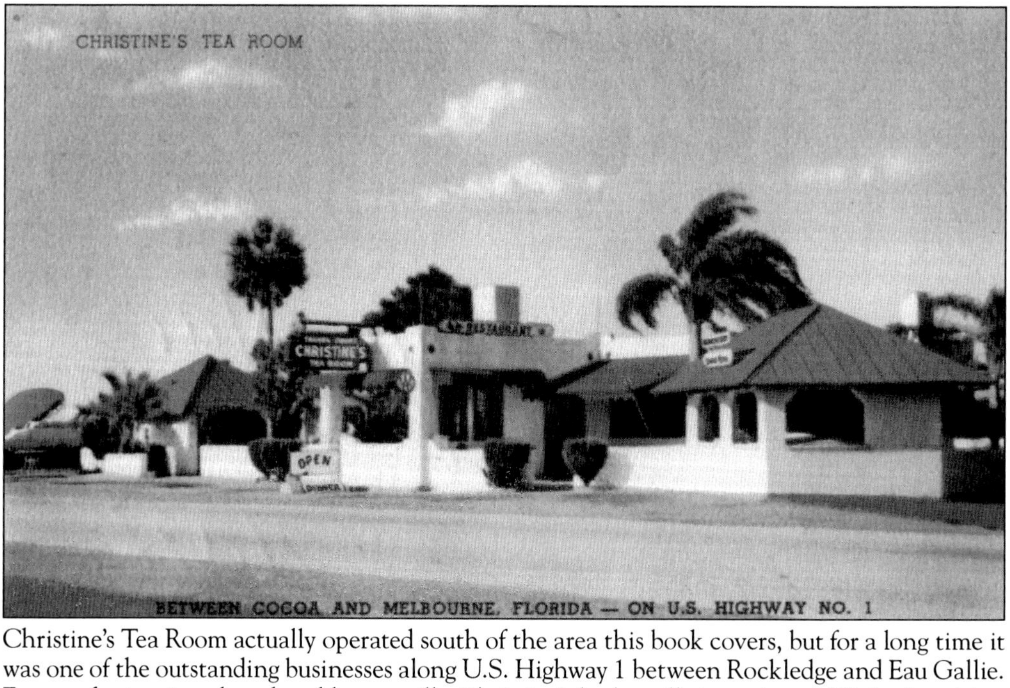

Christine's Tea Room actually operated south of the area this book covers, but for a long time it was one of the outstanding businesses along U.S. Highway 1 between Rockledge and Eau Gallie. Famous for its gingerbread and buttermilk, Christine's had small signs along U.S. 1 advertising its fare.

Five

Sports

Sports have long been a part of the area's pastime. Hunting and fishing brought many people here from the 1800s until the mid-1950s. Pioneers hunted and fished as a means of providing food for their tables. With its early baseball teams, Cocoa lured players here from other states to engage in the game. Many of these young men married local girls and became permanent citizens. Baseball games were a cause for businesses to close on the afternoons they were played. World War II stopped baseball for a while. When the war ended, baseball leagues resumed play but in a rather loose fashion. The teams could play any player there at game time. Wagering did happen. At times the field would be too wet, and to solve the problem, gasoline was poured on the base paths and set afire, and the sand was raked to dry the water. Some days, 50 or more gallons would be burned. This remark was overheard on a rainy day: "I've got too much bet on the game, and on a make-up day we might not be able to get that pitcher from Rollins College."

Boxing, boat racing, and car racing were all part of the sports scene. High school teams of football, boys' basketball, girls' basketball, baseball, and track were all important to the community. Golf also should be mentioned, because at one time there was a golf course on the site of Wuesthoff Hospital.

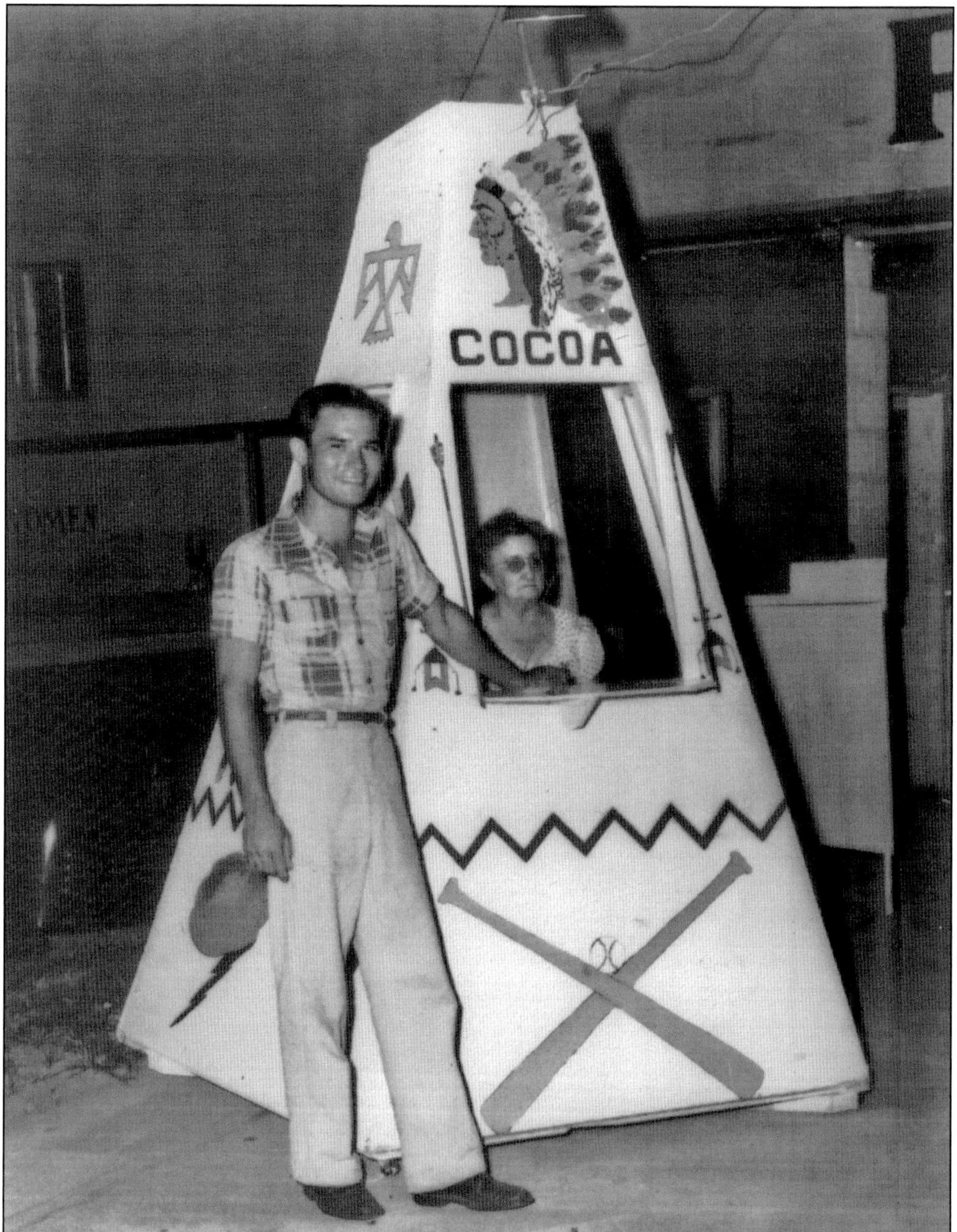

Minor-league baseball was prime entertainment in the pre-television days. Cocoa businesses actually closed to promote attendance at the games. Pictured is the ticket booth for the Cocoa Indians games, where "Miss Susie" Murdock reigned. Posing at the teepee is Harold Murdock.

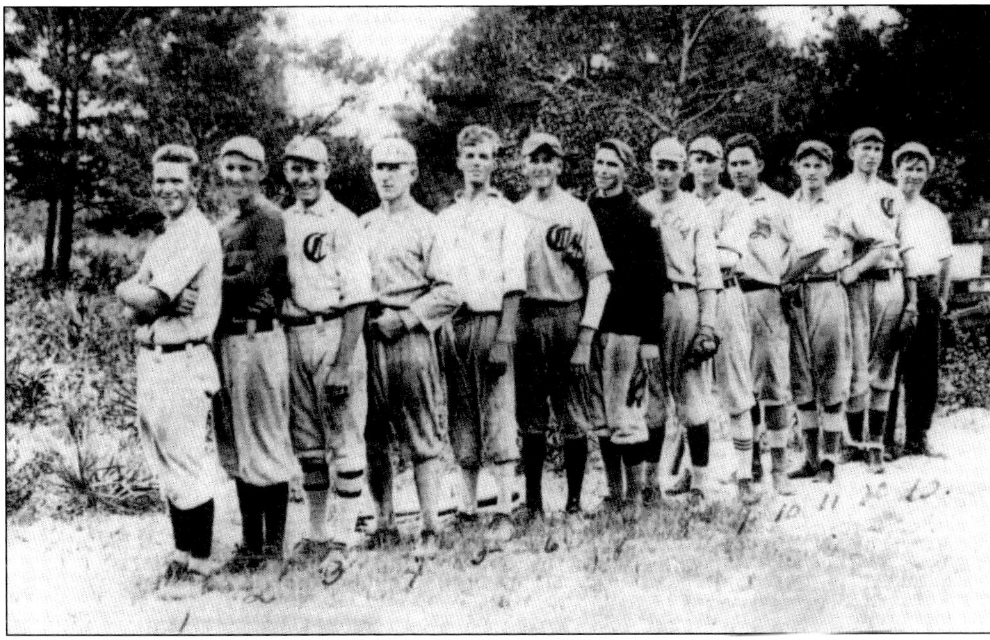

The 1910–1912 Cocoa baseball team included, from left to right, John Paterson, C. Geiger, Speck Jones, Chubby Chalker, Cracker Hindle, unidentified, Lefty Forester, Rex Sosobee, Leland Daniel, Lawrence Abney, Minor Jones, Fred Forester, and Gator Travis.

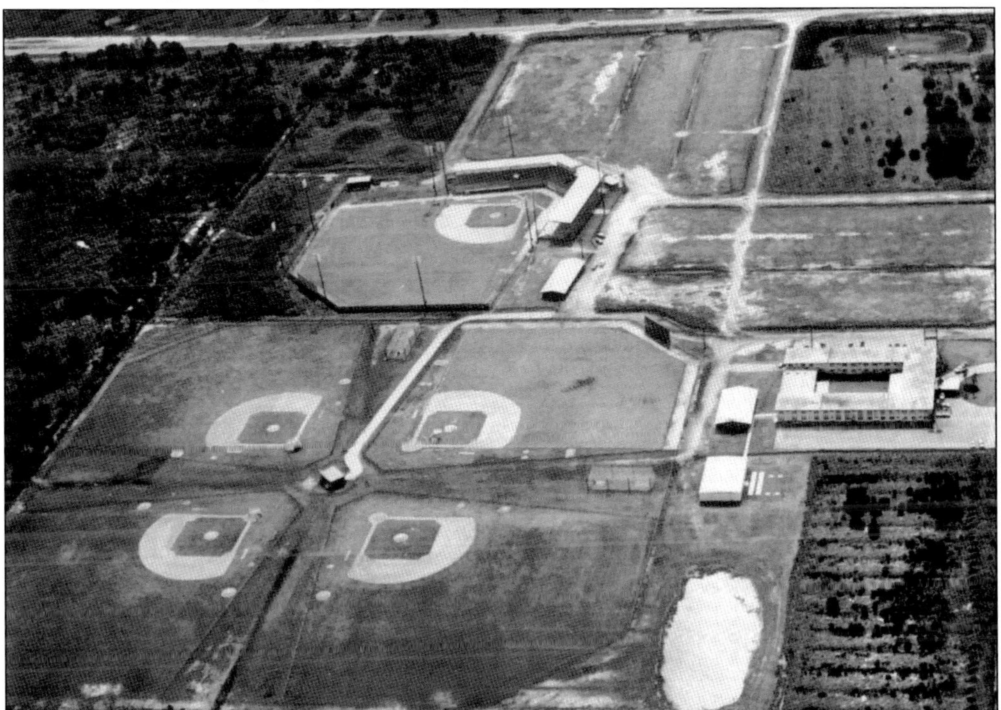

The Houston baseball team, the Colt .45s, and the City of Cocoa built this array of ball fields for the Texas team to stage spring training. The Colt .45s have since become the Houston Astros. Highway 520 is the road shown along the top edge.

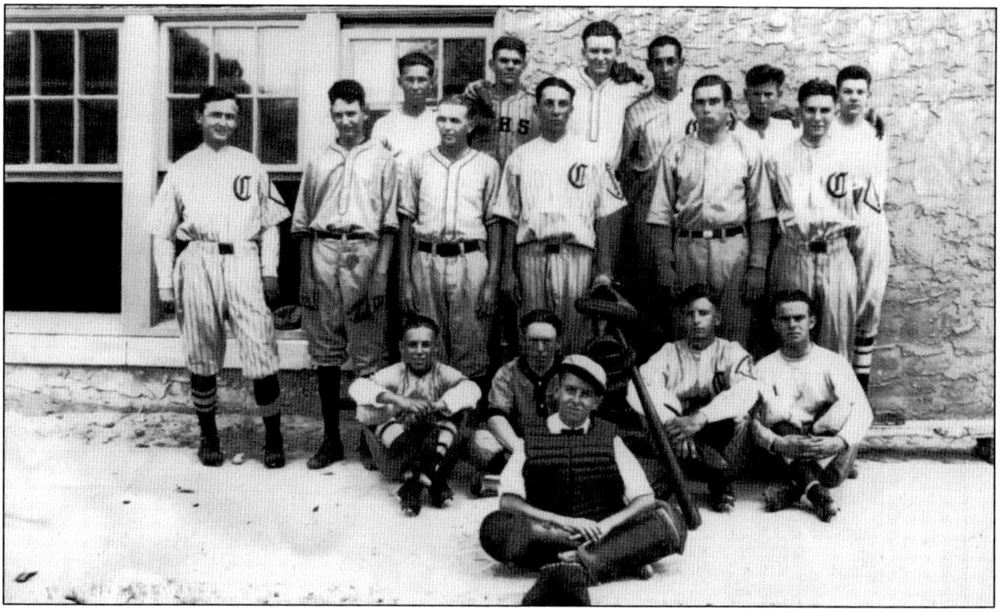

The 1925 Cocoa High School baseball team also excelled. Shown from left to right are the following: (first row) mascot Delmar Gresham; (second row) Bobby Schlernitzauer, Edwin ? (center field), Hugh Gingras (substitute and right field), and Bobby Hill (second base); (third row) coach J. D. Mitchell, ? Sumerland (substitute), Paul Culler (catcher-pitcher), Clive Monts de Oca (catcher-pitcher), James Gray (catcher), and Stanford Marston (right field); (fourth row) ? Alabama (shortstop), Norwood Lockett (left field), John Fiske (first base), William Showalter (substitute), Walter Weeks (substitute), and Eugene "Ice Cream" Sudan (substitute).

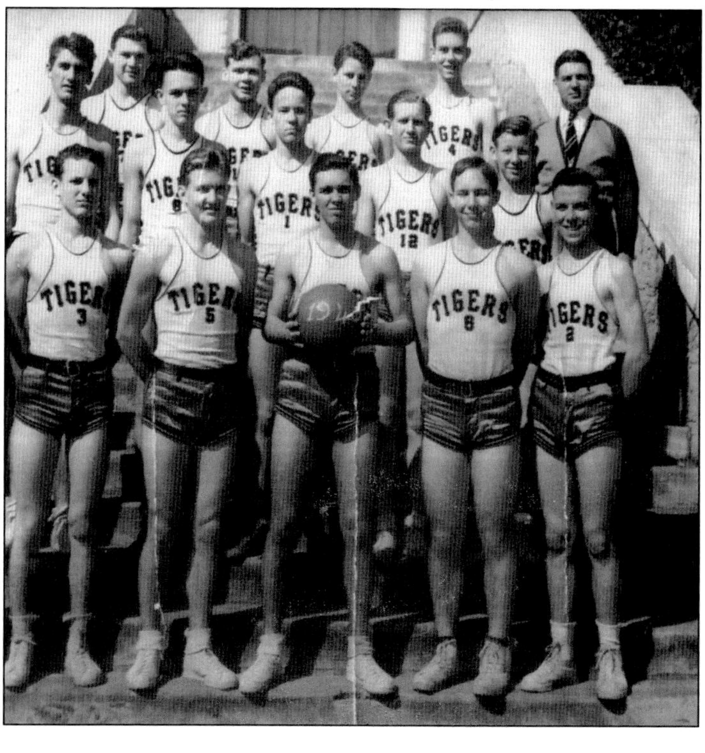

The 1940 Cocoa High Tiger basketball team poses for a group photograph. Pictured here from left to right are the following: (first row) Jimmy Keen, Billy Poole, Sonny Butt, Dick Anderson, and Bunt Travis Fennell; (second row) Coot Furman, Robert Chick, Buddy McGlaun, Don Stradley, and ? Keen; (third row) Bill Aiken, Albert Furman, Ralph Ramsey, Warren Wooten, and coach Ish Brant.

Local trainer C. E. Lucas (left), Gordon Fortenberry (center), and an unidentified fight promoter are pictured in New York in 1934. Fortenberry fought in the heavyweight division in the 1930s.

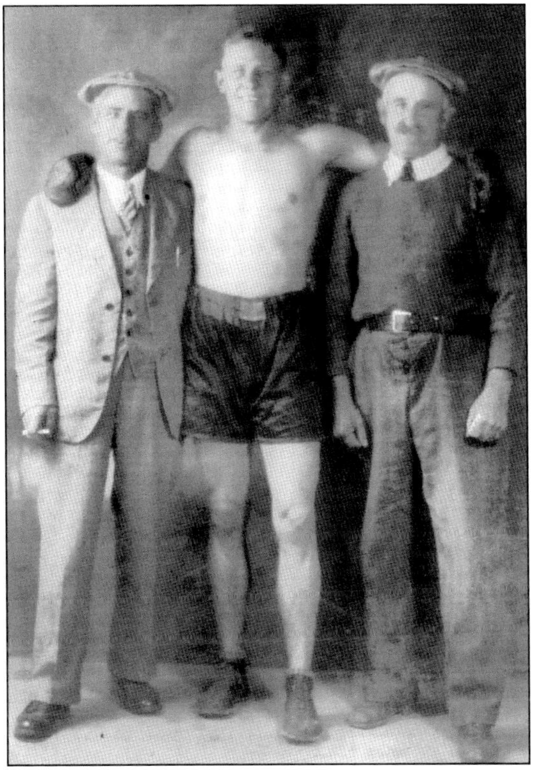

The pride of Cocoa High School in 1925 was its track team. Shown from left to right are the following: (first row) Schyler Hudson, Winston Osteen, Bobby Hill, Ned Morris, and William Morris; (second row) coach J. D. Mitchell, William Akridge, Alfred Robbins, John Fiske, William Showalter, and James Bay.

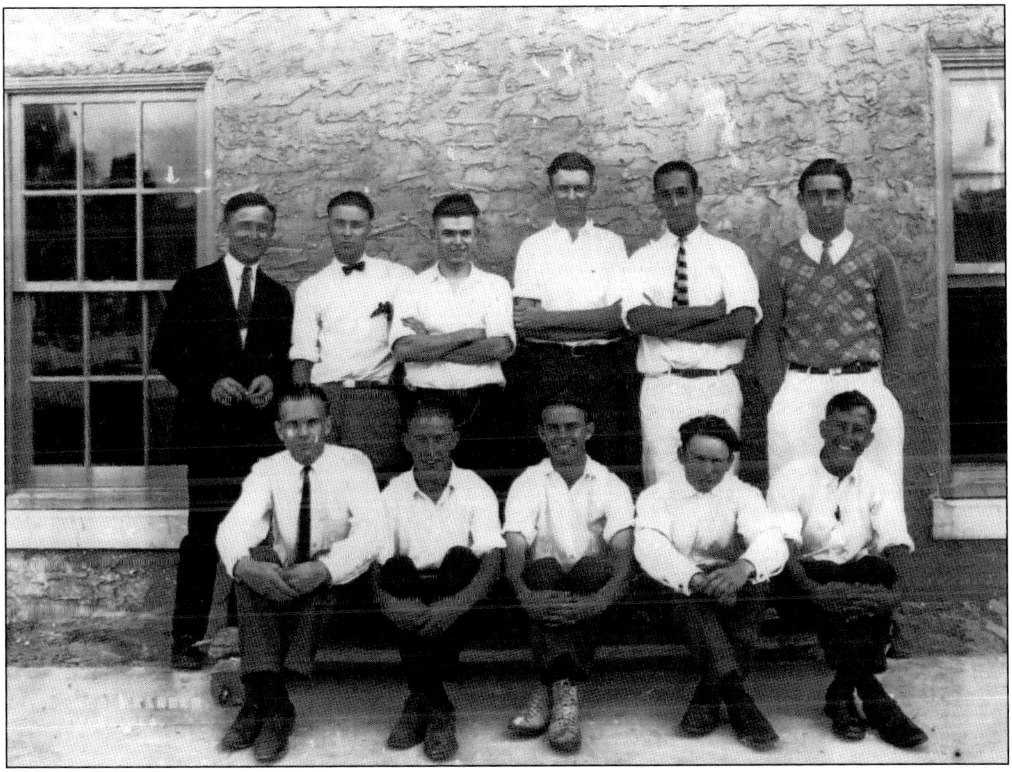

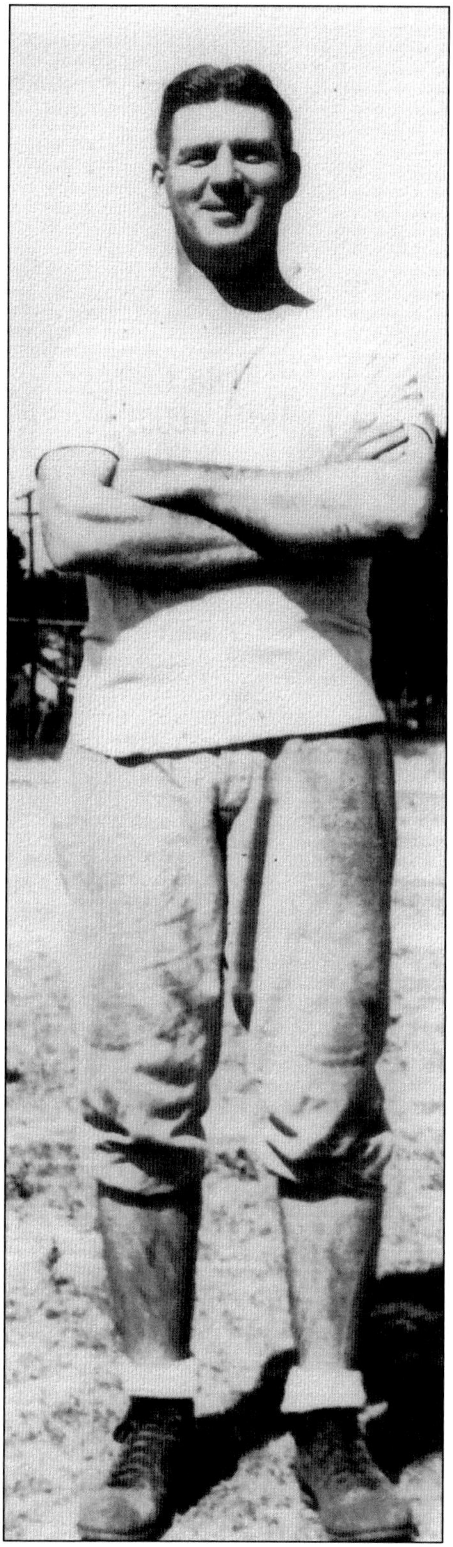

"Ish" Brant was born in Ocala, Florida, and grew into an outstanding high school athlete. He became Cocoa High's football, baseball, and basketball coach and history teacher while also serving as a member of the Rockledge City Council. He left the area when a better job was available as coach at Fletcher High School in Jacksonville. Brant later became superintendent of public instruction for Duval County.

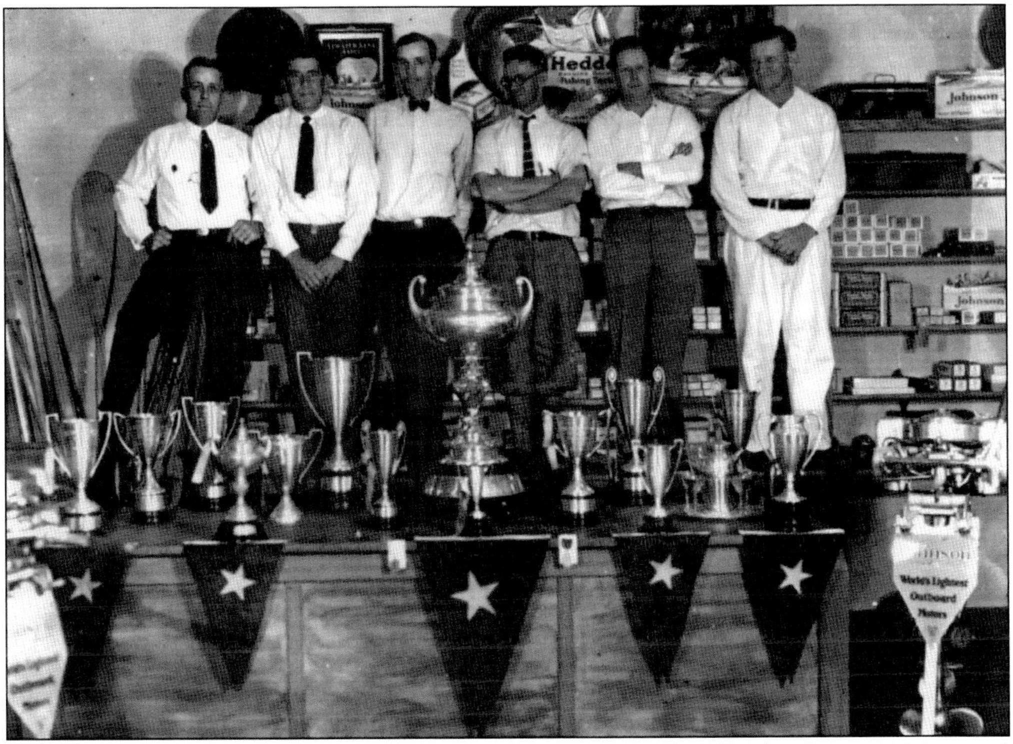

Awards await presentation at an unknown event. They are displayed under the watchful eyes of, from left to right, Barney Allen, Carl Fay, Sleep Hindle, John Paterson, Pete Williford, and Brick Jones. This photograph was likely taken in the late 1920s or early 1930s.

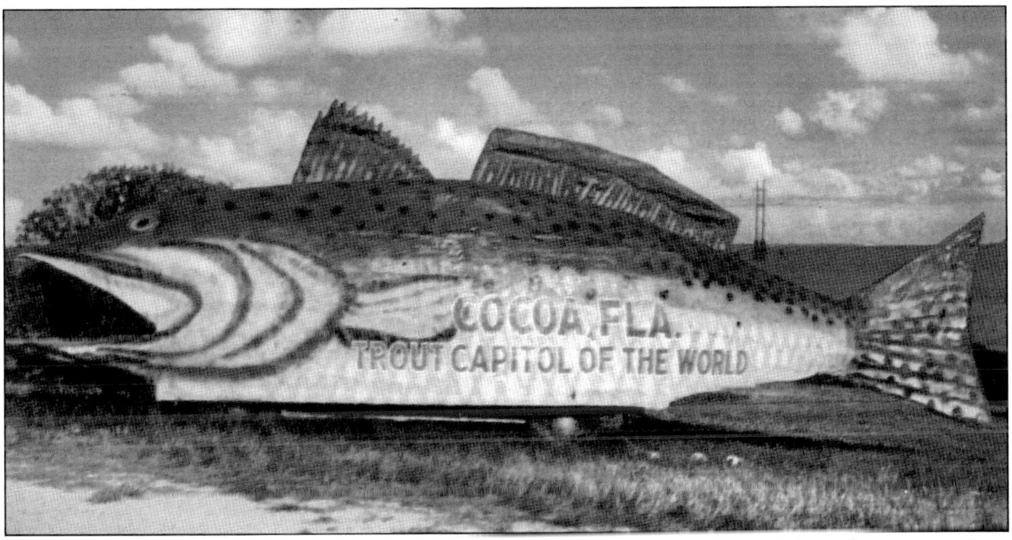

This large float was made for a parade held in Cocoa. Gary Bennett had a fishing business selling fish, tackle, and bait. He asked Dick Granger to build the float using a real trout (spotted weakfish) as a blueprint. The wheels of a full-size Chevrolet truck can be seen under the fish. The claim to be "Saltwater Trout Capitol" was based on the fact that Cocoa had registered more button trout (six pounds or over) than any other location in a *Field and Stream* fishing contest. The float was driven in many parades but eventually burned.

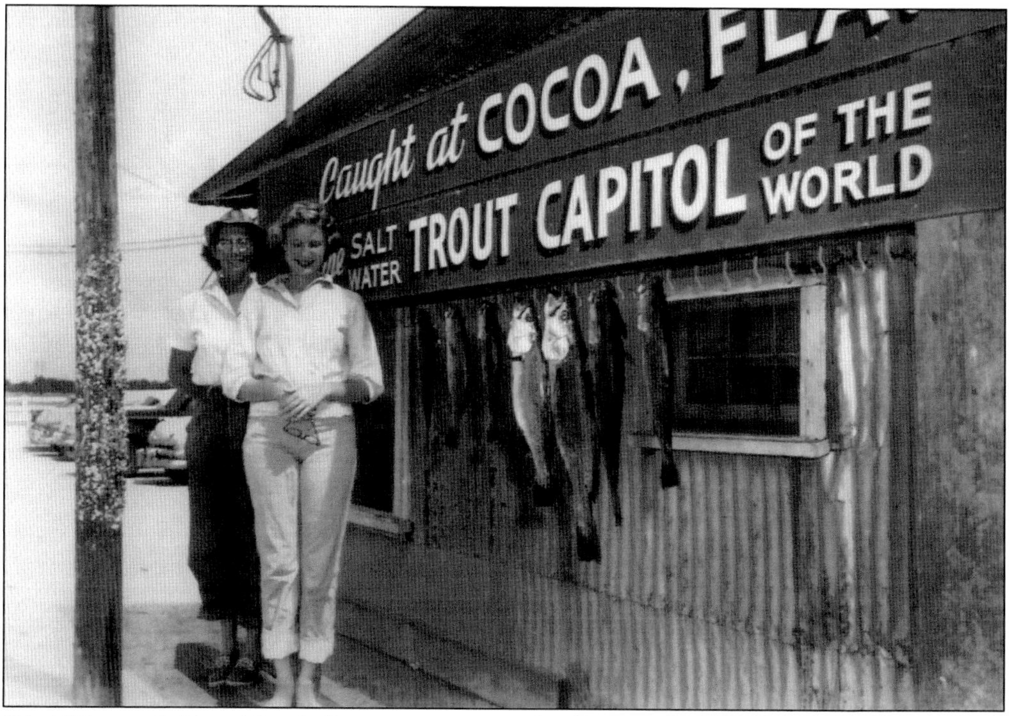

Ethel Watson (left) and Sandy Bennett are pictured at Bennett's Seafood and Tackle Shop. The fish are spotted weakfish, known as saltwater trout.

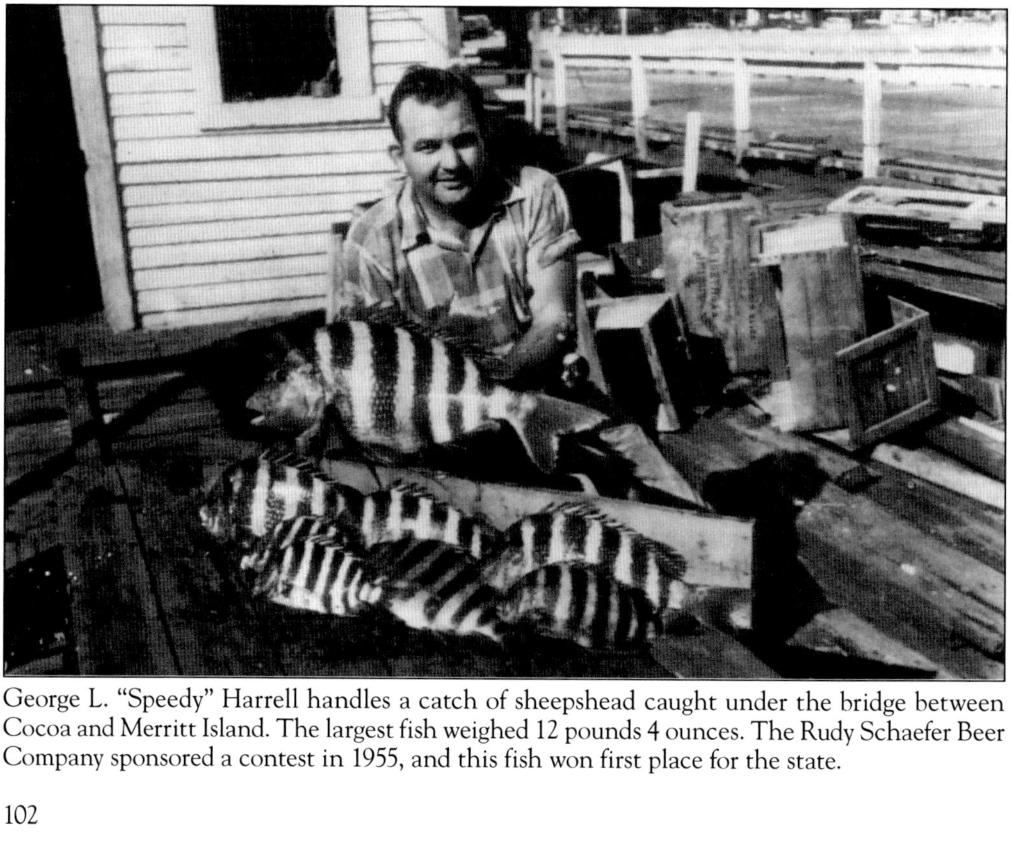

George L. "Speedy" Harrell handles a catch of sheepshead caught under the bridge between Cocoa and Merritt Island. The largest fish weighed 12 pounds 4 ounces. The Rudy Schaefer Beer Company sponsored a contest in 1955, and this fish won first place for the state.

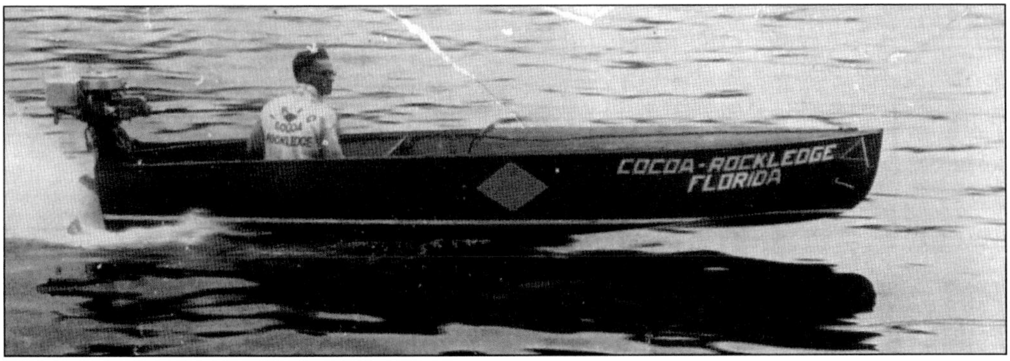

The *Black Diamond* was the name of this race boat, owned by Carl Fay and built by George Gingras. Shown with the boat is John Paterson. Note the diamond on the side.

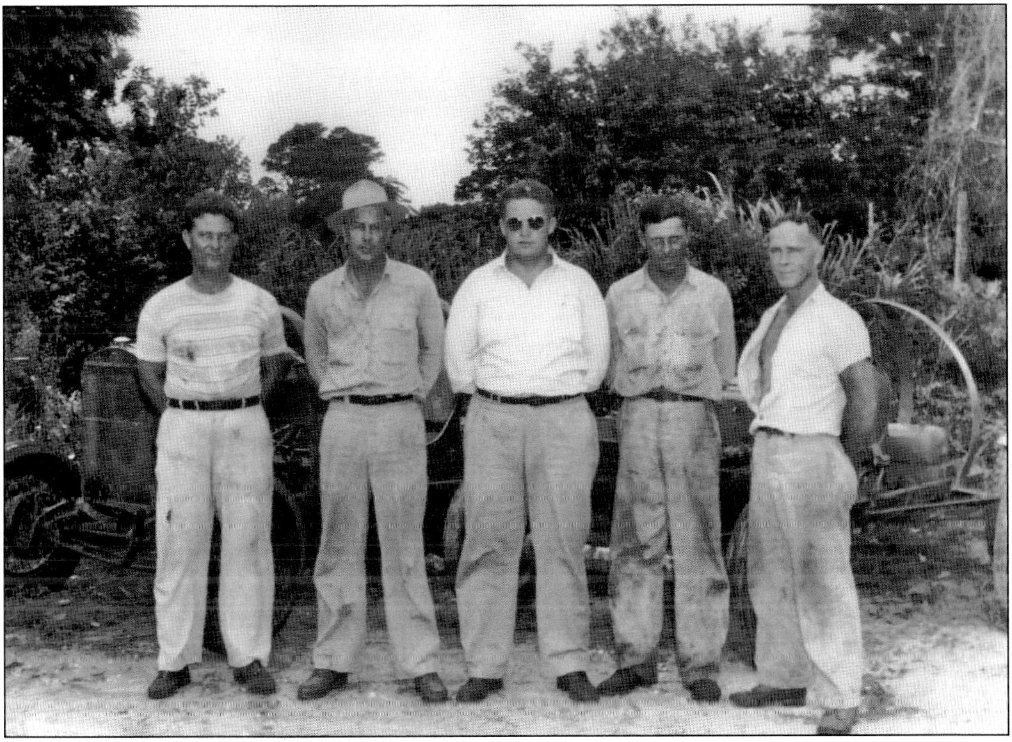

Members of the Cocoa Racing Association stand at attention. Shortly after World War II, a group of young men started racing on Cocoa Beach and later built a quarter-mile dirt track on the east side of Pineda Street in the 400 block. The race cars were mostly Model A Fords reduced to their bare essentials. Seen from left to right are Preston Arnold, Alex Scarborough, Jimmy Thompson, Johnny Fortenberry, and Turk Atkins.

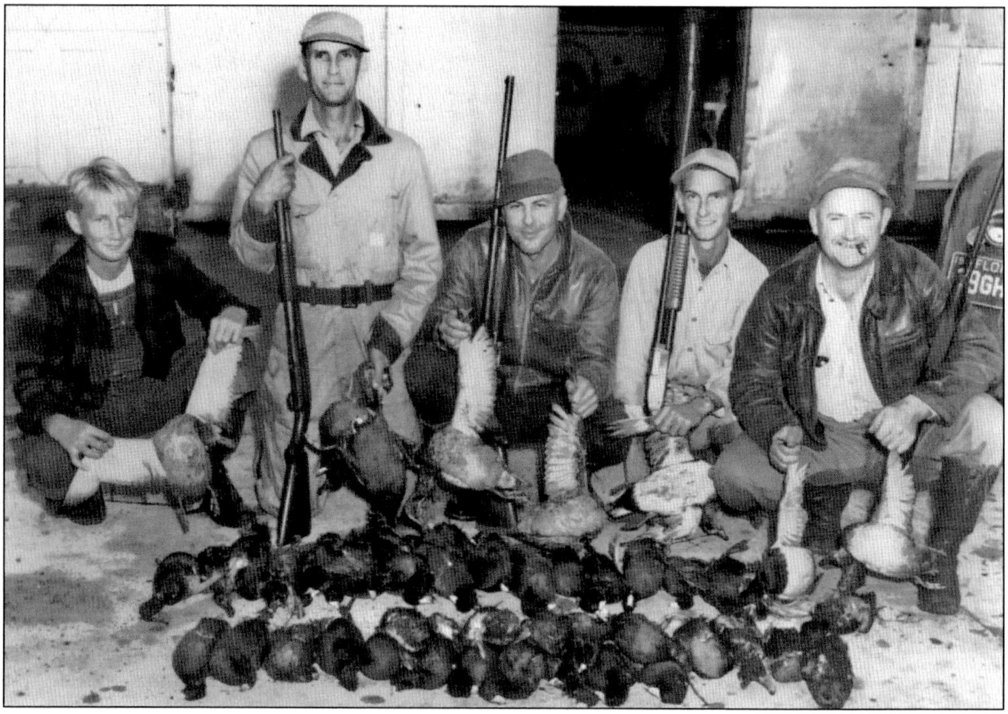

Pictured from left to right are Doug Scarborough, Ovid Scarborough, Alex Scarborough, Ovid "Coot" Scarborough, and E. M. Crisman, with ducks and coots from a morning's hunt. Shooting migratory birds was a major sporting event until loss of habitat stopped the birds from coming to this area.

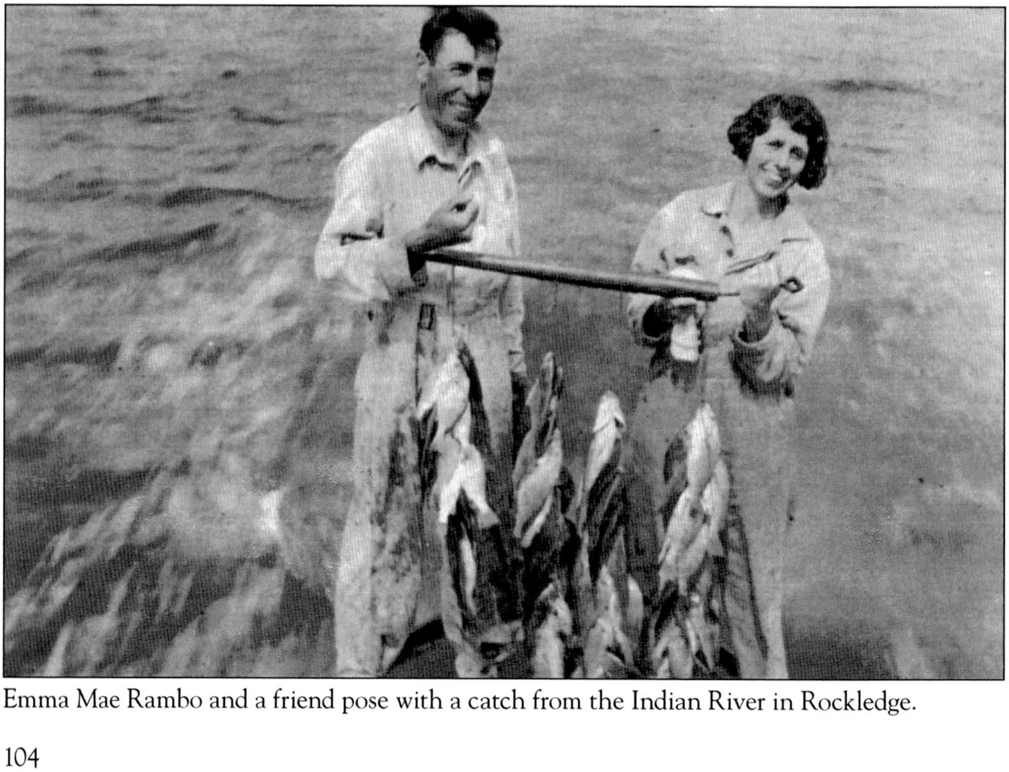

Emma Mae Rambo and a friend pose with a catch from the Indian River in Rockledge.

Six

People

From the early Native Americans of the area to the present-day missile scientists, Cocoa-Rockledge has had its portion of outstanding residents. Very few pioneers came to this region before the Civil War. After the war, however, a number of people from Georgia moved because their homes had been destroyed or they felt Florida would be safer, away from the "Yankee carpetbaggers." Many new arrivals sent word back home as to how wonderful the Cocoa and Rockledge area was. Cocoa's love for baseball brought players and attracted more settlers. The construction of the Banana River Naval Air Station in 1939 accounted for another rise in population. The missile program and NASA also brought people. This chapter contains images of the people who influenced this section of Brevard County.

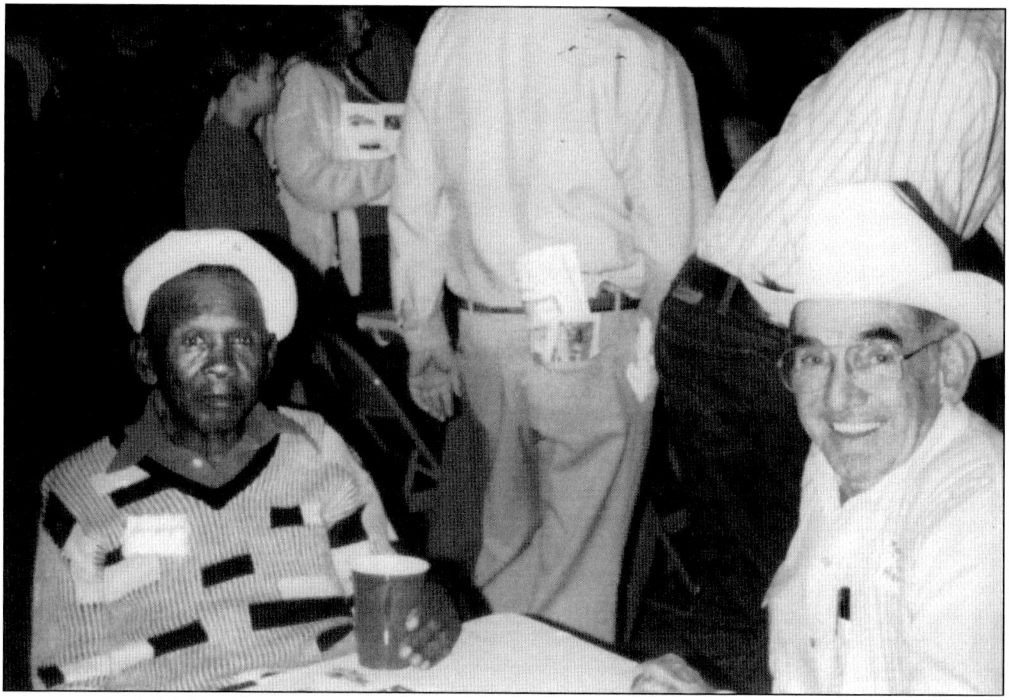

Harry Whitfield (left) and Marion "Little Speedy" Harrell attend the 1995 Mosquito Beater gathering. Whitfield came to Cocoa with the Bazemore family, who opened the Indian River Furniture Store. He later owned Whitfield's Taxi. Harrell is probably best known for plowing up the nightclub parking lot of Nort Kurlan at Cocoa Beach.

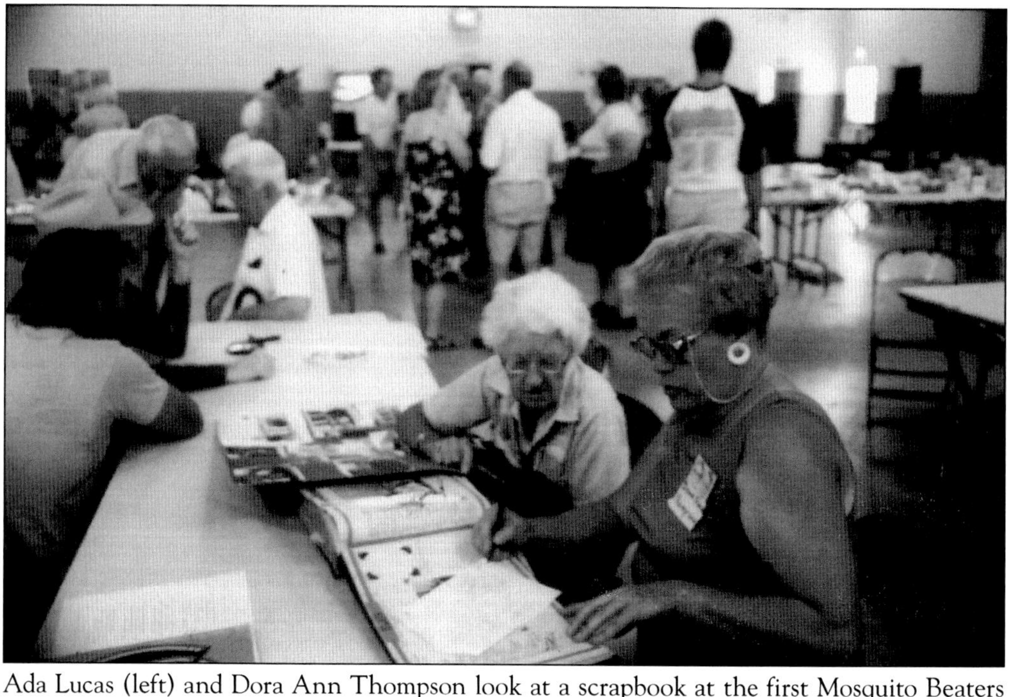

Ada Lucas (left) and Dora Ann Thompson look at a scrapbook at the first Mosquito Beaters gathering, in 1986. The people in the background are unidentified.

The late Mercer Livermore (left) talks to Speedy Harrell (center) and Tommy Gregal, with John Dixon on the right. Livermore was known for her radio program "Cocoa Chatter."

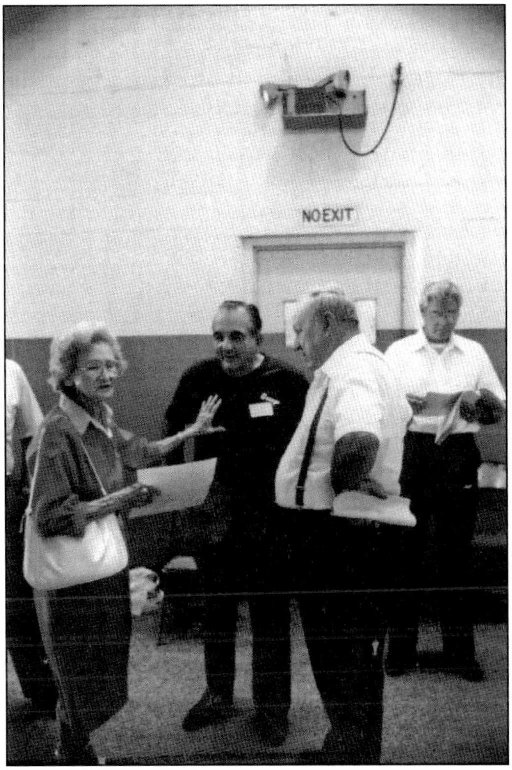

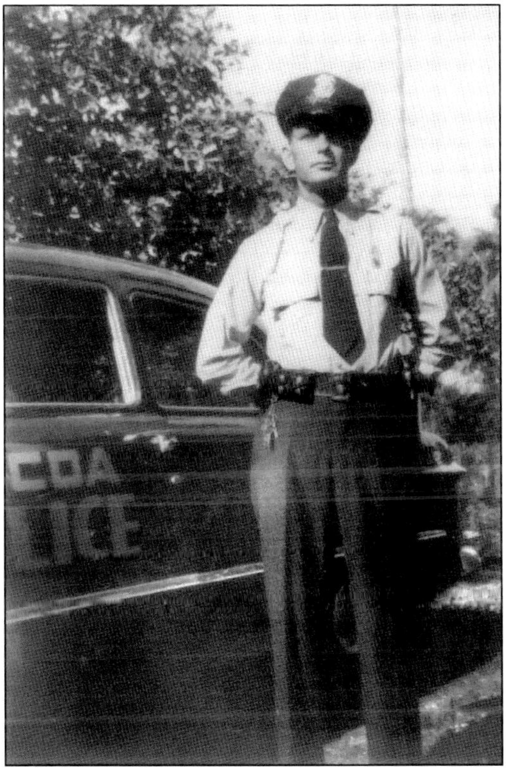

Ed Dempsey served the citizens of Brevard County for many years, holding several different positions: cop on the beat, Rockledge police chief, and Brevard County sheriff's deputy.

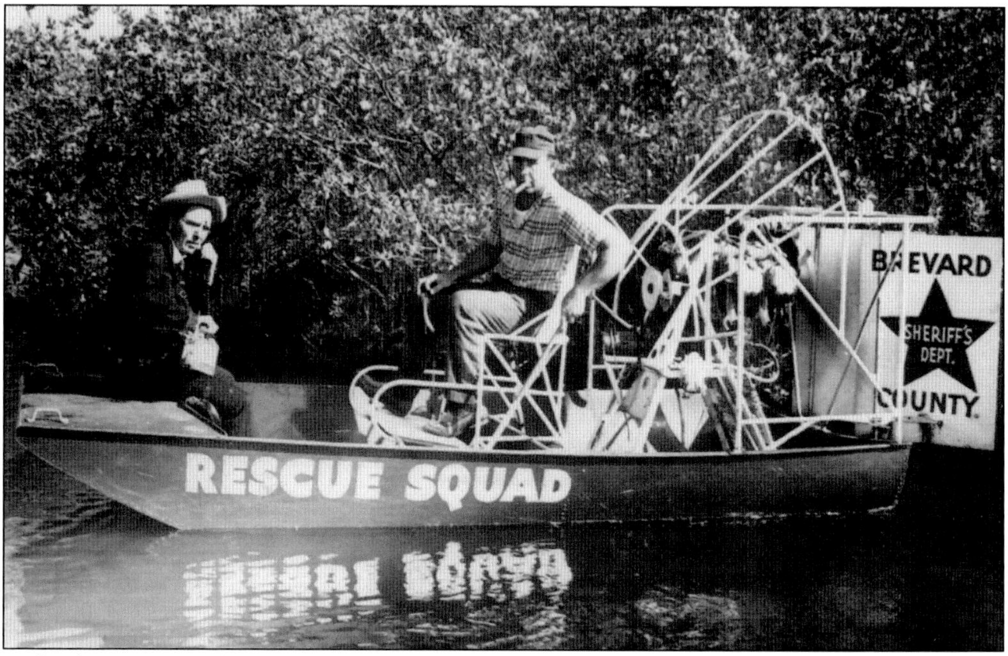

Willard Winnett and Dick Granger both served as deputy sheriffs. Winnett later became chief of police for Cape Canaveral. Granger, a former marine, was born on Merritt Island at Lotus and had an outstanding knowledge of the county.

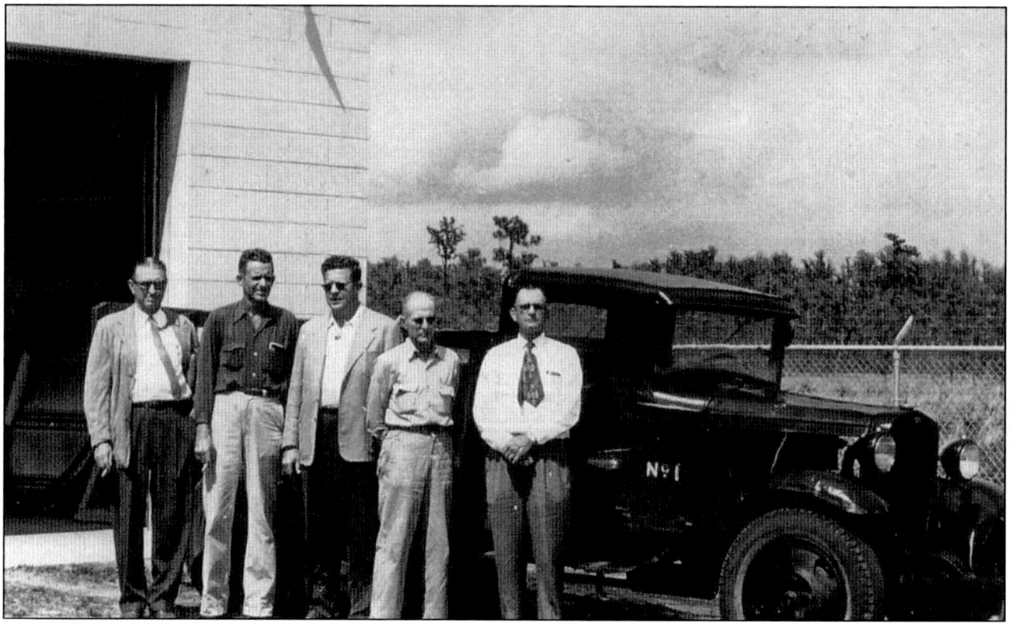

Shown here from left to right are Arthur Ogle, superintendent of the water department; Jerry Sellars, superintendent of the water plant; Gary Bennett, mayor of Cocoa; Lewis Crowe, superintendent of construction for the water department; and Otha Scarborough, superintendent of public works. The truck in the background, maintained today as an antique, is used in parades. This photograph was taken in the mid-1950s, when Cocoa began to receive water from Orange County, a much better source than Clear Lake.

Trigger Griggs, Brevard County deputy, patrolled the entire county and was well known in the Cocoa-Rockledge area. Boys throughout the county wanted to be a motorcycle policeman.

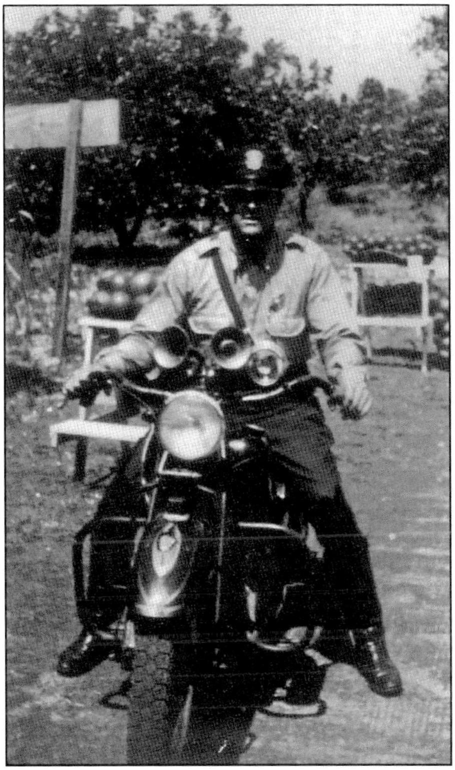

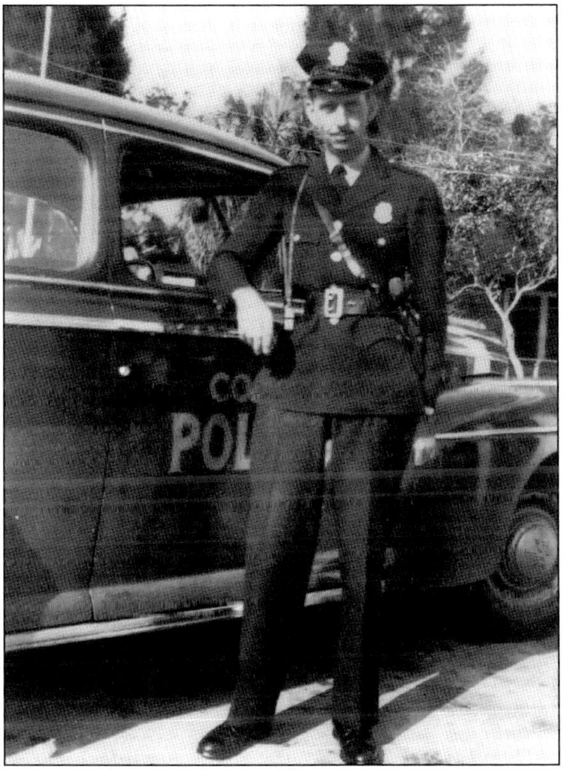

An inquest was held following the death of Lt. Roy D. Blake of the Cocoa Police Department in July 1954. The coroner's jury determined that the fatality was accidental and had occurred in the line of duty. The verdict read that Blake had died due to "an unavoidable discharge of his service revolver falling from an open holster" on his belt. Lieutenant Blake was acting as chief during the absence of G. E. Dempsey, who was undergoing a checkup at the Duke University Hospital.

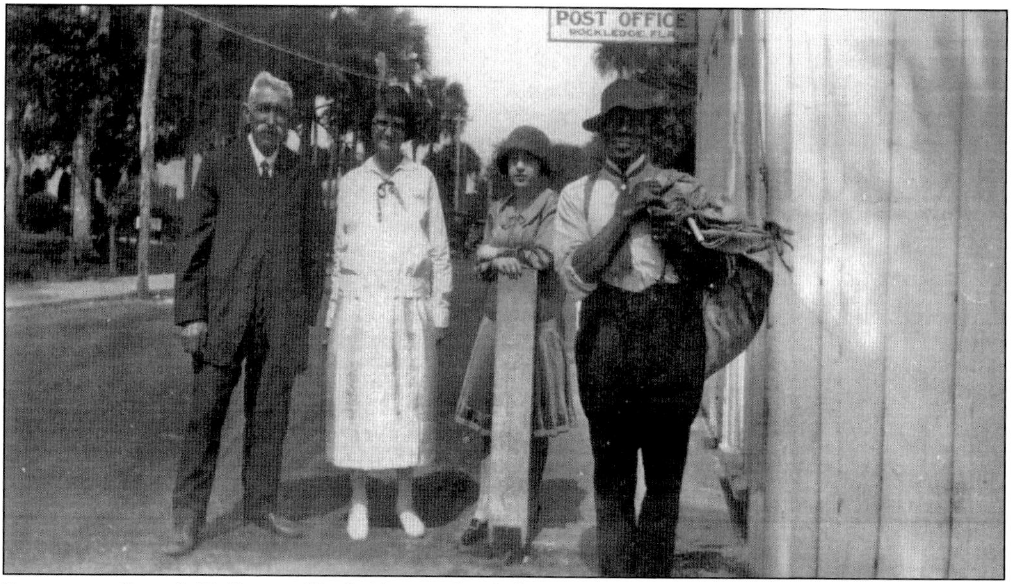

Postmaster Joseph B. Bower (far left) was the father of Hervey Bower, a well-known builder in Rockledge during the 1920s and 1930s. The elder Bower served as postmaster at the Coquina Post Office, three or four miles south of Rockledge. When that office closed on February 25, 1901, Bower became postmaster at Rockledge. The Rockledge Post Office was located on the east side of Rockledge Drive just north of Barton Avenue.

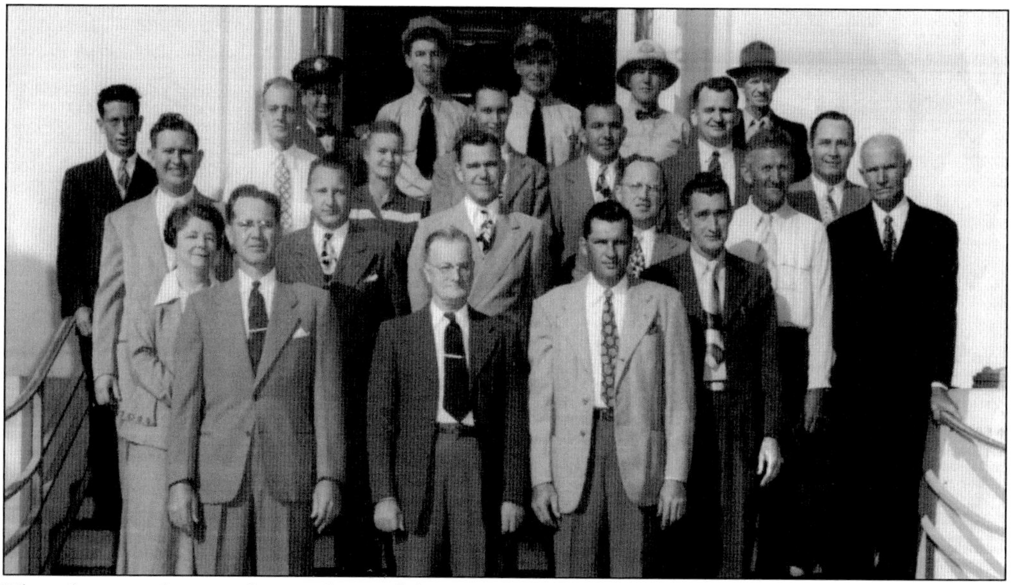

This photograph was taken in front of the Cocoa Post Office about 1950. Built in 1939 at a cost of $70,000, the office opened for business at 435 Brevard Avenue on April 21, 1940. Pictured from left to right are the following: (first row) assistant postmaster Frank Johnston, postmaster A. E. Booth, superintendent of mails Ivan Townsend, Eva Powell Ford, custodian Leon Garvin, Delbert Krepps, Bill Speith, Carroll Booth, Charlie Johnston, A. V. Yancy, Don Stradley, unidentified, George Leighty, Vic Edwards, Charles LaRoche, Speedy Harrell, Hoke Holmes, Jim Caldwell, and Ashley Buck; (second row) Carl P. "Rinky" Geiger, Felton Butler, Bart O'Hara, and Harvey A. White.

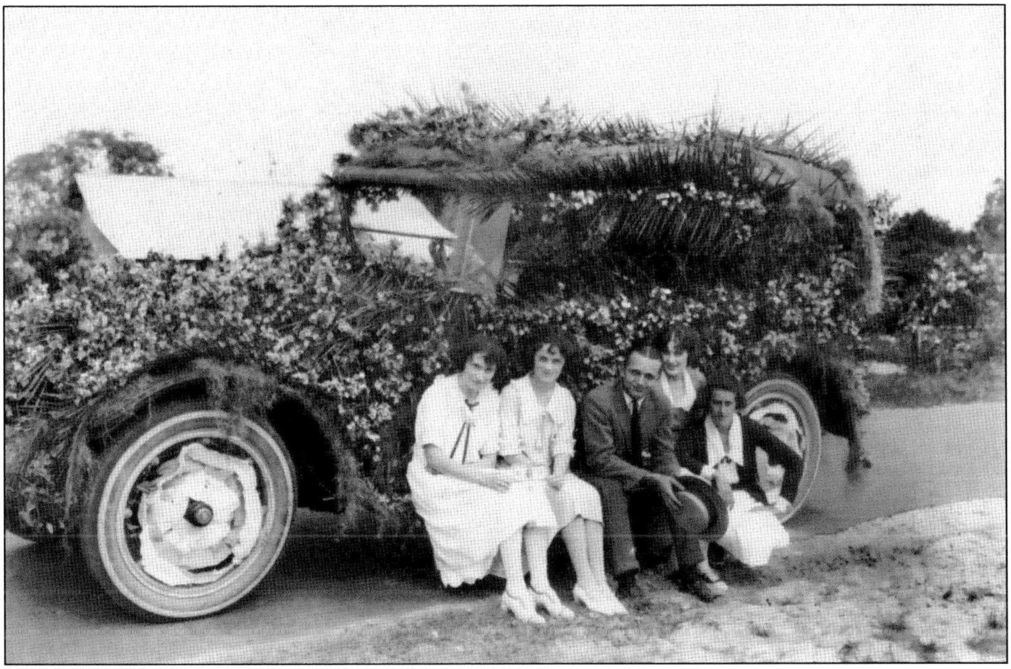

This car is decorated for the Orange Jubilee around 1926. Seen from left to right are unidentified, Myrtis Porcher, Lewis Andrews, Ruth Skelly, and Anita Daniels. Myrtis and Lewis married in 1929 and lived in the Porcher House until 1947.

"I came to Cocoa to practice medicine in 1924," recalled Dr. Hughlett in an interview. "My uncle, Dr. William L. Hughlett, was the physician in the area at the time and the older Hughlett was looking forward to retirement with his nephew and namesake taking over his practice." Young Dr. Hughlett came to Cocoa and met and married a local girl, Violet Packard, in 1927. The couple, active in the Methodist church, accepted a call to become missionaries in what was then the Belgian Congo for 5 years, but somehow the mission call lasted 40. Dr. Thomas Kenaston took the place vacated by Dr. Hughlett.

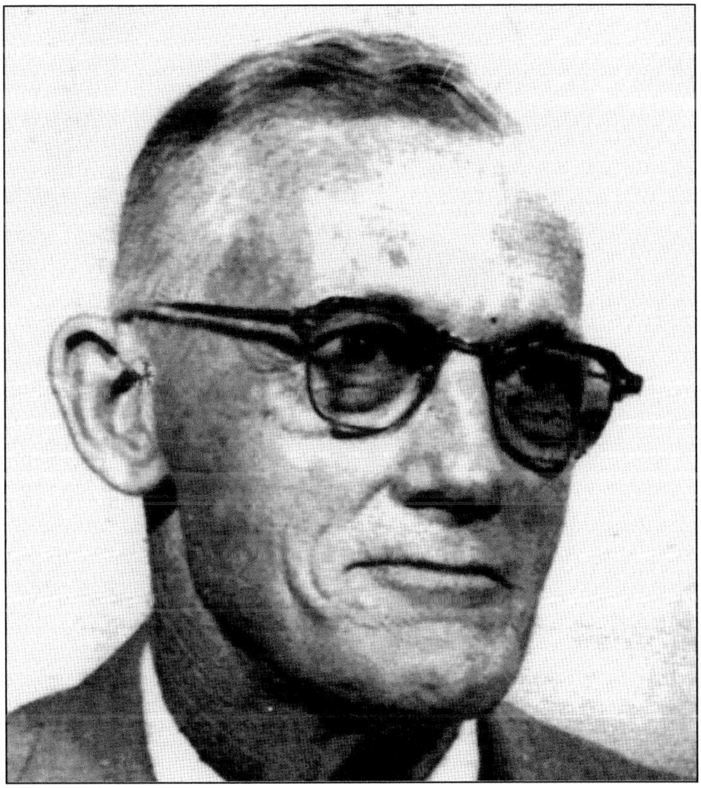

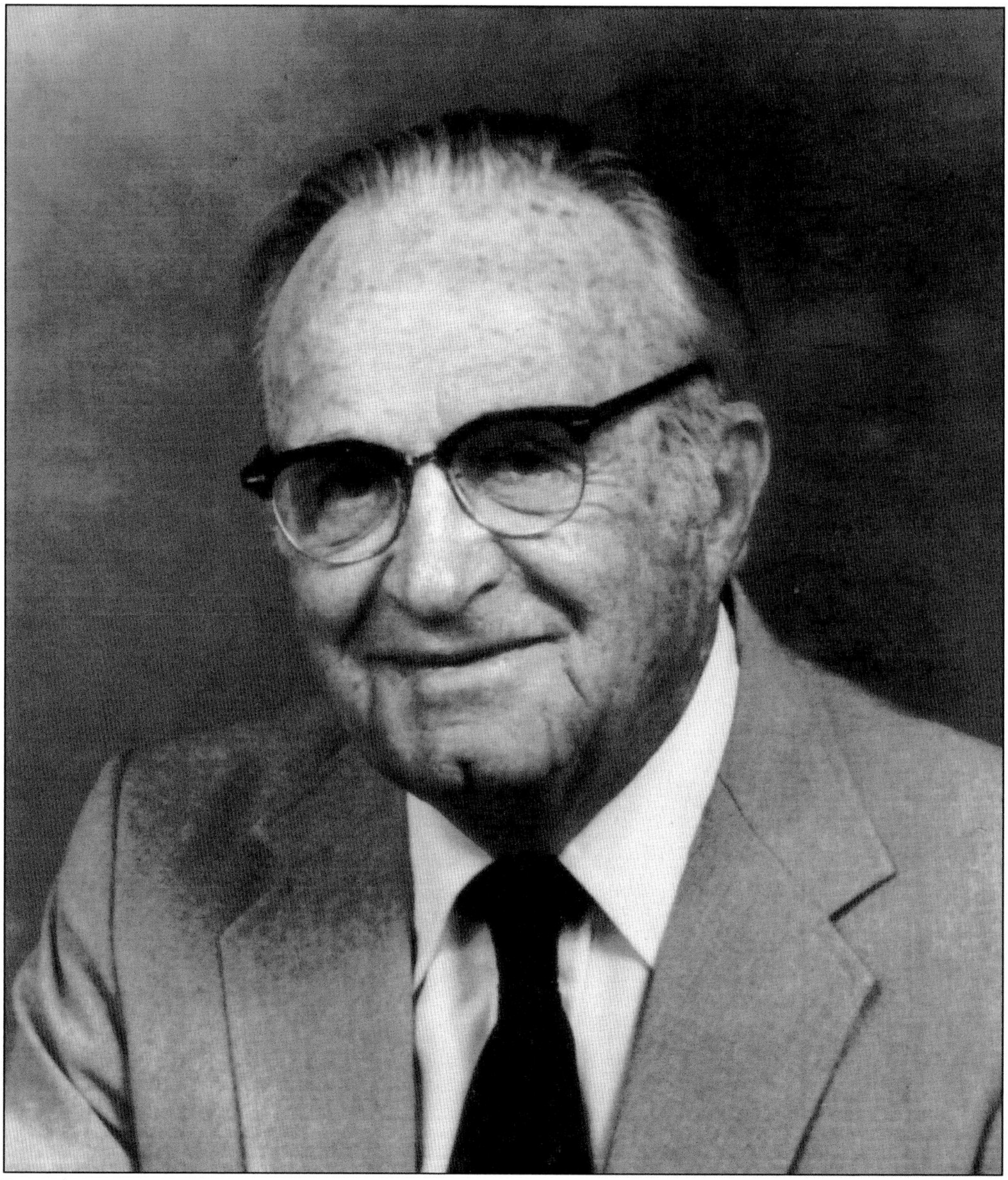

Dr. Thomas C. Kenaston Sr., a native of Nebraska, served his internship at St. Luke's Hospital in Jacksonville, Florida, and then started back to Nebraska. Having gotten sand in his shoes, however, he did not want to leave Florida. He stopped in the panhandle town of Bonifay and entered the office of Dr. Paul, asking about a location in Florida to set up practice. Dr. Paul was the brother of Flave (Ora Lee) Alderman of Cocoa; he visited his sister often and knew that the young Dr. Hughlett would be going to Africa as a missionary. That is how Cocoa had the good fortune of having Dr. Kenaston as a physician for many years.

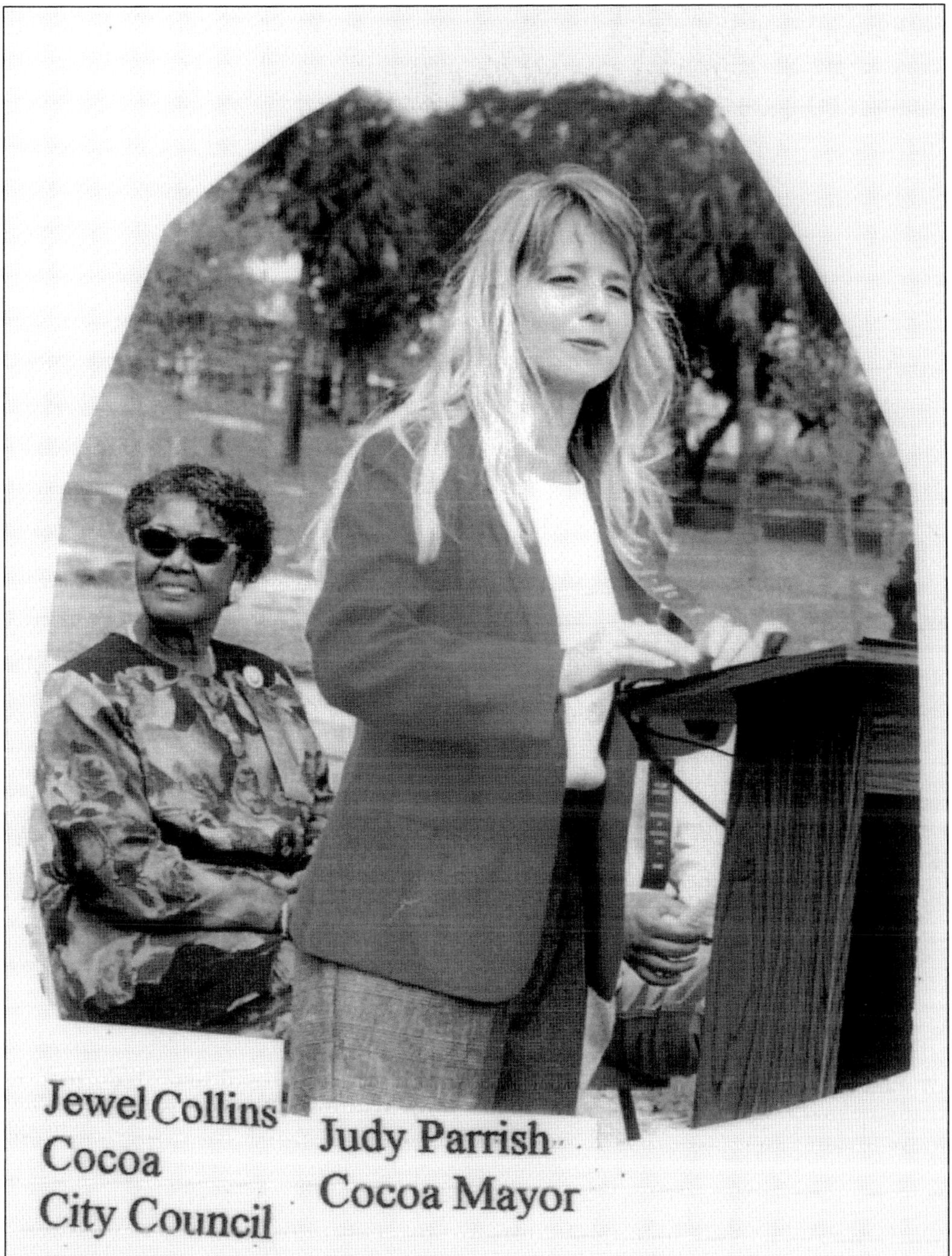

Mayor Judy Parrish (right) and councilwoman Jewell Collins attend the rededication of Hilltop Cemetery on March 4, 2000. Hilltop Cemetery is located in the 300 block of North Cocoa Boulevard.

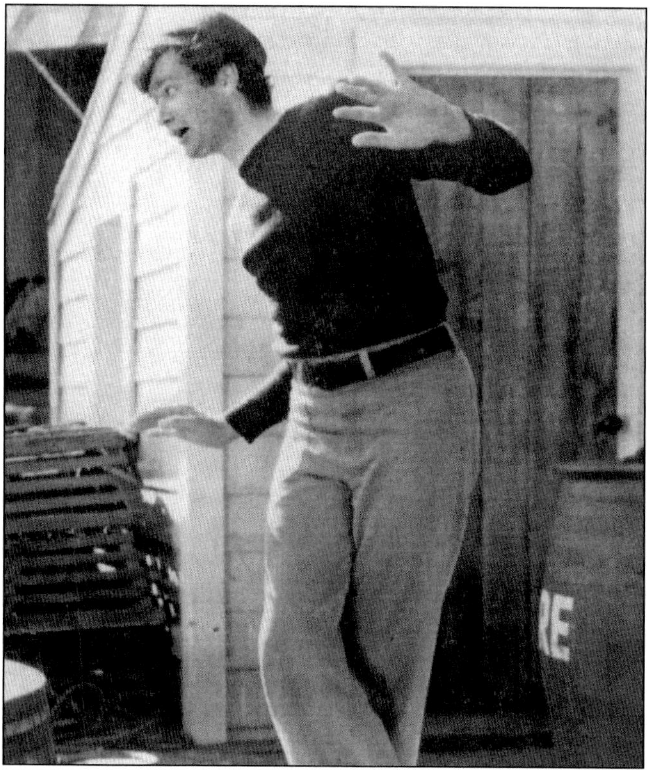

Buddy Ebsen, star of stage, screen, and television, was no stranger to Cocoa. The Ebsen School of Dance was located in Orlando, but before achieving fame in New York and Hollywood, Buddy and his sister Helga endeavored to teach the local girls and boys some deportment and dancing. The school is known to have been active in the late 1930s and early 1950s—often furnishing the dancers for the Orange Jubilee Pageant. Buddy is probably best known for his role as Jed Clampett in the series *Beverley Hillbillies*. One student of the 1940s fondly remembers learning the foxtrot and "the Big Apple."

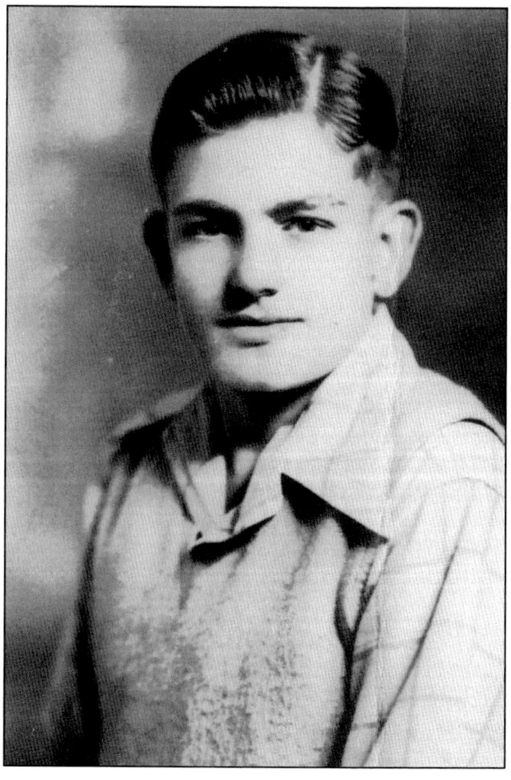

Emory Bennett was a 1948 graduate of Cocoa High School. After high school, he served his country in the Korean War, where he sacrificed his life so that his company could affect an orderly withdrawal. He was awarded the Congressional Medal of Honor posthumously, and a statue of his likeness now stands in Riverfront Park in his honor.

The statue's plaque reads, "Emory Laurence Bennett—For conspicuous gallantry and intrepidity at the risk of his life above and beyond call of duty in action with the enemy."

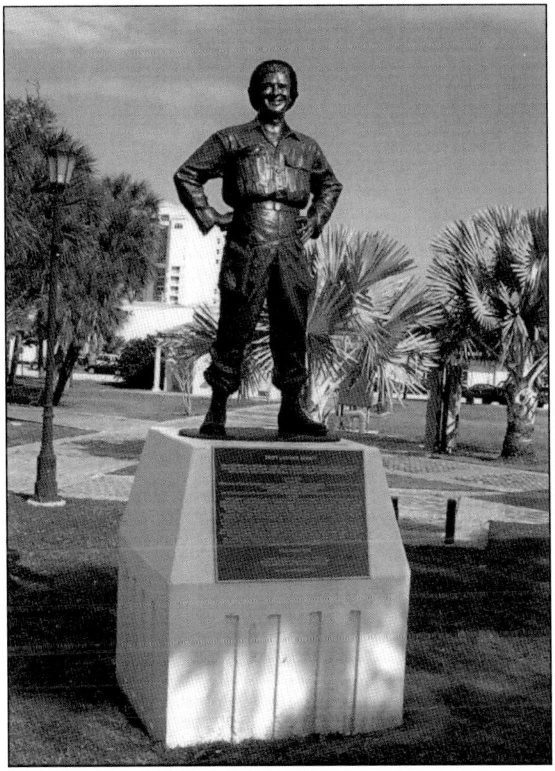

Shown here is the wording at the bottom of the statue shown above.

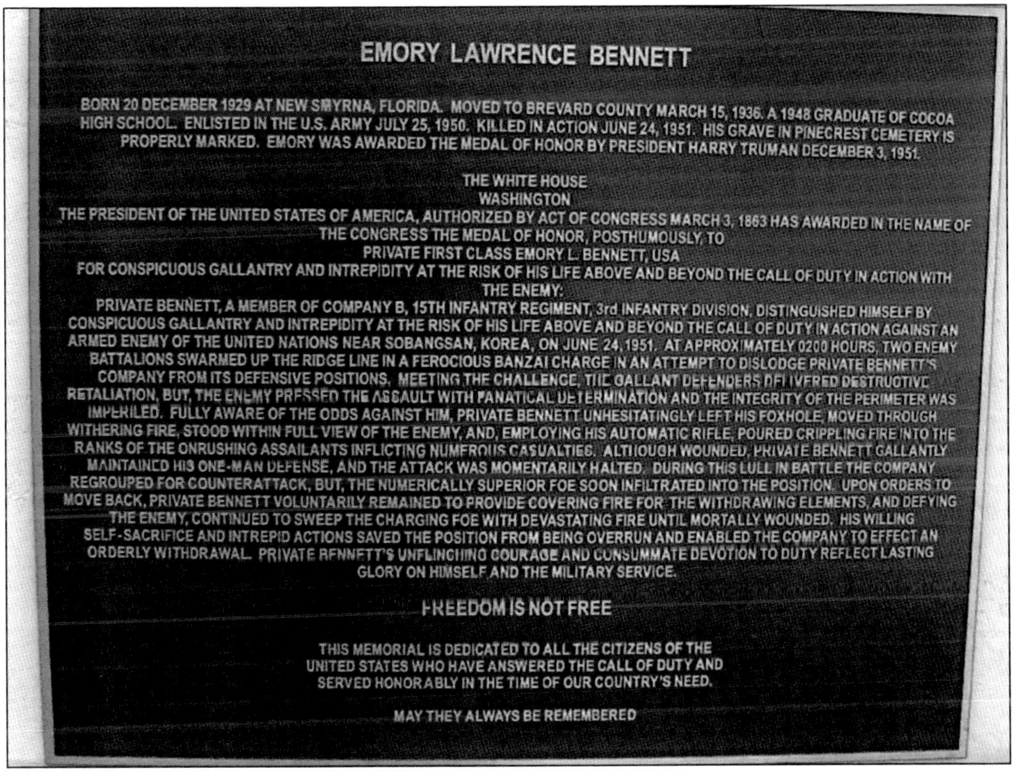

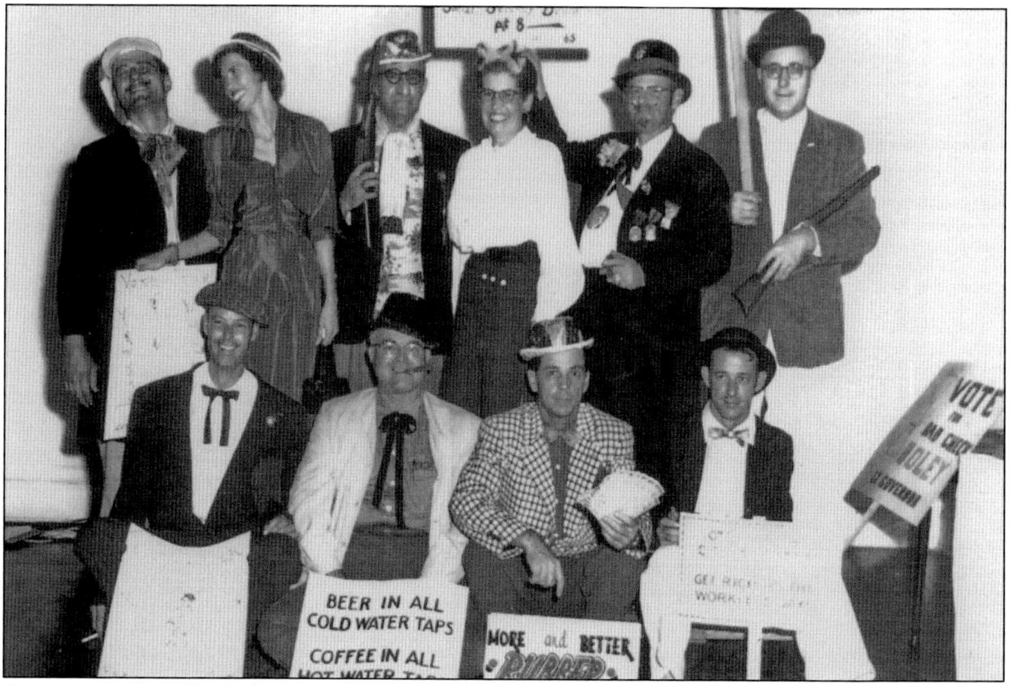

A representative for Dale Carnegie's seminars on "How to Win Friends and Influence People" arrived in Cocoa in the early 1950s to recruit a class. The members of the class at one point formed teams and campaigned for their causes. Shown from left to right are the following: (first row) Ed Newkirk, Luke Blair, John Boley, and J. L. "Jim" Smith; (second row) unidentified, Vadna Beale, unidentified, Halcie Dooley, D. J. Stansfield, and unidentified.

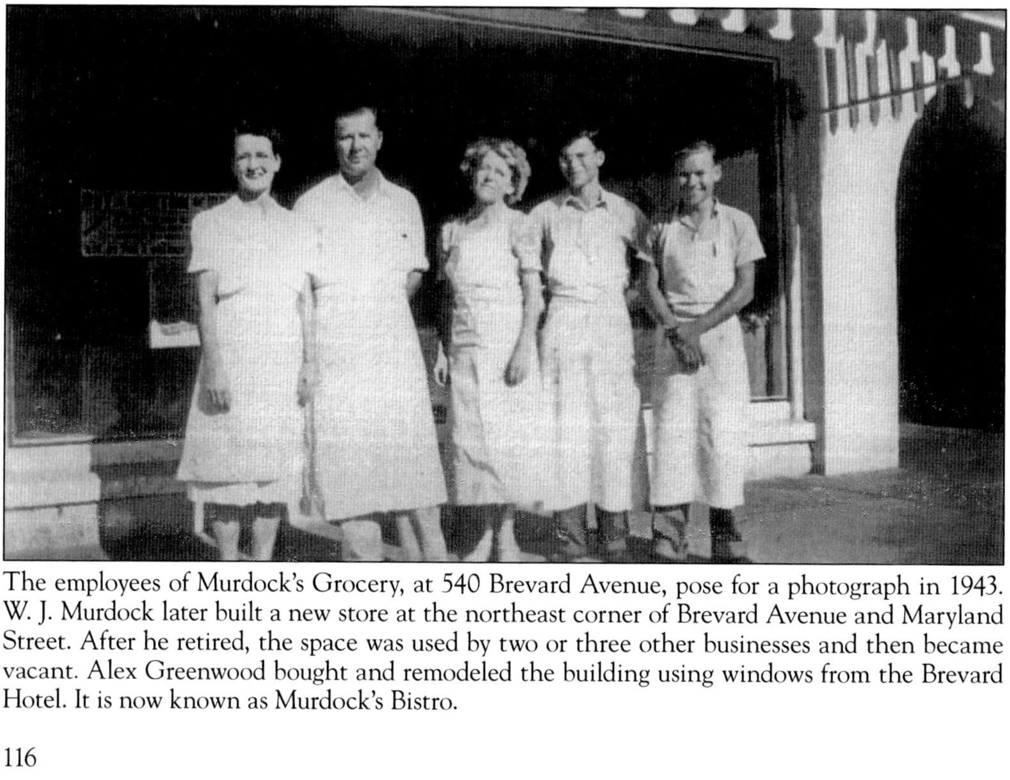

The employees of Murdock's Grocery, at 540 Brevard Avenue, pose for a photograph in 1943. W. J. Murdock later built a new store at the northeast corner of Brevard Avenue and Maryland Street. After he retired, the space was used by two or three other businesses and then became vacant. Alex Greenwood bought and remodeled the building using windows from the Brevard Hotel. It is now known as Murdock's Bistro.

Pictured here are Isadore and Anna Rubin. In 1914, Isadore and Ralph Rubin started a small general store in Cocoa, and in 1917, they built and ran Rubin Brothers department store at the corner of Harrison and Delannoy Avenues. A member of the city council, Isadore was active in community affairs. After the store closed, the family moved to Miami in 1934. The Rubins were the first and only Jewish family in Cocoa at that time.

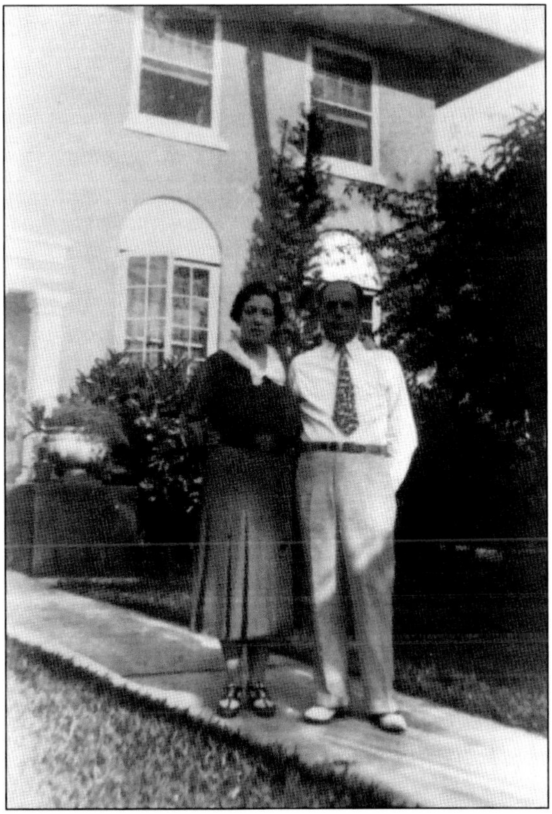

According to the *Cocoa Tribune* of September 16, 1947, Ada Spiller and her sister Elvira Watkins entertained several pioneer ladies of the area with a dinner in their home. In attendance were the following, from left to right: (seated) Frances Hendry, Dell Carter Munson, Mrs. J. E. Pound, "Aunt Barbara" Faber, Gertrude Wilson Honeywell, and Martha Southern; (standing) Louise Salton, Ada Spiller, Cora Goodrich, Julia Jarvis, and Elvira Watkins. Mrs. Spiller was a music teacher, and Miss Watkins directed the Hillside School.

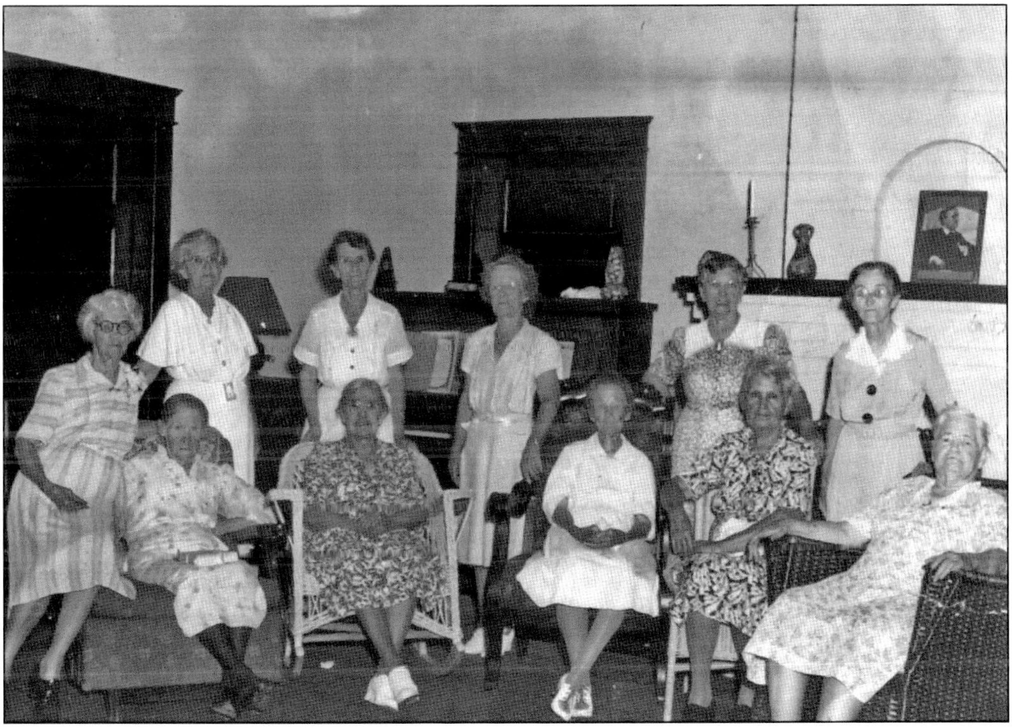

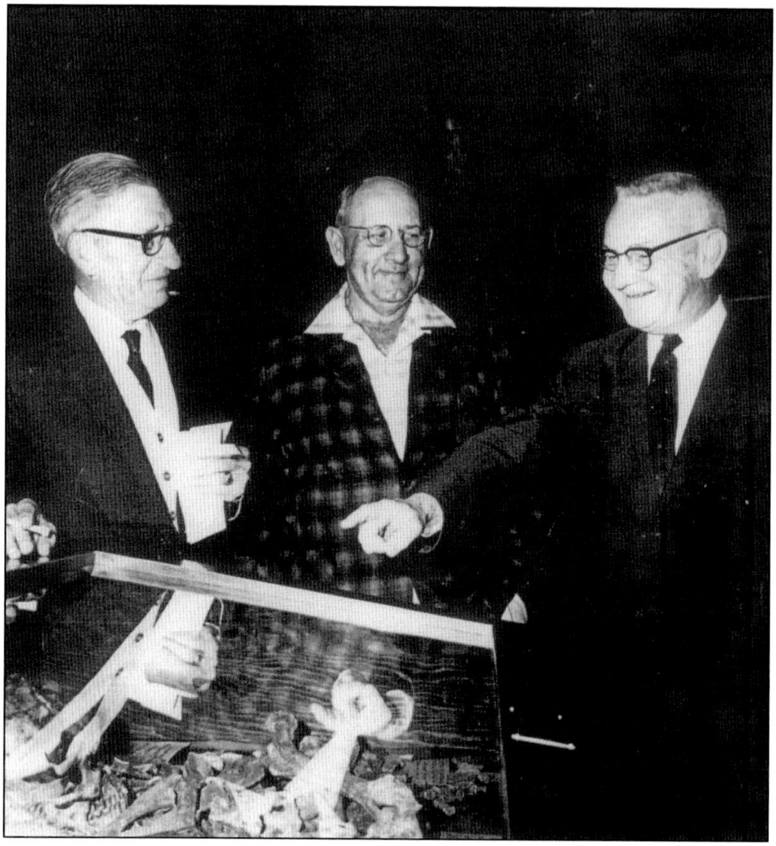

John Pound, editor of the *Cocoa Tribune*; archaeologist Bud Knoderer; and Ed Erdman, president of the Central Brevard National Bank; look over some artifacts.

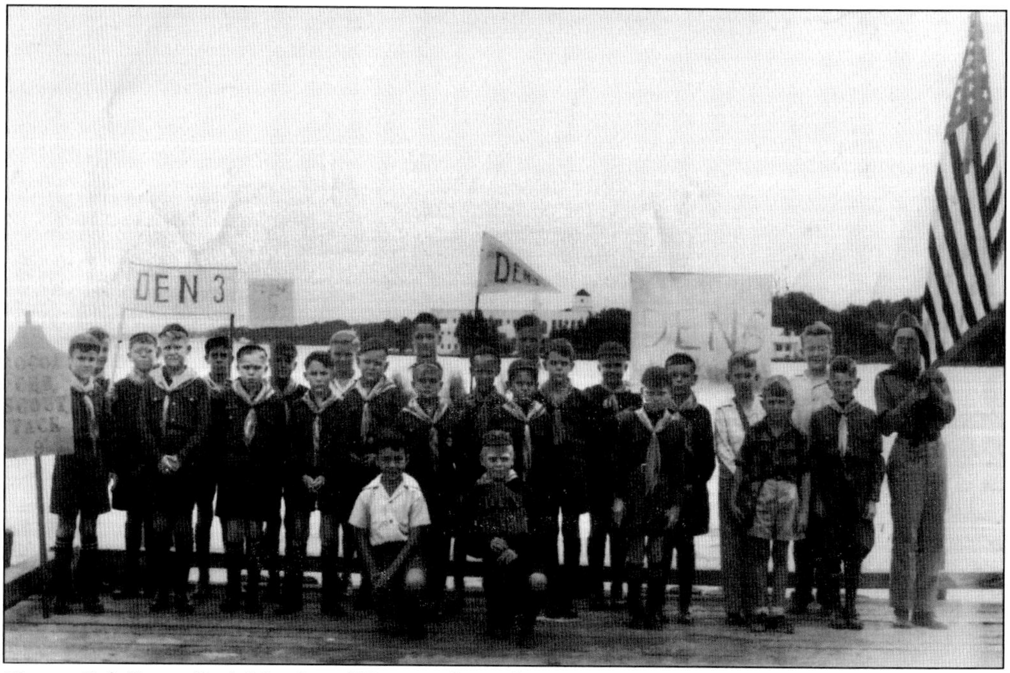

Cocoa Cub Scout Pack No. 9 and Dens 1 through 5 certainly were "prepared."

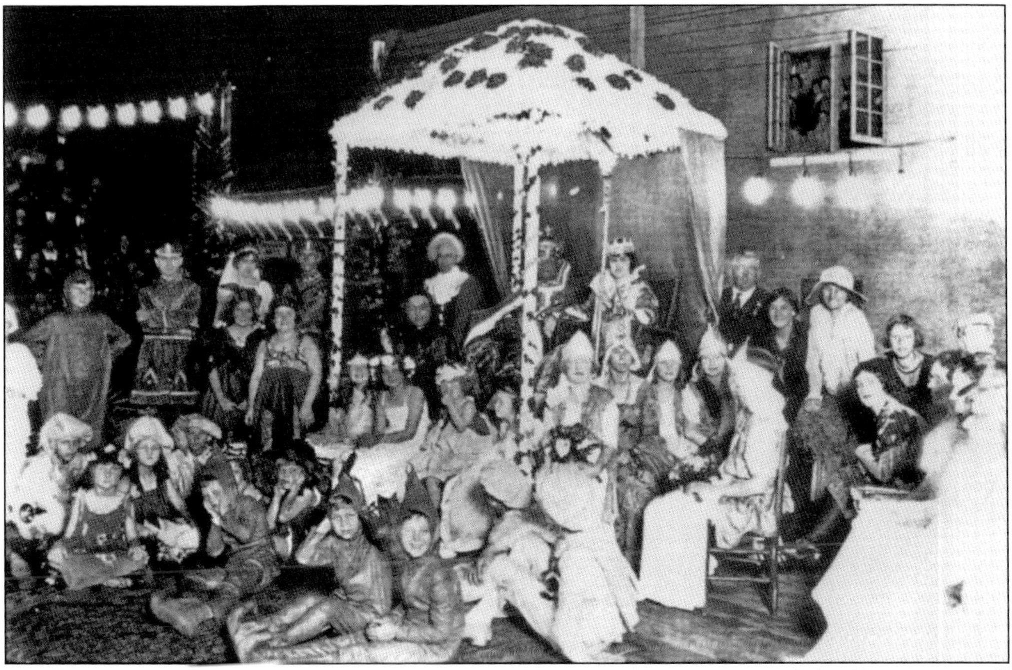

The highlight of the winter season in Cocoa was the now-defunct Orange Jubilee. Tourists as well as inhabitants of neighboring communities were duly impressed with the professional staging of the coronation pageants. Businesses and professionals took off from work to participate in the golf tournaments, boat races, and other events. The celebration culminated when King Street between Brevard and Delannoy Avenue was closed off for the pageant, which ended in the coronation of the king and queen (who had been elected secretly).

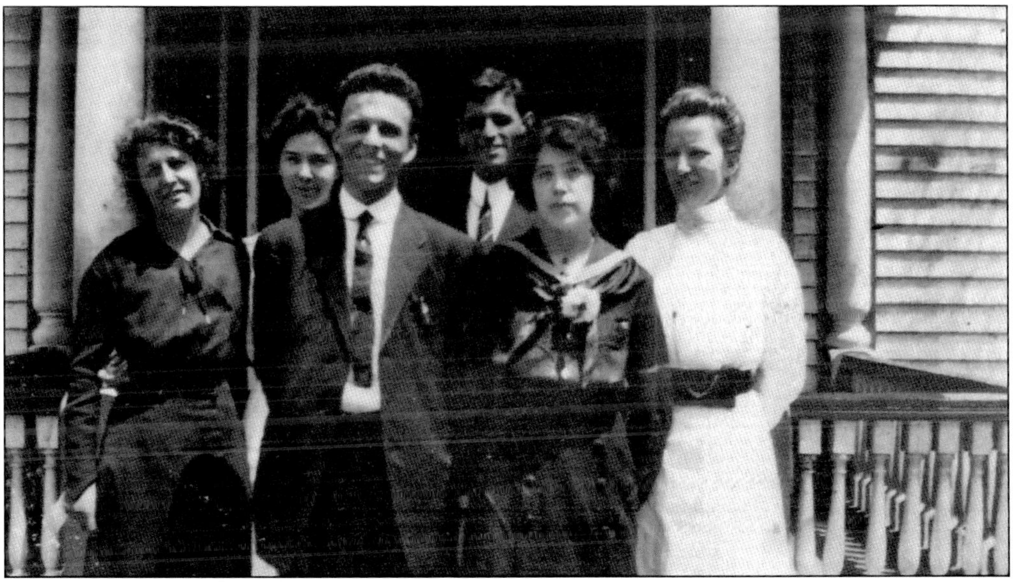

Robert Golding, shown here, served as principal of Cocoa schools at one time. These teachers, though unidentified, instructed both elementary and high school grades. When Golding arrived to take over his duties, he had to fight one of the older high school boys to assert his authority. He later authored a history of Florida.

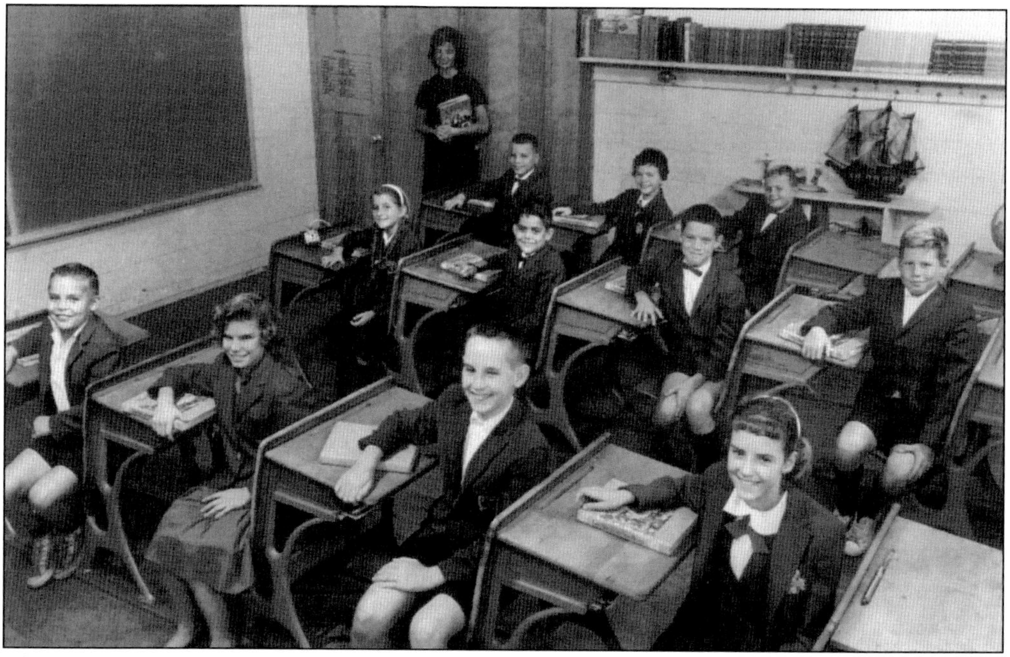

These students attended St. Mark's Episcopal Day School in Cocoa during the 1962–1963 year.

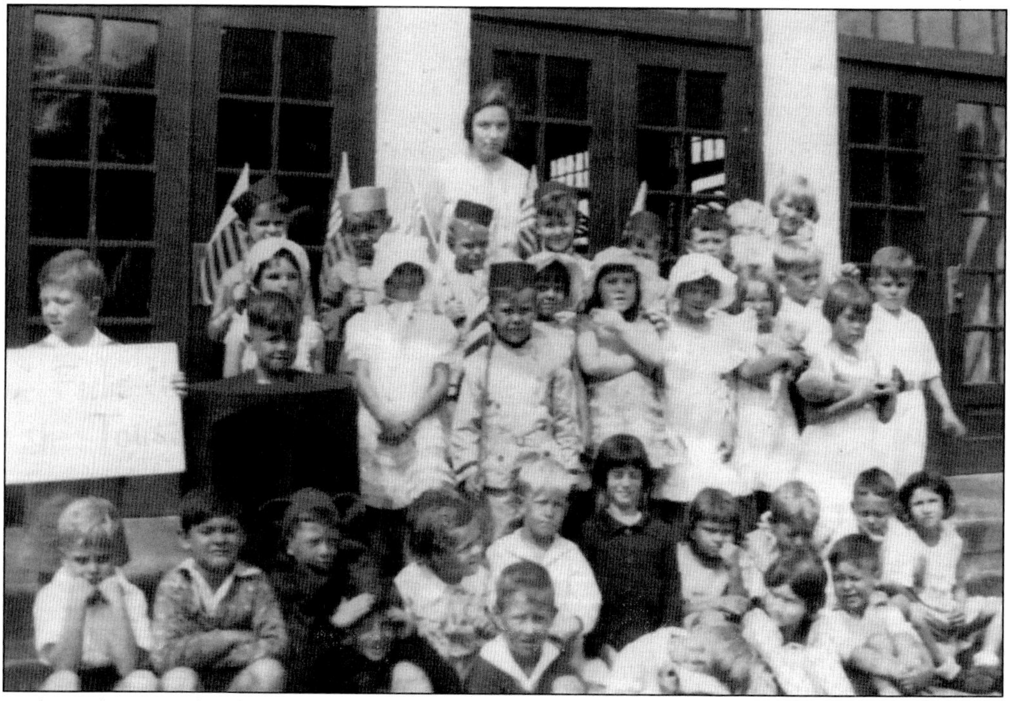

In the early 1930s, the play *Toyland* was presented by Miss Roberts and part of the Cocoa Elementary School first grade. Ashley "Hoot" Ringo holds the sign. Next to him is Jimmy Brady. Behind Jimmy, from left to right, are the following: (first row) Marilu (Shepard) Thistle, unidentified, Franklin Wooten, two unidentified girls, Eleanor Kinsey, and two unidentified girls; (second row) unidentified, Oliver Bossom, Henry "Hugh" Parrish, three unidentified, Margaret (Booth) Cox, and two unidentified boys. The children in the foreground provided the audience for the drama.

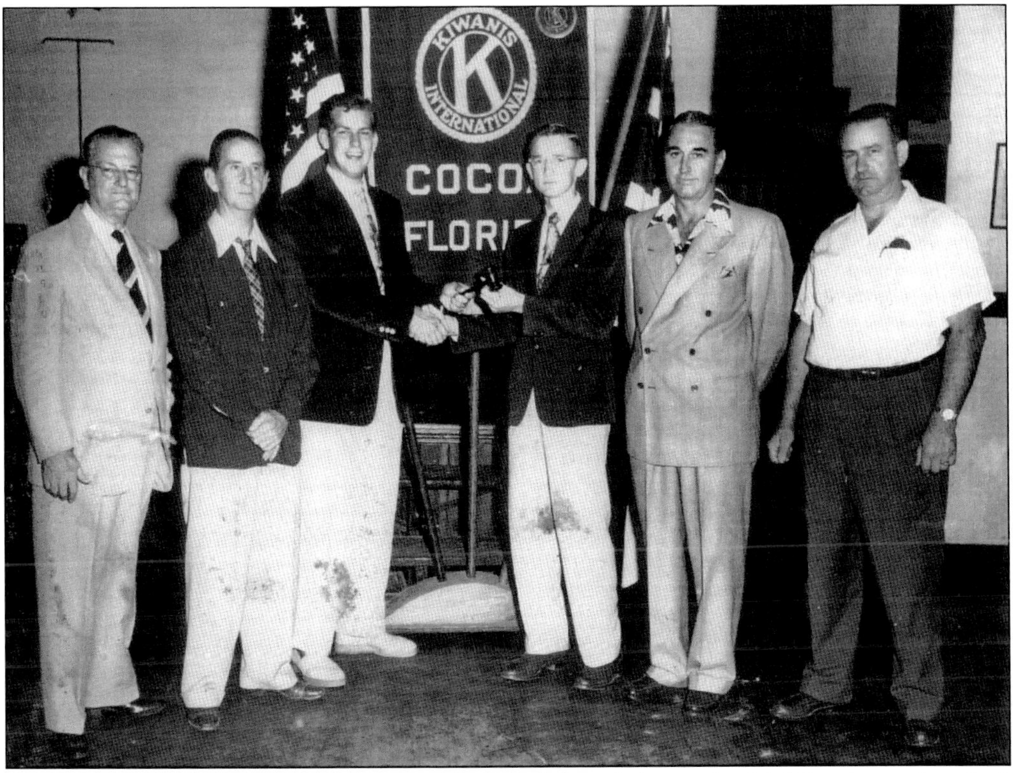

Members of Cocoa Kiwanis International included, from left to right, Ted Booth, unidentified, Dewitt Matthews, Ed Bramlet, Arthur Ogle, and Earl Gray.

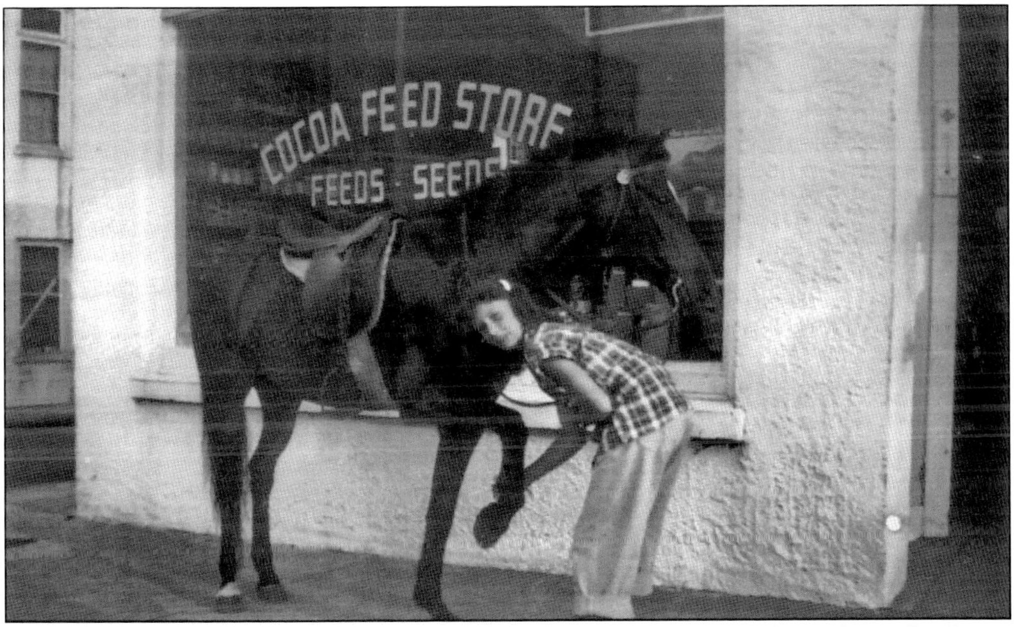

Barbara Ashmore Ellison poses with her horse Beauty in front of her father's shop. The Cocoa Feed Store was located on the southwest coroner of Magnolia (now Stone) and Brevard Court. It was not unusual to see Barbara and Beauty within a five-mile radius of the store.

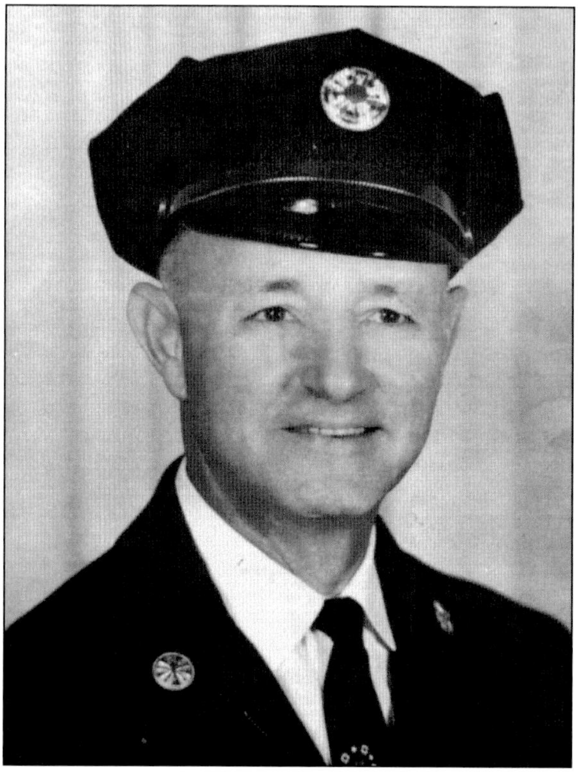

In July 1959, fire chief J. F. MacMillan was honored for 32 years of dedicated service.

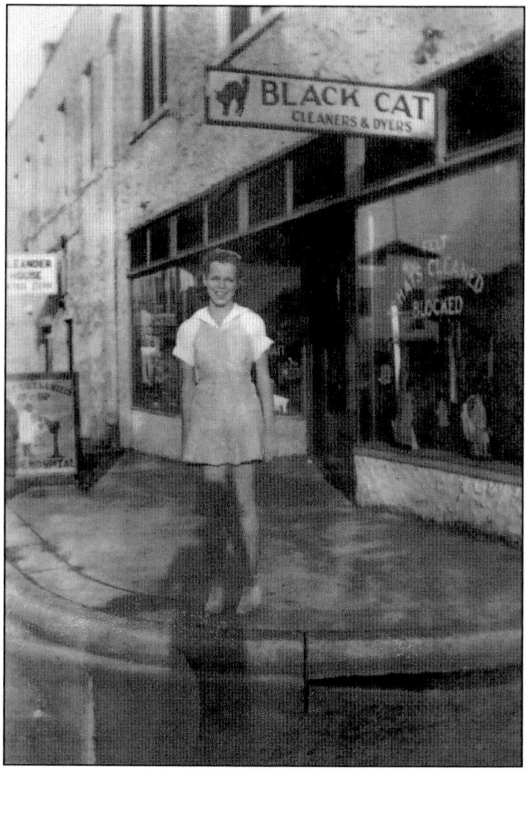

Marion Paterson Jackson poses in front of Black Cat Cleaners and Dryers on Oleander Street.

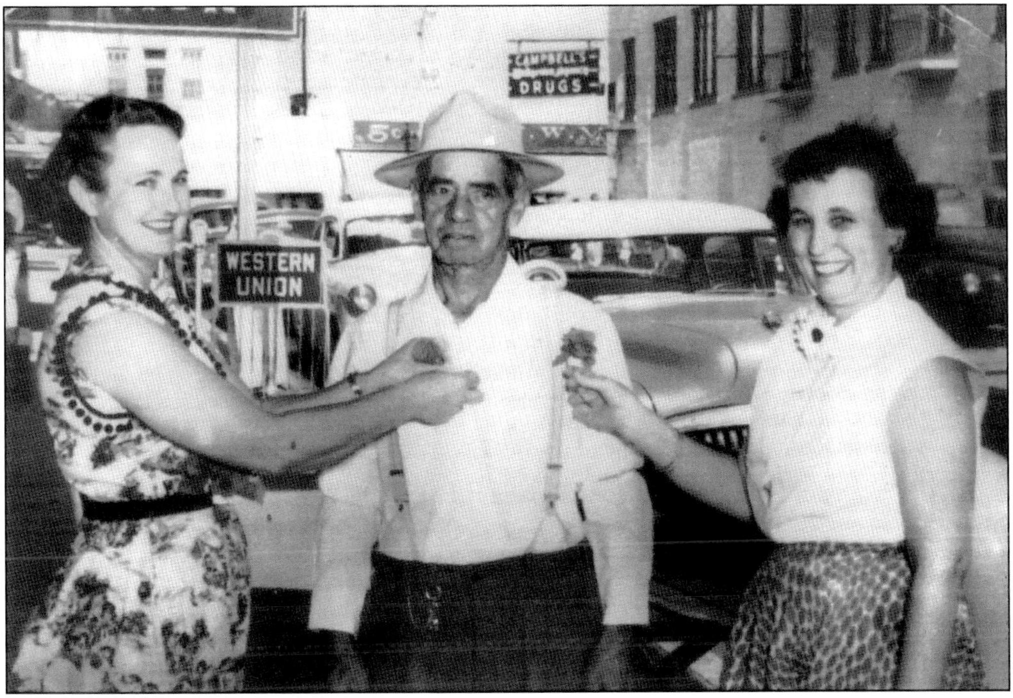

Zelma Seawright (left), C. E. Lucas, and Leota Shackleford are shown on Harrison Street in Cocoa. Zelma and Leota were active in the American Legion Auxiliary. A World War I veteran, Lucas became the principal dock builder in the area for many years.

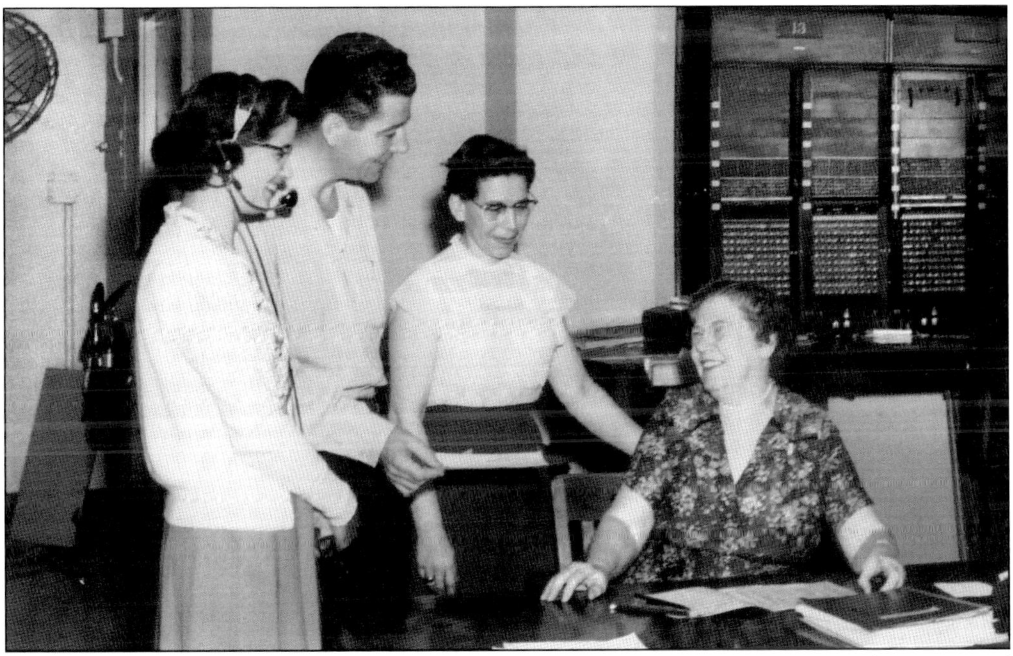

The interior of the Cocoa Telephone Office, situated on Delannoy Avenue, is pictured here. Pictured from left to right are Laura Mae Dewey Crosby, unidentified, Ann Harris, and Edna Tucker.

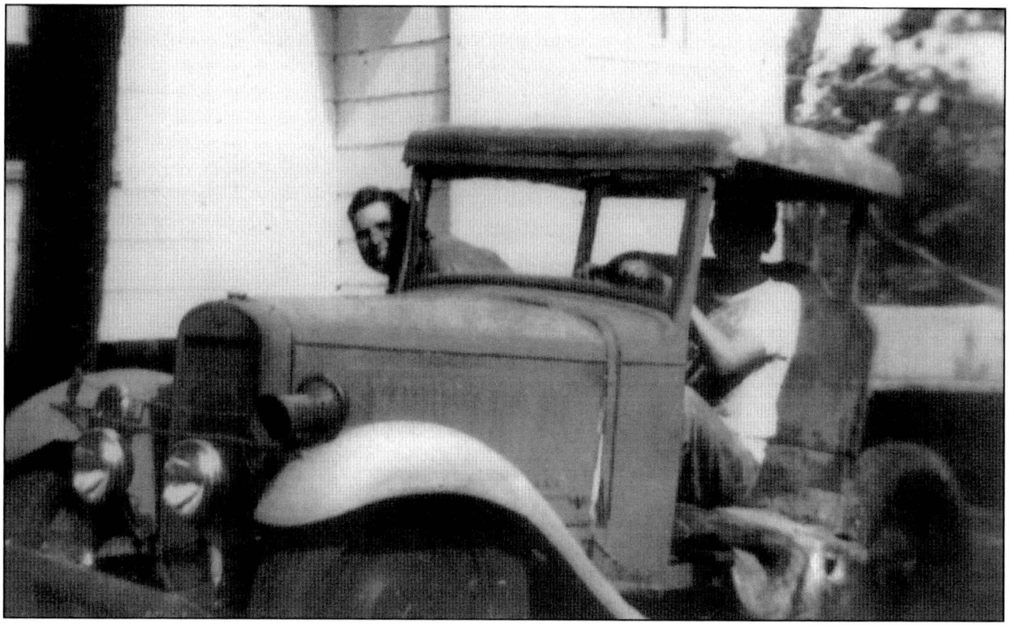

In 1949, James Branch (left) and his son Tommy sit in a "cut down" Austin car used to spray for mosquitoes. The mosquito control district provided residents with diesel fuel containing DDT that would be injected in the hot exhaust, creating a white smoke to kill or repel mosquitoes.

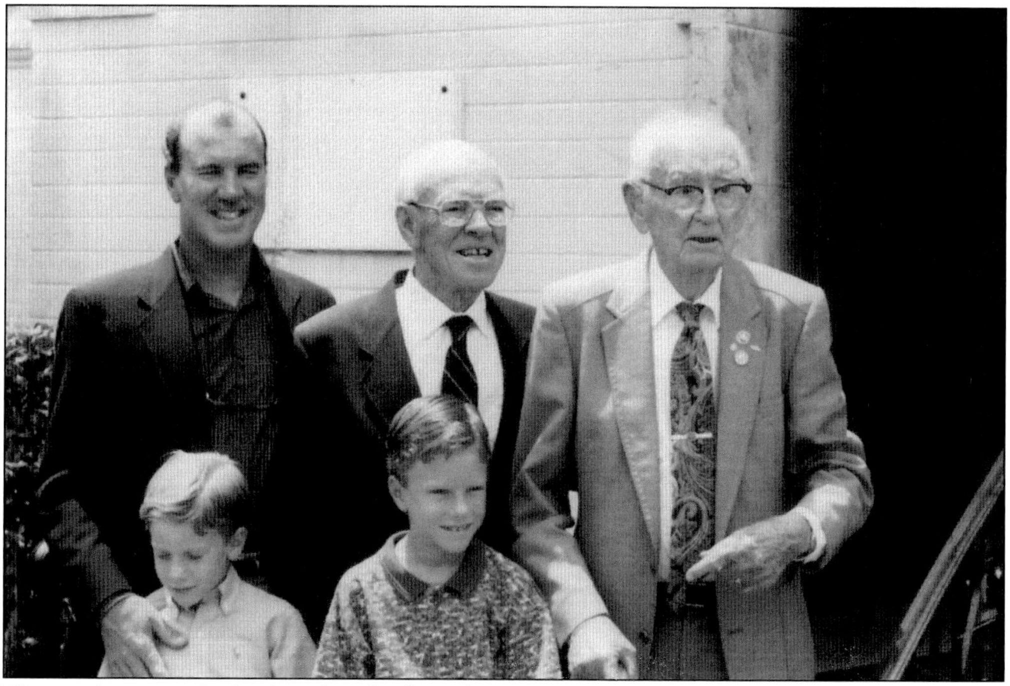

The gentleman at the back and to the far right is Roy W. Wall, 105 years old in this photograph. He lived to be 107. Roy Wall Boulevard was named for him. The other four pictured are members of the Harvey family. In the first are the sons of Larry Harvey of Harvey's Groves, Bryan (left) and Chris Harvey. In the second row from left to right are Larry Harvey; his father, George Harvey; and Roy Wall.

Mike Froh, seen in the 1928 Cocoa High School annual, cared for the school buildings and grounds. Taking a personal interest in each student, he continued his good work until the early 1950s.

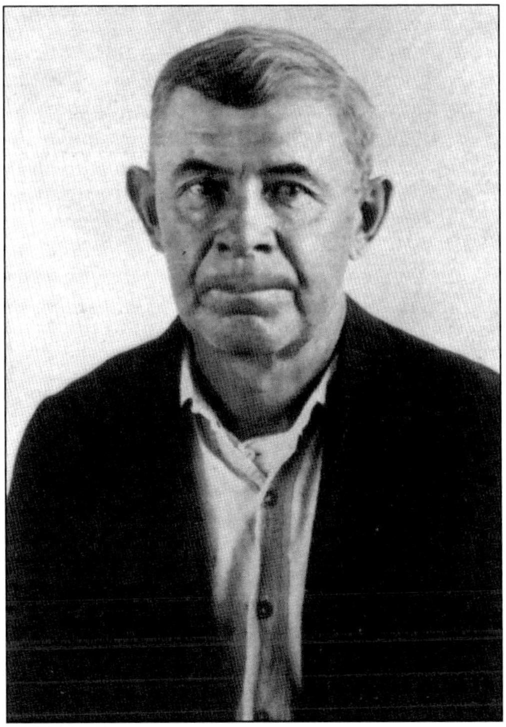

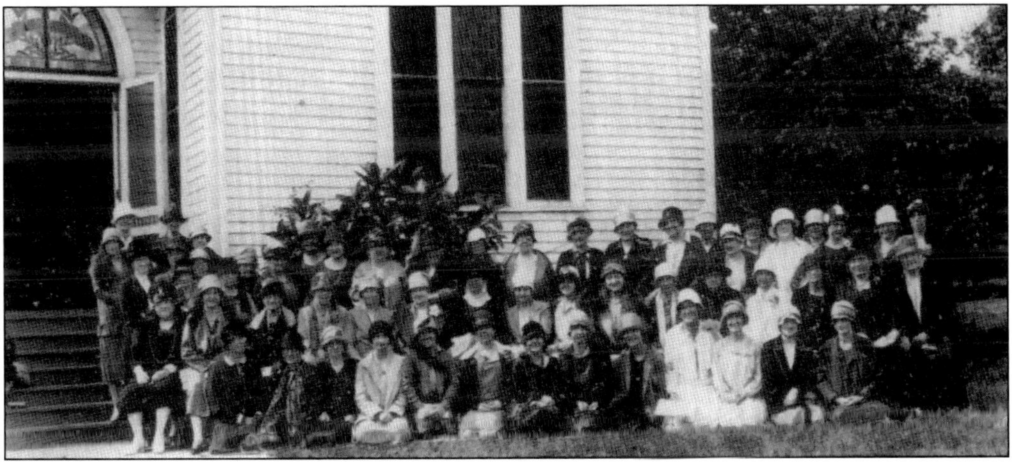

The women's class of the Rockledge Presbyterian Church poses in front of the Orange Avenue church in 1927. Shown from left to right are the following: (first row) Rita Ketcham, Nellie Herkimer, Luella Stark, Mary Sue Sherrod, Mrs. J. C. McLeod, Clara Moore, unidentified, Vida McGill, Katherine Maxwell, Mrs. McFadden, Helen Gotshall, Amy Jones, and Kate Thompson; (second row) Mrs. Eastwick, unidentified, Mrs. Kling, Mrs. D. C. Williams, unidentified, Mrs. Herbert Cogswell, Frances Moore, Mrs. John Wilton, Mrs. Charles Bovard, Mrs. Sheffield, Mrs. Ronald, Mrs. McLeod Sr., Mrs. Enoch Tompkins, and Mrs. Strong; (third row) Sallie Gotshall, unidentified, Clara Longman, Mrs. Louis Mayer, Mrs. E. E. Stark, two unidentified women, Mrs. J. E. Gotshall, Mrs. Brigden, unidentified, Jennie Whitney, two unidentified women, Mrs. Coy, Mrs. Sam Witz, Mrs. Apley, unidentified, Mrs. Chapman, unidentified, Bertha Childs, two unidentified women, Mrs. Plank, and Mrs. Whitcomb; (fourth row) Hulda Gotshall, Mrs. Maxwell, unidentified, and Mrs. Towers.

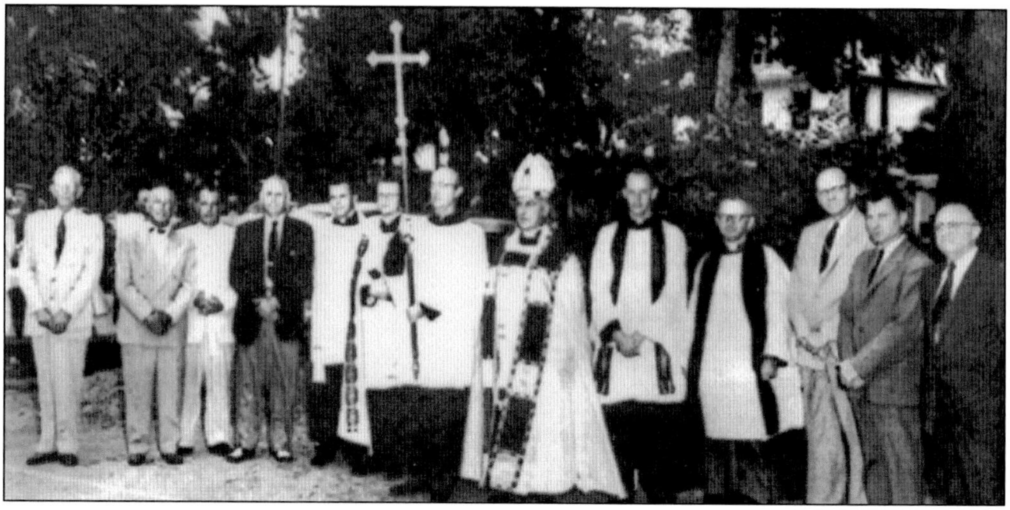

A ground-breaking ceremony is conducted for a new classroom at St. Mark's Academy in April 1957. Enjoying the festivities are, from left to right, J. W. Canfield, Newt Argabrite, Tom Winner, R. L. Schlernitzauer, Rev. W. L. Fulbell, Rev. Edward B. King, James Munroe, Bishop W. F. Moses, Reverend Cuthbertson, Rev. William Hargrave, Dabney Davis, John J. Bryant, and Dr. Tom Kenaston Sr.

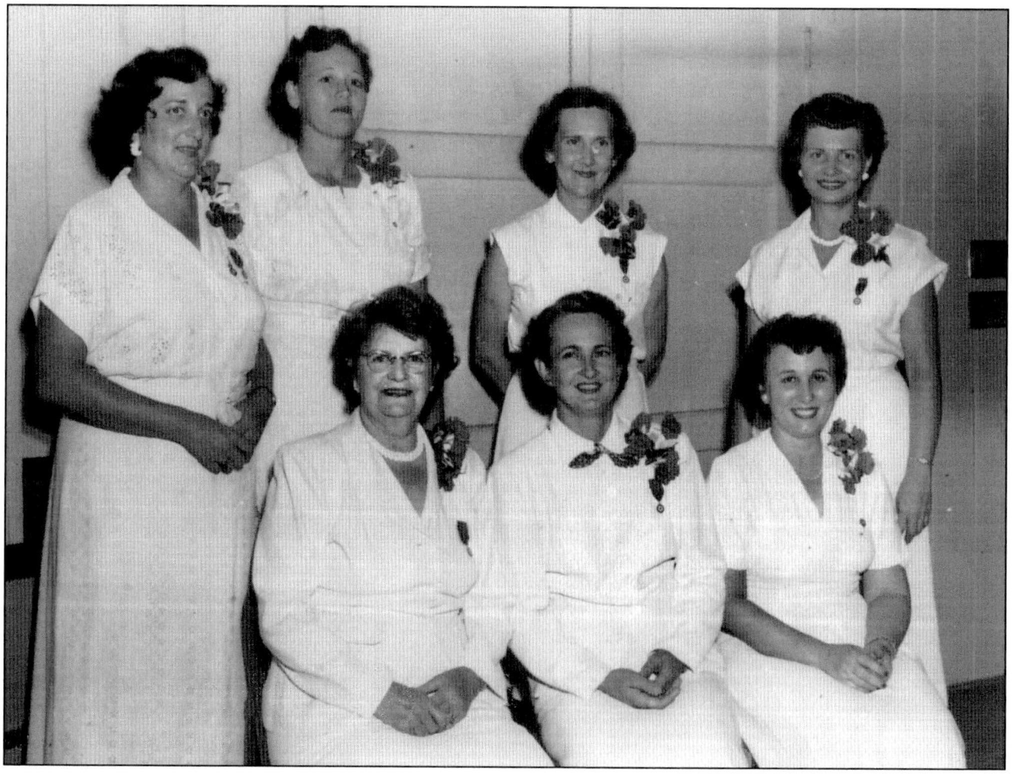

The local post of the American Legion sponsored a glee club in the 1950s. The club's officers included the following, from left to right: (first row) Mae Fenner, Zelma Seawright Burdick, and Leota Shackleford; (second row) Doris DeWitt, Iris Avant Sullivan, Pat Seawright Cannon, and Meda Heider.

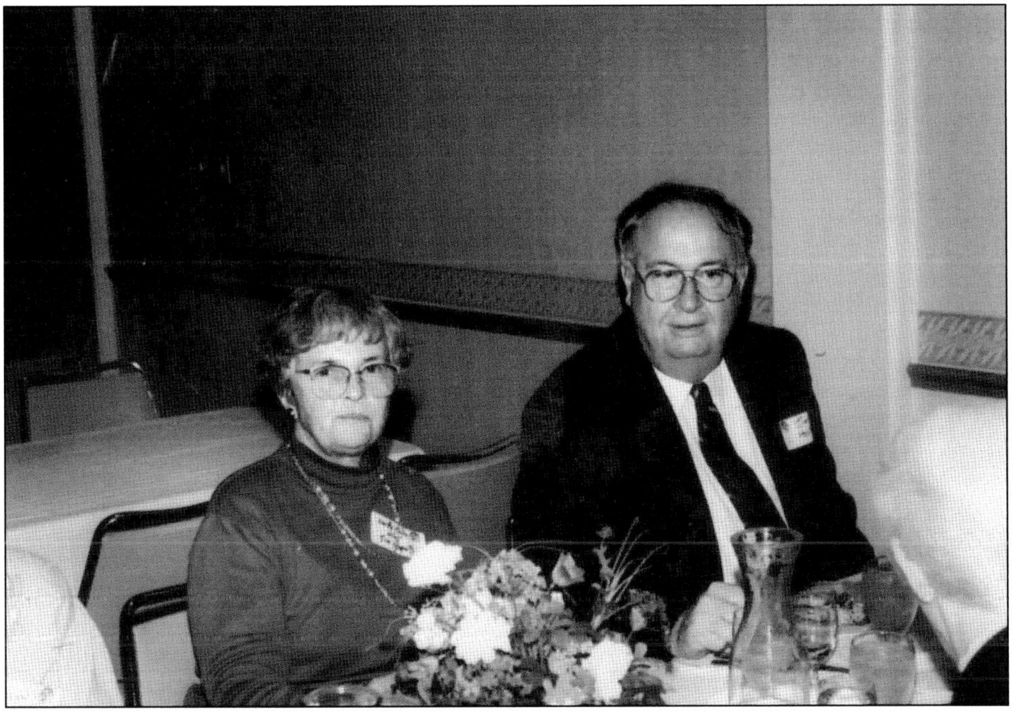

Marilyn "Smitty" and Jimmy Hooper attend the 50-year class reunion of Cocoa High School in 1995. A native of Cocoa, Jimmy inherited the dealership for the Chrysler line of cars, along with Hooper Groves. These businesses employed many people in the area.

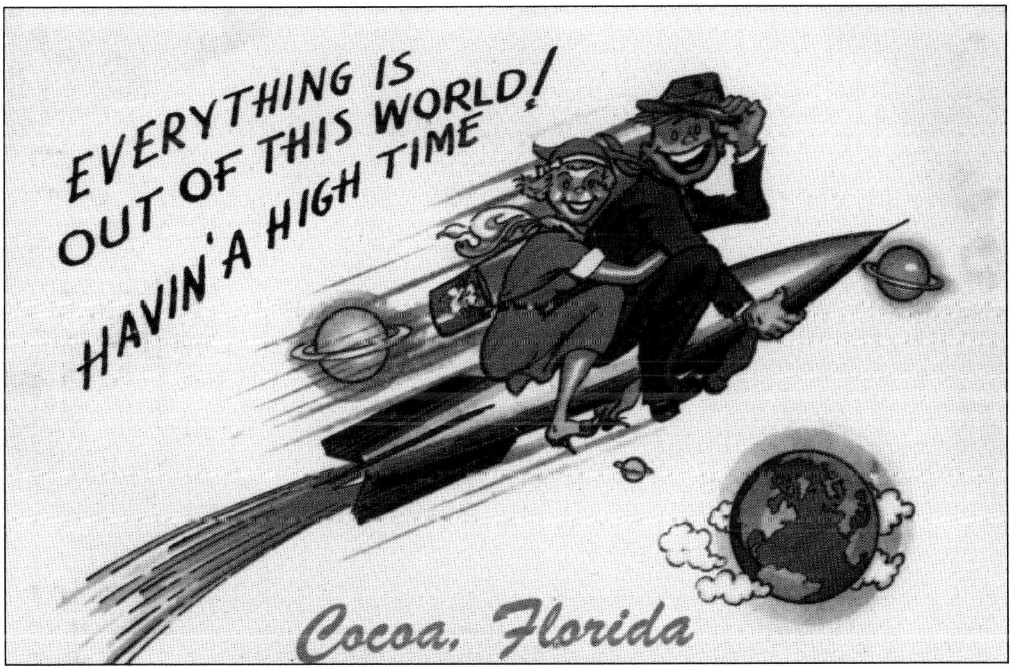

Cocoanuts? Or Coconauts! Which nickname would you choose?